THE POLITICS OF LANGUAGE
IRELAND 1366–1922
A Sourcebook

'A very impressive work . . . I would recommend it with enthusiasm. It is lucidly organised, well informed and comprehensible both to a specialist and non-specialist audience.'
Seamus Deane, *Keogh Professor of Irish Studies, University of Notre Dame, USA*

'A useful and illuminating survey of many centuries of cultural debate. . . . A book on such a hotly-contested topic will surely add to the controversies which it records, but its generation of further debate will be a sure sign of the value of Tony Crowley's contribution.'
Professor Declan Kiberd, *Department of Anglo-Irish Literature and Drama, University College Dublin, Ireland*

For almost a thousand years language has been an important and contentious issue in Ireland. The story of the relations between the English and Irish languages is a complex one full of unexpected alliances, strange accounts of historical origins, and peculiar forms of cultural identity. Above all it reflects the great themes of Irish history: colonial invasion, native resistance, religious and cultural difference.

Collected here for the first time are texts on the politics of language from the date of the first legislation against Irish, the Statute of Kilkenny of 1366, to the constitution of the Free State in 1922. Crowley's introduction connects these texts to current debates, taking the *Belfast Agreement* as an example, and illustrates how the language debates continue to have historical resonance today. Divided into six historical sections with detailed introductions, this unique sourcebook includes familiar cultural texts such as Spenser's *View of the Present State of Ireland* and essays and letters by Yeats and Synge, alongside less familiar writings, from introductions to the first Irish-English and English-Irish dictionaries to the Preface to the *New Testament* in Irish (1602).

Providing direct access to original texts, this is an historical resource book which can be used as a case study in the relations between language and cultural identity both in the present and the past.

THE POLITICS OF LANGUAGE
Series editors: Tony Crowley
University of Manchester
Talbot J. Taylor
College of William and Mary, Williamsburg, Virginia

In the lives of individuals and societies, language is a factor of greater importance than any other. For the study of language to remain solely the business of a handful of specialists would be a quite unacceptable state of affairs.
Ferdinand de Saussure

The Politics of Language series covers the field of language and cultural theory and will publish radical and innovative texts in this area. In recent years the developments and advances in the study of language and cultural criticism have brought to the fore a new set of questions. The shift from purely formal, analytical approaches has created an interest in the role of language in the social, political and ideological realms and the series will seek to address these problems with a clear and informed approach. The intention is to gain recognition for the central role of language in individual and public life.
Other books in the series include:

BROKEN ENGLISH
Dialects and the Politics of Language in Renaissance Writings
Paula Blank

VERBAL HYGIENE
Deborah Cameron

LINGUISTIC ECOLOGY
Language Change and Linguistic Imperialism in the Pacific Region
Peter Mühlhäusler

LANGUAGE IN HISTORY
Theories and Texts
Tony Crowley

LINGUISTIC CULTURE AND LANGUAGE POLICY
Harold F. Schiffman

ENGLISH AND THE DISCOURSES OF COLONIALISM
Alastair Pennycook

THE POLITICS OF LANGUAGE IN IRELAND 1366–1922

A Sourcebook

Tony Crowley

London and New York

First published 2000 by Routledge
11 New Fetter Lane, London EC4P 4EE

Simultaneously published in the USA and Canada
by Routledge
29 West 35th Street, New York, NY 10001

Routledge is an imprint of the Taylor & Francis Group

Typeset in Garamond by
BC Typesetting, Bristol
Printed and bound in Great Britain by
St Edmundsbury Press, Bury St Edmunds, Suffolk

British Library Cataloguing in Publication Data
A catalogue record for this book is available from the British Library

Library of Congress Cataloging in Publication Data
A catalogue record for this book has been requested

ISBN 0–415–15717–X (hbk)
ISBN 0–415–15718–8 (pbk)

IN MEMORIAM
CON CROWLEY
1936–1998

CONTENTS

CONTENTS

CONTENTS

CONTENTS

CONTENTS

CONTENTS

PREFACE

There are a number of points of information which will help the reader in the use of this text. 'Gaelic' and 'Irish' are used interchangeably to refer to the Irish language (an Gaeilge), not least because many of the authors included do so and it thus avoids confusion. English spelling has been left unaltered except where it affects sense or makes understanding difficult for a non-specialist reader. There is a particular problem with Irish spelling since there is no systematic orthography of Old, Middle and Early Modern Irish and the spelling system of Modern Irish (post *c*.1600) though mostly stable can also vary. Contemporary Irish was codified in 1958. I have striven to remain faithful to original spellings of text titles and names whenever possible.

There are a number of references to State Papers or municipal records in the earlier sections of the text and I have abbreviated them for convenience (in the order in which they occur) as follows:

Stat.Ire. *The Statutes at Large Passed in the Parliaments Held in Ireland* (1310–1761).

S.P.Hen. VIII. *State Papers, Henry VIII.*

Cal. pat. rolls Ire., Hen. VIII–Eliz. *Calendar of the Patent and Close Rolls of Chancery in Ireland, Henry VIII to 18th Elizabeth.*

Cal. S. P. Ire., 1509–73 [etc.] *Calendar of the State Papers Relating to Ireland, 1509–73 [etc.].*

Cal. pat. rolls Ire., Jas I *Irish Patent Rolls of James I.*

Anc. rec. Dublin *Calendar of Ancient Records of Dublin.*

At the end of the textual selections I have given an alternative to chronological or period-based approaches by suggesting thematic paths through the material. These are offered simply as ways of making sense, but I hope that the sheer oddness, coherence, zest, desperation, political importance and humour of the writings remain. I hope too, and have no doubt, that readers will replace my themes with their own.

ACKNOWLEDGEMENTS

I am grateful to the following for permission to reproduce material: Institiúid Ard-léinn Bhaile átha Cliath/Dublin Institute for Advanced Studies for the selection from *Pairlement Chloinne Tomáis*, ed. N. J. A. Williams, 1981; Oxford University Press for the text taken from 'The Irish Masque at Court', *Complete Works of Ben Jonson*, ed. C. H. Herford Percy and E. Simpson, 1941; *The Aran Islands*, J. M. Synge, ed. R. Skelton, 1979, and *J. M. Synge, Collected Works*, vol.II, ed. A. Price; Blackwell Publishers for material from *A Proposal for Correcting the ENGLISH TONGUE, Polite Conversation, Etc.*, ed. H. Davis with L. Landa, 1973.

I am grateful to the British Academy, the Leverhulme Trust and the John Rylands University Library Manchester, for their financial support.

The staff at the National Library of Ireland, and Trinity College Dublin, were always extremely helpful and courteous, as were the staff at the John Rylands University Library in Manchester, particularly those at Deansgate. I thank Stella Halkyard especially for her unfailing cheerfulness, efficiency and friendship; this book couldn't have been written without her help. I am indebted to both Seamus Deane and Declan Kiberd for their helpful comments and suggestions.

I wish to express my appreciation to a number of individuals: Ann and Peter McKee for their generosity and their introduction to the complications of Irish history a long time ago; Dr. Ian Adamson gave me access to his work freely; my editor at Routledge, Louisa Semlyen, and her editorial assistants, Miranda Filbee and Katharine Jacobson, have my gratitude for their patient support. I would also like to thank the following for their comradeship and intellectual stimulation (though none of it was ever formal or planned, which made it even more special): Kath Burlinson, Hugo Donnelly, Maud Ellmann, Paul Hamilton, Ken Hirschkop, Maria Lauret, John McGavin, Bella Millett, Edmund Papst, John Peacock, Jonathan Sawday and Robert Young. Isobel Armstrong made my experience at Southampton both possible and enjoyable; I owe her a great deal. My recent cohort of Ph.Ds have constantly challenged me and made me think again; I have very much enjoyed working with them. They are: Kevin Sullivan, Veronica Spencer, Maria Kuteeva, Karin Evans, Rachael Gilmour and Paul Young.

Neet knows what she means to me.

As ever I also give thanks to Jackie, Terry, Collette and Nicky Crowley, as well as all the kids: Jack, Ellie, Rory, Erin, Roisín, Tom, Matty, and our new one, Helen. Finally, my gratitude to the person to whom this book is dedicated, our dad and grandad, Con Crowley. As was said of him, he didn't just live life to the full, he did it with style; he's missed by everyone who knew him.

INTRODUCTION
Familiar and foreign

The language in which we are speaking is his before it is
mine . . . His language, so familiar and so foreign, will
always be for me an acquired speech . . .
Damn the dean of Studies . . . What did he come here for to
teach us his own language or to learn it from us?
(James Joyce, *Portrait of the Artist as a Young Man*)

Irish is spoken in the West Indies. English is a colonial language. Irish is the
language of the soul. English offers freedom from superstitious immorality.
Irish is the guarantor of Irishness. English is the language of poetry. Irish is
the key to the Protestant salvation of Ireland. English is the language of
modernity. Irish is the language which was used in Eden. English is the
only language of use to Irish emigrants. Irish is a philosophical language.
English is a bastardised, mongrel language. Irish is the language of the
past. English is the language of mundane commerce. Irish is a national
language. English is the language of intellectual rigour. Irish is familiar;
English is foreign. English is familiar; Irish is foreign.

The story of the relations between the two main languages of Ireland over
the past 600 years is quite as complicated as the history of the political relations between Ireland and England (and later, Ireland and the United Kingdom). Quite as tortuous and characterised just as much by rivalry, confusion,
misapprehension and bitterness, *as well as* fascination, apparently inevitable
attraction, and striking achievement. The sheer complexity of the story is
indicated by the assertions and claims set out above, all of which were
made during the period covered in this text. It is, by any standards, an extraordinary history and the aim of this collection is to provide access to it. This
has been attempted not so much by way of explicit guidance as by the selection of those materials which best illustrate both the ways in which arguments about the languages in question have developed, and the cultural
and political significance of those developments. Of course any selection is
already an interpretation – there is no way out of that particular bind –

1

but the intended achievement is the presentation of material, some of which may be familiar to students in the field, most of which will not, in such a way as to pose questions of received orthodoxies and modes of understanding. This is not to say, however, that the research for this collection consisted in a quest for heterodox, arcane or bizarre items which could be used to undermine an established history (or histories). Rather the research focused upon work with texts such as legal documents, religious works, grammar books, dictionaries, treatises on language, political pamphlets, newspapers and journals, and records of State, to name but a few of the sources. The result of that work, not previously available in this form, does in fact confirm a number of the claims made by dominant accounts of the history. Just as importantly, however, those accounts are challenged, sometimes opposed, and on occasion contradicted, by other material. This *is* a strange, unfamiliar and thus surprising story; perhaps its importance lies in that fact alone, but there is more to learn.

Simple versions of history are dangerous, though not quite as pernicious as the belief that all versions of the past are equally acceptable (a claim which rests on a misunderstanding of the nature of the criteria for validation and objectivity). In the case of the history of the relations between the languages of Ireland, however, the intent of the selection is to show that the reality has been much more difficult, convoluted and, that word again, complex, than has often been thought. To take the most obvious example, and this is a controversy which is bound to appear, the selected texts do not confirm the view held by traditional Irish nationalists that the near-death of the Irish language was simply the result of a crude policy implemented by the colonists as part of a plan to stamp out both the Irish nation and Catholicism in Ireland. A good deal of evidence to support this view will be found below since that is a major part of the story. The Tudor monarchs executed policy to this effect; Sir Richard Bingham advised Buckingham, pithily that the Irish were 'never tamed with words, but with swords'. And at the beginning of the eighteenth century and the end of the nineteenth, there were those who argued precisely for the extermination of the Irish language as part of a larger political project. But there are other elements to the story too. The first legislation proscribing the use of Gaelic was enacted against the English colonists rather than the native speakers of the language. The Statute of Kilkenny (1366) banned Irish in the Pale (the relatively small area of English rule); *de facto* the Statute recognised the Brehon (native Irish) code of law in the rest of the country. Protestantism itself has a long, inflected and interesting record of promoting the use of Gaelic as well as, sometimes at the same time as, arguing against it. Queen Elizabeth I sent a Gaelic fount to Ireland for the purpose of printing a translation of the Bible; she also expressed a desire to learn the language and she may, or may not, have been pleased to be presented with a Gaelic primer for the purpose. The complete Catholic version of the Bible only appeared in the late twentieth century. There are other apparent oddities in this history. Daniel O'Connell, the greatest leader of nineteenth-century Irish nationalism, spoke of seeing the demise of Gaelic without a sigh, despite the fact that he was a native speaker. He was opposed in that view by his contemporary nationalist ally, Thomas Davis, the Young Irelander from a Protestant backgound. Later in the century the most important figure in Irish cultural nationalism and the language wing of the Gaelic revival was Douglas Hyde, a firm Church of Ireland man. Irish political nationalism of the day was reluctant to engage with the language question, and apart from initial support in Counter-Reformation Europe, and the work of isolated clerics, the institutional Catholic Church was *very* late to get in on the act. Maynooth, the principal seminary for training priests and effectively the centre of Catholic intellectual life in Ireland after its foundation in 1795, used the English language. This was a confirmation of an already existing attitude, a point which was not lost on poets, commentators and the flock.

The history presented in this text, with all its shifting trends and manifestations, shows language often to be the vehicle for debates concerned with cultural identity and therefore political legitimacy. It is a story which resists simplicity, though as with most arguments which deal with these issues, there is a good deal of it about. Cultural identity (in all its differing forms) and the modes of political legitimacy which attach to it, are of course central to our sense of who we are, where we are, what we have a right to claim and expect, and what others have a right to ask and receive from us. How much more important will these issues have been, and continue to be, in lives and places which have had long experience of division, bitterness and, often enough, war? In those lives and places questions of identity and legitimacy have been and, again, continue to be, crucial; and for better or worse many of those questions do centre upon language. Models of language, which one way or another are models or definitions of community, are, as the texts will make clear, the basis upon which central acts of contestation have been played out. Tradition, innovation, purity, heterogeneity, civility, barbarity, origins, ends, foreignness, familiarity: these are amongst the things which have been at stake in the language debates which this text seeks to illustrate. It may even be that the presentation of these debates of the past will be a contribution to the ongoing arguments in the present. At the very least it will show historical difference, and that, if successful, can lead to a sense of our own historicity; which is as good a place as any to start thinking. The debates are not yet finished, however, and those which were seemingly concluded still resonate. Limitations of space have prevented a treatment of the politics of language in Ireland (by which is meant in this specific context the *island* of Ireland) in the period after the formation of the Saorstát (Free State) and Northern Ireland. It is intended that the developments of this later history will be considered in a later edition of this text, or in a companion volume to it. It is instructive to note briefly, however, a few examples from Ireland in the period after 1922 in order to see both the significance and the difficulty of questions around language.

There is little doubt that the revolution which gained for Ireland at least partial independence from colonial rule was inspired by the Irish language movement, of which, from 1893, the Gaelic League was the mainstay. Though dogmatically 'non-political' until 1915, the League served as the means by which Ireland's history was validated, its language celebrated and its national distinctiveness asserted. Having played such an important role in the shift in cultural and political thought which stimulated the struggle for independence, it could only be expected that the language would be elevated in the new State, and that it would be protected and promoted, and a start made on reversing the disastrous decline in the use of Gaelic which the nineteenth century had witnessed. And at first sight, once the Saorstát had been declared in 1922, and the Republic constituted in 1937, it appeared that such a policy was to be pursued. In the 1920s, for example, the simple presumption that fluency in Irish would be sought eagerly by all (a belief which flew in the face of the lessons of nineteenth-century history) played a part in the decline of the Gaelic League. After all, why rely on a self-funded voluntary organisation when the State itself could be relied upon to facilitate the good cause? And indeed the State did intervene in language policy: Irish became a compulsory subject in public examinations and a prerequisite for entry to the Civil Service and professions such as the law. The effect of this, as both Thomas Davis and Douglas Hyde had foreseen, was significant alienation from the language not simply amongst the Northern Unionists, but also, and more damagingly, amongst generations of Irish schoolchildren faced with imposed tuition in a language which was not that of their home, their playground or, for the vast majority, their adult life. There is a clear parallel with the crude imposition of the doctrine of Standard English on the schoolchildren of the United Kingdom in the same period. In both cases damage was done not simply to the children involved, but also to the cause of education in Irish and English respectively. It is hard to foster an interest, or facilitate empowerment, in a language which is seen as alien; it is impossible to cultivate a love for such a language if those who don't speak it are told that they are simply 'inauthentic' or 'inferior', to cite just two common epithets in the language debates which took place in both Ireland and the United Kingdom.

In *Bunreacht na hÉireann* (*Constitution of Ireland*), 1937, we find:

Article 4
The name of the State is Éire, or in the English language, *Ireland.*

Airteagal 4
Éire is ainm don Stát nó, sa Sacs-Bhéarla, *Ireland.*

With regard to the status of the English and the Irish languages the constitution is clear:

Article 8

1 The Irish language as the national language is the first official language.
2 The English language is recognised as a second official language.
3 Provision may, however, be made by law for the exclusive use of either of the said languages for any one or more official purposes, either throughout the State or in any part thereof.

Airteagal 8

1 Ós í an Ghaeilge an teanga náisiúnta is í an phríomhtheanga oifigiúil í.
2 Glactar leis an Sacs-Bhéarla mar theanga oifigúil eile.
3 Ach féadfar socrú a dhéanamh le dlí d'fhonn ceachtar den dá theanga sin a bheith ina haon-teanga le haghaidh aon ghnó nó gnóthaí oifigiúla ar fud an Stáit ar fad nó in aon chuid de.

In the case of any conflict of intrepretation between the two versions of the text, under the article concerned with the signing and promulgation of laws, the constitution is again explicit:

Article 25

4 In case of conflict between the texts of any copy of this Constitution enrolled under this section, the text in the national language shall prevail.

Airteagal 25

4 I gcás gan na téacsanna d'aon chóip áirithe de Bhunreacht seo a bheidh curtha isteach ina hiris faoin alt seo a bheith de réir a chéile, is ag an téacs Gaeilge a bheidh an forlámhas.

This seems to show that the makers of the new Ireland did decide to do exactly what had been asked of them by those who had campaigned with such vigour for the language in the thirty-odd years between 1890 and 1922; that is, to achieve the dream of placing the language at the centre of Ireland's political and cultural life.

As has already been noted, however, the reality was different, and it is apparent even from the relative ordering of the English and Irish versions of the constitution (verso and recto respectively). Despite the fact that the Gaelic text was given legal precedence, the English text was presented first not least because without it the Gaelic version did not make sense. As Breatnach observed, 'the Irish text contains a very large number of specially invented terms which can scarcely be said to have any legal or other connotation except by virtue of being equated with English legal terms' (Breatnach, 1956: 42). This was not the worst of the disappointments for language revivalists in the twentieth century. In the same way that the Gaelic League numbered hundreds of thousands in its membership rolls, but only a very small number of students who actually became fluent in the language, likewise the efforts of the State in halting the decline of Irish have failed dismally. Irish Independence did not bring a revival of Gaelic; if anything, it appears to have hastened its decay. It certainly led to a curious form of double vision typified in the attitude of that well-known oxymoron, the 'average individual', as given in the report of the Committee on Irish Language Attitudes in the mid-1970s:

> The average individual . . . has rather negative views about the way Irish has been taught in school and has a rather low or 'lukewarm' personal commitment to its use, although in this latter case, the average person has not sufficient ability in the language to converse freely in it. On the other hand, he strongly supports nearly all government efforts to help the Gaeltacht, but at the same time feels that the language is not very suitable for modern life.
>
> (Committee on Irish Language Attitudes, 1975: 24)

This ambivalence resulted from the combination of the *de jure* recognition given to the importance of the language in national life, and the *de facto* use of the English language as the sole medium of communication by the vast majority of the population. Indeed there was formal resistance to compulsory Irish: Yeats spoke against it, and in the 1960s the Language Freedom Movement (a title which eerily echoes the rhetoric of the nineteenth-century campaign for the restoration of Irish) opposed it. The State fudged the issue in the nineteen-seventies by retaining Irish as a compulsory subject of study but conceding the requirement of a pass in Irish in order to pass State or professional exams.

Things were not even this simple; the story twists again. For although the Gaeltacht (Irish-speaking) areas have grown ever smaller in the course of the century, they have successfully forced the Irish State to give more than rhetorical support to the survival of Irish. Material support for industrial initiatives, the introduction of political responsibility for the development of the Irish-speaking areas, and the creation of media outlets – a radio and television station – have significantly improved the prospects of the Gaeltacht. In addition there have been mini-revivals in the urban centres of Galway, Cork and Dublin, as evinced by the appearance of scoileanna Gaelacha (Irish-speaking schools). The greatest irony, however, is that the major upsurge of interest in the language, both institutional and personal, has taken place outside the Republic of Ireland and without the support

of the Irish State. It has grown in fact in the nationalist areas of Northern
Ireland over the past twenty-odd years and was stimulated to a great
extent (though not entirely) by the use of the language as a political issue
by republican prisoners and Sinn Féin activists; *An Lá* is a daily paper in
West Belfast. The wag who made the crack about the Gaeltacht becoming
the Jailtacht, though, was telling an old joke: Aodh MacCruitín (Hugh Mac-
Curtin) was imprisoned by Sir Richard Cox for satirising Cox's *Hibernia
Anglicana* (1690), particularly its denunciation of Irish. Being the recidivist
that he was, MacCruitín passed his time working on an Irish Grammar (*The
Elements of the Irish Language*, 1728).

The Gaelic revival in Northern Ireland is, again, clearly an aspect of the
continuing struggle there over cultural identity and political legitimation.
Sinn Féin's position is articulated by Ó Maolchraoibhe, a representative of
the party's Cultural Department (set up in 1982):

> When the men in the H-Blocks of Long Kesh jail and the women in
> Armagh prison were stripped of everything, they realised that the
> most Irish thing they had was their Irish language. Learning it,
> speaking it all day, was a way of resisting, of asserting your identity.
> (Ó Maolcraoibhe 1984: 9)

The party's President, Gerry Adams, stated his own position in arguing:

> that the restoration of our culture must be a crucial part of our
> struggle and that the restoration of the Irish language must be a
> central part of the cultural struggle.
> (Adams 1986: 143–4)

Adams supported his contention with reference to the words of Máirtín Ó
Cadhain (IRA activist, Professor of Irish at Trinity College Dublin, and
one of modern Ireland's major writers in Gaelic): 'Tosóidh athghabháil na
hÉireann le hathghabháil na Gaeilge' (The reconquest of Ireland will
begin with the reconquest of the Irish language) (ibid.: 144).

That Sinn Féin should see the Irish language as having a role to play in
contemporary political debate is hardly surprising given its historical lineage.
That one of its political opponents should dispute the same ground with
them is more striking, but this is the tactic employed by the Loyalist politician and intellectual Ian Adamson. Adamson takes on the nationalist claim
to cultural ascendancy which is based on the assertion of the historical continuity of Gaelic identity, by countering with an appeal to an even earlier
form of civilisation:

> The ancient British Cruthin or 'Cruithne' formed the bulk of the
> population of both Ulster and North Britain in early Christian

times and they are therefore the earliest recorded ancestors not only of the people of Ulster but those of Scotland as well.

(Adamson 1982: 1)

Needless to say, of course, this people had their own language (Brittonic, or Old British) and identity: 'Gaelic did not arrive in Ireland until *even later*, at a time when the ancient British and Gaels thought of themselves as distinct peoples.' When Gaelic did arrive, it became the vehicle of colonial dispossession: 'Old British was displaced in Ireland by Gaelic just as English later displaced Gaelic' (ibid.).

But if this intervention in the war of words is striking, there are others which illustrate how unpredictable and historically specific these debates have been – and are. The first was voiced in the magazine of another group opposed to the nationalist and republican agenda, the Loyalist paramilitary group the Ulster Volunteer Force. In a note on the first edition of Ó Snodaigh's *Hidden Ulster: Protestants and the Irish Language*, the anonymous reviewer acknowledged that 'the majority of Ulster Protestants equate Gaelic and Irish culture with Roman Catholicism' and that they believed that 'no "good prod" would have anything to do with such Popish traditions'. The writer argued, however, that this was a misconception:

> The truth of the matter is, Ulster Protestants have as much claim, if not more in some cases, to the Gaelic culture as the Roman Catholic population. Someone once said that the Irish language was stolen from the Protestant people by the Papists; it would be more correct to say that the Protestant people gave their culture away to the Roman Catholics.
>
> (Ó Snodaigh 1995: 130)

There are two remarkable points here which are worth noting. One is that this claim was made in 1974, at a time when the war in Northern Ireland was at its bitter sectarian height. A second is that the rebuke to the Protestant community for giving away their linguistic heritage is remarkably similar to that delivered by Stephen Dedalus to the young Irish nationalist Davin in *A Portrait of the Artist as a Young Man*.

If this contribution to the debate is surprising, or at least certainly not well known, then the final example, given the historical context, is remarkable. There has been conflict in Ireland for over eight hundred years, starting with colonial invasion and ending, it has to be hoped, with a political settlement. It is a conflict which has taken various forms at specific points, but which can in general terms be described as a struggle for political status, recognition and legitimacy by different communities under particular historical conditions. The complications of that struggle, and its multifarious manifestations, are illustrated in the texts selected in this book.

Here, however, it may be interesting to note a similarity and distinction between an early phase of that struggle and what may, with any luck, turn out to be one of its latter stages. The similarity is evident in the attitude taken by the ruling power towards Gaelic culture in an area of the island of Ireland in which English, later British, writ was upheld. Among other proscriptions, the Statute of Kilkenny ordained that 'if any English, or Irish living among the English, use the Irish language among themselves', and were convicted of the offence, then the offender should lose either their property or their liberty. Likewise, until recently, the practice of the British State in Northern Ireland towards the use of the Irish language was at best simply negative and at worst actively hostile. Speaking in Gaelic, for instance, to give a name and address to a policeman, soldier or member of the judiciary in Northern Ireland, invited prosecution for the obstruction of justice (though a thump was more likely).

In war, life is the first casualty, truth may be the second, but respect for cultural difference is up there with them. In peace, however, tolerance of cultural difference must come to the fore as a crucial element of any settlement. And language, once more, will figure as an important factor in the resolution of the conflict in Ireland. Perhaps no more than five years ago, the speaking of Gaelic in particular contexts in Northern Ireland would have been enough to provoke serious consequences. Of all the strange twists and turns of the language debates covered in this text, it may be that the final example is the oddest of all. The *Belfast Agreement* was subscribed to by almost all shades of political opinion, from the Irish nationalism of the Irish Government to the Unionism of the British Government, and, at least as significantly, from Loyalist paramilitary groups to Sinn Féin; it was also overwhelmingly supported by the majority of the electorate both North and South. As part of the accord, under the heading of 'Rights, Safeguards and Equality of Opportunity: Economic, Social and Cultural Issues', it was declared that

> All participants recognise the importance of respect, understanding and tolerance in relation to linguistic diversity, including in Northern Ireland, the Irish language, Ulster Scots and the languages of the various ethnic communities, all of which are part of the cultural wealth of the island of Ireland.
>
> (*Belfast Agreement* 1998: 19)

The British Government further committed itself, 'in relation to the Irish language, where appropriate and where people so desire it', to

> take resolute action to promote the language;
> facilitate and encourage the use of the language in speech and writing in public and private life where there is appropriate demand;

seek to remove, where possible, restrictions which would discourage or work against the maintenance or development of the language; make provision for liaising with the Irish language community, representing their views to public authorities and investigating complaints;

place a statutory duty on the Department of Education to encourage and facilitate Irish medium education in line with current provision for integrated education;

explore urgently with the relevant British authorities, and in co-operation with the Irish broadcasting authorities, the scope for achieving more widespread availability of Teilifís na Gaeilige in Northern Ireland; and seek more effective ways to encourage and provide financial support for Irish language film and television production in Northern Ireland.

(Ibid.)

The status of Irish as a language of danger, of defensive assertiveness, of an embattled identity, has been altered: now it is the British State which promises to encourage it, maintain it, and of course pay for it. Moreover, the British Government has also decreed that the Irish language can be a subject in the National Curriculum in the United Kingdom from 1999. Whatever the eventual outcome in practice, and a year after the *Agreement* there have already been republican complaints of slow movement in the implementation of the language policies it promised, the irony of this enormous shift can best be appreciated in the context of the history explored in this collection of texts.

A final twist in the story is easy to miss, not least because of the remarkable new status given to the Irish language. But it is important to note, since it is possible that in the end it may be more significant. For as well as its commitment to Gaelic, the *Belfast Agreement* also pledged to respect linguistic diversity in relation to 'Ulster Scots and the languages of the various ethnic communities', on the basis of their formation of part of the cultural riches of the whole island of Ireland. Such a declaration was in fact simply catching up with recent developments in the recognition and validation of forms of language and the identities which go with them (developments which had been prefigured in various ways in texts such as those of Boorde in 1547, Swift in 1735, and the anonymous author of the 'Dialogue in the Ulster Dialect' in 1858). In *A New Look at the Language Question*, published by Field Day in 1983, Tom Paulin issued an appeal for a dictionary of Hiberno-English; his call was met by the publication of Dolan's *Dictionary of Hiberno-English* in 1998. The year of 1996 saw the appearance of *A Concise Ulster Dictionary*, published by that long-standing institution of linguistic codification, Oxford University Press. Thus whatever the consequences of the recognition of Gaelic, the promise to accord respect to the other languages of Ireland – Ulster Scots, Ulster English, Hiberno-English (and its varieties) – may prove to be a more radical measure in the long run.

To reiterate: the aim of this selection is to present the peculiar history of the main languages of Ireland with two purposes in mind. The first is to show the historically shifting allegiances, loyalties, identities – and their attendant political implications – gathered around language, or forms of language, in Ireland from the Statute of Kilkenny to the declaration of the Saorstát. The second, which is dependent upon the first, is to demonstrate that the history is much more complicated than is often thought, and that received versions are on occasion unnecessarily divisive precisely because they are too simple. Language(s), rather than being disputed territory, might turn out to be the common ground upon which both agreement and disagreement are possible.

1

1366–1534

INTRODUCTION

The Anglo-Norman invasion of Ireland, which began in 1169 with the official purpose of bringing the Irish Church and State to order (hence the Papal support of *Laudabiliter*) rapidly became a more extensive project. Henry II's arrival in Ireland in 1171 achieved three distinct but related ends: recognition from the Irish bishops, the assertion of lordship over his Norman subjects, and the submission of several important Gaelic chieftains. Whether this was what Henry intended is in fact doubtful but, once completed, this series of events altered radically the link between the English Crown and Ireland and set off events that were to continue for eight hundred years or more. One of the immediate legacies of the invasion was the creation of a complex linguistic situation. Gaelic culture, despite the Viking raids and settlements and the ecclesiastical contacts with Europe, was relatively self-contained. The native population spoke Irish and there was already a written heritage in Old and Middle Irish (the oldest vernacular tradition in western Europe) as well as in Latin. The invaders brought to this culture a number of languages: the ruling group spoke Norman French; there were Welsh-speaking bowmen and Flemish men-at-arms; the general soldiery used English. Welsh and Flemish were to be of negligible import, but Norman French was retained for almost two centuries after the conquest as the medium (with Latin) of officialdom – commerce, civil government and law. Indeed one of the ironies of the Statute of Kilkenny, one purpose of which was to ordain that 'every Englishman do use the English language', was that it was written in Norman French. Gradually, however, it too faded under pressure from both Gaelic and English as medieval Ireland settled into a confrontation between, and interpenetration of, the cultures of *Gaedhil* and *Gaill*.

The initial success of the invaders, though slow, was extensive. A century after the invasion they had attained secure bases in Leinster and parts of Ulster and Munster, the towns in particular being strongholds; the rest of the country remained Gaelic. With the decay of Norman French (Normandy was lost to the English Crown as early as 1204) English began to emerge as the language of the Anglo-Norman settlements, though Irish was also clearly in use in them. During the thirteenth century, discord among the Anglo-Norman nobles, added to an increasing distance from the interests of the English Crown, inaugurated a period of decline in their power. As a corollary what was to become known as the Gaelic recovery took place, beginning in the mid- to late-thirteenth century and lasting to the start of the sixteenth. One of the practical consequences of the recovery was the Gaelicisation of the Anglo-Normans, or to put it another way, their assimilation into Irish society. For present purposes the most important aspect of this process was its cultural effect; it is here that the history presented in this *Reader* begins.

Ireland has long been afflicted by a particularly irritating nuisance known to historians as the cultural observer. Giraldus Cambrensis (Gerald of Wales) is the earliest and most notorious. Historian and apologist for the colonial invasion, his *Topography of Ireland* (1188) was enormously influential with later commentators and provided the catalyst for several significant replies in the debates which will be presented later in this book. The Anglo-Irish Chronicles of the Tudor and Stuart periods rely heavily upon Giraldus, and native historians such as Céitinn (Keating), Lynch and MacCruitín (MacCurtin) engage in hostile debate with his text. As one would expect of a polemical justification of the colonisation, his depiction of the Irish was highly negative, accusing them, among other things, of cultural barbarism, political treachery, laziness, paganism, incest, inconstancy and bestiality. Their alleged treachery in particular caused Giraldus to observe a pattern which was later a matter of great concern to the colonial rulers of Ireland:

> the pest of treachery has here grown to such a height – it has so taken root, and long abuse has succeeded in turning it into a second nature – habits are so formed by mutual intercourse, as he who handles pitch cannot escape its stains – that the evil has acquired great force . . . Thus, I say, 'evil communications corrupt good manners'; and even strangers who land here from other countries become generally imbued with this national crime, which seems to be innate and very contagious.
>
> (Giraldus Cambrensis 1863: 137–8)

What Giraldus comments on in passing was a central consideration in the framing of colonial legislation in both medieval and early modern Ireland: how to stop the Gaelicisation of the descendants of the Anglo-Norman invaders. Law, as often a guide to the fears (real or imagined) of the powerful, was intended to prevent the English from becoming *Hiberniores Hibernis ipsis* (more Irish than the Irish themselves).

The Gaelic recovery, political and cultural, meant that colonial governance moved to a defensive strategy of consolidating its power and keeping the native Irish at bay. In time this was to create the English Pale, a term first used in the

1490s to refer to the relatively small area around Dublin in which English writ ran and English culture and language were supposed to be practised. So strong was the recovery that by 1500 Irish had displaced English in all but the major towns, the Pale itself, and the Baronies of Forth and Bargy in Wexford. This process, and the reaction to it, is explored in the texts presented in this first chapter. It is worth noting the penalties stipulated in the legal orders as an indication of the colonial view of the gravity of the threat. The extent of the use of Irish is shown by the arrangement permitting legal proceedings to be held in Gaelic if necessary (this has added significance in this case given Waterford's attested loyalty to the English Crown). The success of legislative attempts to halt Gaelicisation is demonstrated by the exclusion of the language issue from the reconfirmation of the Kilkenny Statute in 1495; the Statute was, however, invoked again in 1588.

1.1 *The Statute of Kilkenny*, 1366

Whereas at the conquest of the land of Ireland, and for a long time after, the English of the said land used the English language, mode of riding and apparel, and were governed and ruled, both they and their subjects called Betaghes, according to the English law, in which time God and holy Church, and their franchises according to their condition were maintained [and themselves lived] in [due] subjection; but now many English of the said land, forsaking the English language, manners, mode of riding, laws and usages, live and govern themselves according to the manners, fashion, and language of the Irish enemies; and also have made divers marriages and alliances between themselves and the Irish enemies aforesaid; whereby the said land, and the liege people thereof, the English language, the allegiance due to our lord the King, and the English laws there, are put in subjection and decayed, and the Irish enemies exalted and raised up, contrary to reason; our Lord the King considering the mischiefs aforesaid, in consequence of the grievous complaints of the commons of his said land, called to his Parliament held at Kilkenny, the Thursday next after the day of Cinders, in the fortieth year of his reign, before his well-beloved son, Lionel Duke of Clarence, his lieutenant in the parts of Ireland, to the honour of God and of His Glorious Mother, and of holy Church, and for the good government of the said land, and quiet of the people, and for the better observation of the laws, and punishment of evil doers there, are ordained and established by our said Lord the King, and his said lieutenant, and our Lord the King's counsel there, with the assent of the archbishops, bishops, abbots, and priors (as to what appertains to them to assent to), the earls, barons, and others the commons of the said land, at the said parliament being and assembled, the ordinances and articles under written, to be held and kept perpetually upon the pains contained therein. . . .

I. First, it is ordained, agreed to, and established, that holy Church shall be free, and have all her franchises without injury, according to the franchises ordained and granted by our Lord the King, or his progenitors, by statute or ordinance made in England or in Ireland heretofore. . . .

II. Also, it is ordained, and established, that no alliance by marriage, gossipred, fostering of children, concubinage or by amour, not in any other manner, be henceforth made between the English and the Irish of one part, or of the other part; and that no Englishman, nor other person, being at peace, do give or sell to any Irishman, in time of peace or war, horses or armour, nor any manner of victuals in time of war; and if any shall do to the contrary, and thereof be attainted, he shall have judgement of life and member, as a traitor to our lord the King.

III. Also, it is ordained and established, that every Englishman do use the English language, and be named by an English name, leaving off entirely the manner of naming used by the Irish; and that every Englishman use the English custom, fashion, mode of riding and apparel, according to his estate; and if any English, or Irish living among the English, use the Irish language amongst themselves, contrary to this ordinance, and thereof be attainted, his lands and tenements, if he have any, shall be seized into the hands of his immediate lord, until he shall come to one of the places of our Lord the King, and find sufficient surety to adopt and use the English language, and then he shall have restitution of his said lands, by writ issued out of said places. In case that such person shall not have lands and tenements, his body shall be taken off by any of the officers of our Lord the King, and committed to the next gaol, there to remain until he, or some other in his name, shall find sufficient surety in the manner aforesaid: And that no Englishman who shall have the value of one hundred pounds of land or of rent by the year, shall ride otherwise than on a saddle in the English fashion; and he that shall do to the contrary, and shall be thereof attainted, his horse shall be forfeited to our Lord the King, and his body shall be committed to prison, until he pay a fine according to the King's pleasure for the contempt aforesaid; and also, that beneficed persons of holy Church, living amongst the English, shall use the English language; and if they do not, that their ordinaries shall have issues of their benefices until they use the English language in the manner aforesaid; and they shall have respite in order to learn the English language, and to provide saddles, between this time and the feast of St Michael next coming.

IV. Also, whereas diversity of government and different laws in the same land cause difference in allegiance, and disputes among the people; it is agreed and established, that no Englishman, having disputes with any other Englishman, shall henceforth make caption, or take pledge, distress or vengeance against any other, whereby the people may be troubled, but that they shall sue each other at the common law; and that no Englishman be governed in the termination of their disputes by March law nor Brehon law, which reasonably ought not to be called law, being a bad custom; but they shall be governed, as right is, by the common law of the land, as liege subjects of our Lord the King; and if any do to the contrary, and thereof be attainted, he shall be taken and imprisoned, and adjudged as a traitor; and that no difference of allegiance shall henceforth be made between the English born in Ireland, and the English born in England, by calling them English hob, or Irish dog, but that all be called by one name, the English lieges of our Lord the King; and he who shall be found to the contrary, shall be punished by imprisonment of a year, and afterwards fined, at the King's pleasure. . . .

VI. Also, whereas a land, which is at war, requires that every person do render himself able to defend himself, it is ordained, and established, that the commons of the said land of Ireland, who are in the different marches at war, do not, henceforth use the plays which men call hurling, with great sticks [and a ball] upon the ground, from which great evils and maims have arisen, to the weakening of the defence of the said land, and other plays which men call quoit; but that they do apply and accustom themselves to use and draw bows, and throw lances, and other gentlemenlike games, whereby the Irish enemies may be the better checked by the liege people and commons of these parts; and if any do or practise the contrary, and of this be attainted, they shall be taken and imprisoned, and fined at the will of our Lord the King.

1.2 *Stat.Ire.* An Act that the Irishmen Dwelling in the Counties of Dublin, Meath, Uriel, and Kildare, Shall Go Apparelled like Englishmen, and Wear their Beards after the English Manner, Swear Allegiance, and Take English Surname, 1465.

At the request of the commons it is ordained and established by authority of said Parliament, that every Irishman, that dwells betwixt or amongst Englishmen in the county of Dublin, Meath, Uriel and Kildare, shall go like to one Englishman in apparel and shaving of his beard above the mouth, and shall be within one year sworn the liege man of the king in the hands of the lieutenant or deputy, or such as he will assign to receive this oath, for the multitude that is to be sworn, and shall take him to an English surname of one town, as Sutton, Chester, Trim, Cork, Kinsale: or colour, as white, black, brown: or art or science, as smith or carpenter: or office, as cook, butler, and that he and his issue shall use this name, under pain of forfeiting of his good yearly, till the premisses be done to be levied two times by the year to the King's wars, according to the direction of the lieutenant of the King or his deputy.

1.3 *Archives of the Municipal Corporation of Waterford*, 1492–3

Also, in the said day and year, it was enacted that no manner of man, free-man nor foreign, of the city or suburb dwellers, shall plead nor defend in the Irish tongue against any man in the court, but that all they that any matters shall have in court to be ministered shall have a man that can speak English to declare his matter, except if one party be of the country; then every such dweller shall be at liberty to speak Irish.

1.4 *Stat.Ire.* An Act of Confirmation of the Statutes of Kilkenny, 1495

Item, pray the commons, that forasmuch as the statutes of Kilkenny were made and ordained for the public weal of the King's subjects of Ireland to keep them under due order and obeyance, and all the season that the said statutes were set in use, and duly executed, the said land continued in prosperity and honour, and since the time that they were not executed, the foresaid subjects rebelled, and digressed from their allegiance, and the land did fall to ruin and desolation: the premisses considered, that it be ordained, enacted, and established by authority of this present parliament, that all and every of the foresaid statutes (those that will, that every subject shall ride in a saddle, and those that speaketh of the Irish language, only excepted) be authorised, approved, confirmed, and deemed good and effectual in law, duly to be enquired of, and to be executed according to the tenors and pur-port of them, and every of them; any act or ordinance made to the contrary of them notwithstanding.

2

1534–1607

INTRODUCTION

The practice of Tudor and early Stuart rule in Ireland mirrored to a great extent that exercised in England, Wales and, later, Scotland: the centralisation of the State, the running of a relatively efficient bureaucracy, and the consolidation and development of the monarch's powers. In Ireland, in the light of the circumstances set out in Chapter 1, this meant the extension of English rule beyond the borders of the Pale by means of legal dictate, military conquest, sequestration of land, and plantation of a loyal population. This state of conflict was exacerbated by the new factor of religious difference. Henry VIII's break with Rome and the passing of the Act of Supremacy in the Irish Parliament (1537), confirming the King and his successors as supreme Head of the Church of Ireland, began a new phase in Anglo–Irish relations. The distinction which the Statute of Kilkenny had interdicted, between 'the English born in Ireland, and 'the English born in England', was already in use by the beginning of the sixteenth century. It became sharper during this period and developed along religious lines: the *Sean Ghaill* (Old English) aligned themselves increasingly with the Gaelic order and Catholicism, while the *Nua Ghaill* (New English) were firmly Protestant and loyal to the Crown. The split, though significant at this stage, issued in the political confederation of the Gaels and the *Sean Ghaill* only later in the rising of 1641.

Colonial rule in Ireland in this period can be, and was, presented as simply the military conquest of a troublesome, infidel dominion. The Minutes of Council of 1546, for example, reveal the day-to-day concerns of colonial administration which were to be repeated later the world over:

> Mines. Mint. Chancellorship. Exchanges with Ormond. Prisage of wines. Viceregent for the clergy. Judge's salaries. Resident Council. Council at Limerick. Martial Law. McAlister and McClean. Coin and livery. English habit and tongue. Reformation of Leinster. Archbishop of Armagh. Wyse, and Francis Habart to be of the Council. Wm.Keting. Auditors. O'Conor. O'Mulmoy. Money.

The Plantations were the exemplary manifestation of the colonial solution to the political, religious and cultural problems presented in Ireland. Commenced under Queen Mary in the 1550s, Plantation was deployed as an answer to uprising or rebellion until after 1690.

Yet despite this militarist response, attitudes and practices to the Irish language were somewhat ambivalent. The language question evidently remained a problem. Chancellor Gerrard listed the 'evils which annoy the English Pale' in 1580 as

> want of churches, curates, discipline, schools, marrying with the Irish, want of gaols, armour, and musters. Irish speech. Irish habit. Hard setting of lands, increasing cottiers. Want of inclosures.

Even the Bill declaring Henry VIII King of Ireland (1541) had to be presented in Irish to both the Irish Commons and Lords. To remedy the difficulty, legislation was passed against the use of Irish within areas of English rule. At times of political tension the measures suggested to control the threat of Gaelic were severe. Henry Sidney, a less efficient colonial servant than is often argued, recommended the simple abolition of the Irish language together with the martial execution of adherents to the Gaelic order ranging from Jesuits to brehons and bards. Yet even Sidney proposed as part of his drastic policy the extension of education for the purposes of reform. This was a commonplace of the period and included the call for, and granting of, a University College in Dublin (Trinity College was established in 1592) and the reiterated appeal for the erection of schools for the education of children in the English language. Henry VIII's order to this effect was finally put into practice three centuries later with the introduction of the National Schools in 1833.

The uncertain stance of the State towards Irish is clearest in relation to religion. One of the basic tenets of the Reformation was that religious instruction should be delivered in the vernacular, a principle taken seriously by Elizabeth. She sent a Gaelic fount to Ireland, encouraged the translation of The Bible (the *New Testament* was completed in 1602) and accepted a Gaelic primer from Lord Delvin. Her colonial administrators were also prompted to the use of Irish speakers in their clerical relations with the native Irish. Part of this engagement by the State with Irish in the religious domain in the latter part of the century can be attributed to the appearance of the first book printed in Irish, Carsuel's *Foirm na nUrrnuidheadh* (1567), a Presbyterian translation of the *Book of Common Order*. The established Church in Ireland, anxious about the influence of Presbyterianism, responded with the publication in 1570 of Ó Cearnaigh's *Aibidil Gaoidheilge and Caiticiosma* (*Gaelic Alphabet and Catechism*), the first book in Irish to be printed in Ireland, the *New Testament* (1602) and the *Book of Common Prayer* (1608). But the policy of preaching to the Irish in their own language, with all the complications that involved, was seen as a necessary accompaniment to the subjugation of the land.

19

Gaelic culture and the language were, however, subject to hostile treatment at the hands of the Anglo-Irish chroniclers (Campion, Stanihurst and Spenser in this chapter, Davies and Moryson in Chapter 3). Following the lead given by Giraldus, and plagiarising with facility from each other, the chroniclers ridiculed both Irish historiography and the Irish character. Their pet theme was that of 'degeneration', the process by which the English destroyed their 'genus' or 'type' (lost their 'Englishness' would be a modern way of putting this, but that does not convey the negative sense of the original) by becoming Irish. Other targets were the accounts of the origin of the Irish and their language, which in turn drew fierce responses from the Gaelic historians, including in the mid-seventeenth century that of Seathrún Céitinn, one of the Old English. This rejection of the language of the native population, however, has to be set against the representations of both Gaelic (Boorde is the first to attempt a stylised transcription of Irish speech) and the new form of language which had already appeared by this point: Hiberno-English. The appearance of speakers of this language in the drama of the period points to a recognition, albeit indirect, that this is an important development. Indeed, the uncertain representation of MacMorris in *Henry the Fifth* (though he is argumentative, touchy about his identity and loyalty, and unable to pronounce English 'properly', he is not the stage-Irishman type depicted in Jonson's *Irish Masque*) reveals a certain lack of confidence in relation to Gaelic culture rather than colonial arrogance.

In 1500 Irish was clearly the dominant spoken language of Ireland; at the century's end it was still the most extensive mode of speech but it was already under pressure from English.

2.1 *S.P.Hen.VIII.* Henry VIII to the Town of Galway, 1536

Well beloved, we greet you well. Signifying unto you that we, willing of our tender and zeal we bear unto you, to the furthering of your weal, profit and commodity, and the extirpation of all abuses hitherto used or accustomed amongst you, that you firmly and unfeignedly observe the devices and articles ensuing, perpetually. . . .

Item, that every inhabitant within the said town endeavour themselves to speak English, and to use themselves after the English fashion; and especially that you, and every [one] of you, do put forth your child to school, to learn to speak English, and that you fail not to fulfil this our commandment, as you tender our favour, and would avoid our indignation and high displeasure.

2.2 *Cal.pat.rolls Ire., Hen.VIII–Eliz,* 1536

Appointment of Anthony Selenger, George Powlett, Thomas Moyle, and William Barners, Commissioners for letting, for the term of 21 years, such as the King's honours, manors, lordships, lands and tenements as lie waste upon the marches of the English pale; upon condition that the tenants shall use the English tongue, the English habit, and forbear from alliance or familiarity with the Irish.

2.3 *Stat.Ire.* An Act for the English Order, Habit, and Language, 1537

I. The King's majesty, our most gracious and most redoubted sovereign lord, prepending and weighing by his great wisdom, learning, and experience, how much it more doth confer to the induction of rude and ignorant people to the knowledge of Almighty God, and of the good and virtuous obedience, which by his most holy precepts and commandments, they owe to their princes and superiors, than a good instruction in his most blessed laws, with a confirmity, concordance, and familiarity in language, tongue, in manners, order, and apparel, with them that be civil people, and do profess and acknowledge Christ's religion, and civil and political orders, laws and directions, as his Grace's subjects of this part of this his land of Ireland, that is called the English pale, doth; and most graciously considering therewith upon the great love, zeal, and desire, which his most excellent Majesty hath to the advancement of the state of this his said land, and to conveyance and training of his people of the same, to an honest christian civility and obedience, whom his Highness tendreth as his members of this political body, whereof immediately under God, he is supreme head and governor, that there is again nothing which doth more contain and keep many of his subjects of this his said land, in a certain savage and wild kind and manner of living, than the diversity that is betwixt them in tongue, language, order, and habit, which by the eye deceiveth the multitude, and persuadeth unto them, that they should be as it were of sundry sorts, or rather of sundry countries, where indeed they be wholly together one body, whereof his highness is the only head under God, as is aforesaid, of his most noble and princely disposition, and fervent zeal, which his Highness hath and beareth to the advancement of the state of this his land, for a certain direction and order to be had, that all we his said subjects thereof, might the better know God, and do that thing that might in time be and redound to our own wealth, quiet, and commodity, doth not only desire that all such good laws, as by wise, godly and prudent princes, his most noble progenitors, have been heretofore made for the use of the English tongue, habit and order, within this his said land, may be put in due execution, but also that the same may be so established, and in this present Parliament brought to such a perfection, that the said English tongue, habit and order, may from henceforth continually (and without ceasing or returning at any time to Irish habit, or language) be used by all men that will acknowledge themselves according to their duties of allegiance, to be his Highness's true and faithful subjects, his Majesty doth hereby intimate unto all his said subjects of this land, of all degrees, that whosoever shall, for any respect, at any time, decline from the order and purpose of this law, touching the increase of the English tongue, habit, and order, or shall suffer any within his family or rule, to use the Irish habit, or not to use themselves to the English tongue, his Majesty will repute them in his noble heart as persons that esteem not his most dread laws and commandments, but whatsoever they shall at other times pretend in words and countenance, to be persons of another sort and inclination than becometh the true and faithful subjects. . . .

III. And be it enacted by authority aforesaid, That every person or persons, the King's true subjects, inhabiting this land of Ireland, of what estate, condition, or degree he or they be, or shall be, to the uttermost of their power, cunning, and knowledge, shall use and speak commonly the English tongue and language, and that every such person and persons, having child or children, shall endeavour themselves to cause and procure his said child and children to use and speak the English tongue and language, and according to his or their ability, cunning, and power, shall bring up and keep his said child and children in such places, where they shall or may have occasion to learn the English tongue, language, order and condition. . . .

IX. And further be it enacted by authority aforesaid, That every archbishop, bishop, suffragan, and every other having authority and power, to give order of priesthood, deacon, and subdeacon, shall at such time as they or any of them do give to any person or persons, any of the said orders of priesthood, deacon, or subdeacon, give unto every person taking any of the said orders of priesthood, deacon, or subdeacon, a corporal oath that he or they so taking order as is aforesaid, shall to the utmost of his power, wit, and cunning, endeavour himself to learn the English tongue and language, and use English order and fashions, if he may learn and attain the same by possibility, in such place and places, where his cure or dwelling shall be; and further, shall endeavour himself to move, educate, and teach all other being under his order, rule and governance, to accomplish and perform the same, and that also every such archbishop, bishop, suffragan, archdeacon, commissary, and other having power and authority, to admit, install, collate, institute or induct, any person or persons, to any dignity, benefice, office or promotion spiritual, as is aforesaid, shall at the time of the admission, institution, installation, collation and induction of such person and persons, to any dignity, benefice, office or promotion spiritual, give unto the said person and persons, so admitted, instituted, installed, collated, or inducted, a corporal oath, that he and they so being admitted, instituted, installed, collated, or inducted, shall to his wit and cunning, endeavour himself to learn, instruct, and teach the English tongue, to all and every being under his rule, cure, order, or governance, and in likewise shall bid the beads in the English tongue, and preach the word of God in English, if he can preach, and also for his own part shall use the English order and habit, and also provoke as many as he may to the same, and also shall keep, or cause to be kept within the place, territory, or parish where he shall have pre-eminence, rule, benefice or promotion, a school for to learn English, if any children of his parish come to him to learn the same, taking for the keeping of the same school, such convenient stipend or salary, as in the said land is accustomably used to be taken.

2.4 *Cal.S.P.Ire.*, 1509–73, 1537

An abstract of the misorders and evil rule within the land of Ireland. All the English March borderers use Irish apparel and the Irish tongue, as well in peace as in war, and for the most part use the same in the English Pale, unless they come to Parliament or Council.

2.5 *S.P.Hen VIII.* Lord Deputy and the Council of Ireland to Cromwell, 1539

May it please your Lordship to be advertised . . . it hath been openly bruited the King Grace's pleasure to be, that all the monastries within this land should be suppressed. Amongst which, for the common weal of this land, if it might stand with the King's gracious pleasure, by your good Lordship's advertisement, in our opinion it were right expedient, that six houses should stand and continue, changing their clothing and rule into such sort and order, as the King's Grace shall win them: which are named Saint Mary's Abbey adjoining to Dublin, a house of White Monks: Christ Church, a house of Canons, situated in the midst of the city of Dublin; the nunnery of Grace-Dew, in the county of Dublin; Conall in the county of Kildare; Kenlys and Gerepont, in the county of Kilkenny . . . in them young men and children, both gentlemen's children and other, both of mankind and womankind, be brought up in virtue, learning, and in the English tongue and behaviour, to the great charge of the said houses.

2.6 *The First Book of the Introduction of Knowledge,* Andrew Boorde, 1547

I am an Irishman, in Ireland I was born;
I love to wear a saffron shirt, although it be to-torn.
My anger and my hastiness doth hurt me full sore;
I cannot leave it, it creaseth more and more;
And although I be poor, I have an angry heart.
I can keep a Hobby, a garden, and a cart;
I can make good mantles, and good Irish fryce;

I can make aqua vite, and good square dice.
Pediculus other while do bite me by the back,
Wherefore divers times I make their bones crack.
I do love to eat my meat, sitting upon the ground,
And do lie in eaten straw, sleeping full sound.
I care not for riches, but for meat and drink;
And divers times I wake, when other men do wink.
I do use no pot to seethe my meat in,
Wherefore I do boil it in a beast's skin;
Then after my meat, the broth I do drink up,
I care not for my masher, neither cruse nor cup.
I am not new fangled, nor never will be;
I do live in poverty, in mine own country.

In England, and under the dominion of England, be many sundry speeches beside English: there is French used in England, specially at Calais, Guernsey and Jersey: the Welsh tongue is in Wales, the Cornish tongue in Cornwall, and Irish in Ireland, and English in the English pale. There is also the Northern Tongue, which is true Scottish; and the Scots tongue is the Northern tongue. Furthermore in England is used all manner of languages and speeches of aliens in diverse Cities and Towns, specially in London by the sea side. . . .The speech of England is a base speech to other noble speeches, as Italian, Castillian and French; howbeit the speech of England of late days is amended. . . .

Ireland is a kingdom belonging to the king of England. It is in the west part of the world, and is divided into two parts. One is the English Pale, and the other the Wild Irish. The English Pale is a good country, plenty of fish, flesh, wildfowl, and corn. There are good towns and cities, such as Dublin and Waterford, where the English fashion is maintained in meat, drink, other fare, and lodgings. The people of the English Pale are suitably well-mannered, using the English tongue; but naturally they are testy, especially if they are vexed; yet there are many well-disposed people, in the English Pale and among the Wild Irish, virtuous creatures, when grace works above nature. The other part of Ireland is called the Wild Irish; and the Redshanks are among them. That country is wild, wasted, and vast, full of marshes and mountains and little corn; but they have sufficient flesh, and little or no bread, and no ale. For the people there are slothful, not caring to sow and till their land, nor caring for riches. In many places they care not for pot, pan, kettle; nor for mattress, feather bed, nor other such household implements. For this reason it is supposed that they lack manners and honesty, and be untaught and rude; which rudeness, with their melancholy complexion, causes them to be angry and testy without reason. . . .

A talk in Irish and English.

God speed you, sir!	*Anoha dewh sor!*
You be welcome to the town.	*De van wely.*
How do you fare?	*Kanys stato?*
I do fare well, I thank you.	*Tam agoomwah gramahogood*
Sir, can you speak Irish?	*Sor, woll galow oket?*
I can speak a little.	*Tasyn agomee.*
Maiden, come hither and give me some meat!	*Kalyn, tarin chowh, toor dewh!*
Wife, have you any good meat?	*Benitee, wyl beemah hagoot?*
Sir, I have enough.	*Sor, tha gwyler.*
Wife, give me bread!	*Benytee, toor haran!*
Man, give me wine!	*Farate, toor fyen!*
Maiden, give me cheese!	*Kalyn, toor case!*
Wife, give me flesh!	*Benyte, toor foeule!*
Give me some fish!	*Toor yeske!*
Much good do it you!	*Teena go sowgh!*
How far is it to Waterford?	*Gath haad o showh go port laarg?*
It is one and twenty mile.	*Myle hewryht.*
What is it o'clock?	*Gaued bowleh glog?*
It is vi. o'clock.	*She wylly a glog.*
When shall we go to supper?	*Gahad rah moyd auer soper?*
Give me a reckoning, wife.	*Toor countes doyen, benitee.*
You shall pay iii. pence.	*Yeke ke to tre pyn Iny.*
When shall I go to sleep, wife?	*Gah hon rah moyd holowh?*
By and by.	*Nish feene.*
Good night, sir!	*Ih may sor!*
Fare well, fare well!	*Sor doyt, sor doit!*

Thus ends the manner and speech of Ireland.

2.7 *Stat.Ire.* An Act for the Uniformity of Common Prayer and Service in the Church, and the Administration of the Sacraments, 1560

And forasmuch as in most places in this realm, there cannot be found English ministers to serve in the churches or places appointed for common-prayer, or to minister the sacraments to the people, and that if some good means were provided, that they might use the prayer, service, and administration of sacraments set out and established by this act, in such language as they might understand, the due honour of God should be thereby much advanced; and for that also, that the same may not be in their native language, as well for difficulty to get it printed as that few in the whole realm

25

can read the Irish letters. We do therefore most humbly beseech your Majesty that with your Highness's favour and royal assent, it may be enacted, ordained, established and provided by the authority of this present Parliament, that in every such church or place, where the common minister or priest hath not the knowledge or use of the English tongue, it shall be lawful for the same common minister or priest to say and use the matins, evensong, celebration of the Lord's supper, and administration of each of the sacraments, and all their common and open prayer in the Latin tongue, in such order and form, as they be mentioned and set forth in the said book established by this act, and according to the tenor of this act, and none otherwise, nor in other manner.

2.8 *Cal.S.P. Ire.*, 1509–73, 1562

Alexander Craik, Bishop of Kildare, to Cecil. Has received no answer to his petitions. Desires the discharge of 'my first fruits which was promised to be remitted me afore I came from London,' and that he may enjoy his deanery without trouble of the law. Prays to be disburdened of the bishopric of Kildare, as he cannot understand the Irish language.

2.9 *Foirm na nUrrnuidheadh [The Book of Common Order]*, Seon Carsuel (John Carswell) 1567

But there is indeed a great disadvantage and want which we the Gael of Alban (Scotland) and Eireand (Ireland) have ever lain, beyond the rest of the world, that our Gaelic language has never been printed, as have been the languages and tongues of all other nations in the world; and there is a greater want than any other from which we suffer, in that the Holy Bible has never been printed in Gaelic as it has been printed in Latin and in English, and in all other tongues, and besides in that the history of our forefathers and our ancestors has likewise never been printed; but although some of the history of the Gael of Alban and Eireand is written in manuscripts and in the remnants of poets and chief bards, and in the notices of the learned, it is great labour to write with the hand, when men see what has been printed rapidly and in how short a time it can be done, however much there may be of it. And great is the blindness and darkness of sin and ignorance and of understanding among composers and writers and supporters of the Gaelic, in that they prefer and practise the framing of vain, hurtful, lying, earthly stories about the Tuath de Dhanond, and about the sons of Milesius, and about the heroes and Fionn Mac Cumhail with his giants, and about many others whom I shall not number or tell of here in detail, in order to maintain and advance these, with a view to obtaining for themselves passing worldly gain, rather than to write and to compose and to support the faithful words of God and the perfect way of truth. For the world loves the lie much more than the truth, proving how true it is which I say, that worldly men will give a price for the lie but will not listen to the truth when offered them for nothing. Besides a large amount of the want of knowledge and the ignorance of those of whom I have already spoken arise from a want of faithful teaching among us, and of a good book which men could understand generally in their own tongue and in their own native Gaelic language.

But God Almighty and King of all things and of archangels has opened up an excellent path and way and doors for us now, proclaiming to us that we are free to peruse the Holy Scriptures, and to judge of them and declare them to the people. And besides that, the forms and substance of the prayers and administration of the sacraments, and the confession of the Christian faith, are put in order for us by the Christian brethren who are in the city called Geneva. But there is this, if I saw any man of the Gael of Alban and Eireand, that should undertake, in aid of the Church of God, to translate this little book into the Gaelic language in which men could understand it, it would be very grateful to me. And I myself would not undertake this work. But since none such has been found, or if there be such I do not know him, who will undertake it out of love to God and to the Church, with more ability than my means and my power can bring to it. I hope that God will aid me in my defects and my ignorance.

2.10 *Stat.Ire.* An Act for the Erection of Free Schools, 1570

For as much as the greatest number of the people of this your Majesty's realm hath of long time lived in rude and barbarous states, not understanding that Almighty God hath by his divine laws forbidden the manifold and heinous offences, which they spare not daily and hourly to commit and perpetrate, nor that he hath by his holy Scriptures commanded a due and humble obedience from the people to their princes and rulers; whose ignorance in these so high points touching their damnation proceedeth only of lack of good bringing up of the youth of this realm either in public or private schools, where through good discipline they might be taught to avoid these loathsome and horrible errors: it may therefore please your most excellent Majesty, that it be enacted, and be it enacted by your Highness with the assent of the lords spiritual and temporal and the commons in this present Parliament assembled, and by the authority of the same, that there shall be from henceforth a free school within every diocese of this realm of Ireland, and that the schoolmaster shall be an Englishman, or of the English birth of this realm. . . . The schoolhouse for every diocese to be built and erected in the principal shire town of the diocese, where schoolhouses be not already built, at the costs and charges of the whole diocesse.

2.11 The Oration of James Stanihurst, Speaker of the Parliament, 1570

Rather of custom and dutiful humility, than for doubt of your honourable disposition (so well known to us all, and to every one of us in private, that it little needs my praise) we are to request your Lordship in the behalf of ourselves, and our counties, whom we represent in this Parliament, to accept our service and endeavour in driving these conclusions, where by to the uttermost of our skill we have intended without injury, the Crown to enrich, treasons to chastise, to better the state, traffic to further, learning to cherish, and in brief, to maintain with our best advice those benefits, which the Prince has conferred upon this Realm by you, and you with your sword and wisdom have performed. An ordinary suite it is, in the end of such assemblies to crave executions of law, for it suffices not, to keep a statute *tanquam inclusum in tabulis*, as a thing shut up in parliament rolls, but law must speak and walk abroad, to the comfort and behoof of good subjects. . . . In particular the zeal which I have to the reformation of this Realm, and to breed in the rudest of our people, resolute English hearts, moves me to pray your Lordship's helping hand for the practice, namely of one statute which is for the erecting of Grammar Schools, within every diocese, the stipends to be levied in such proportion, as in the late act has been devised, whereunto the royal assent is already granted, and yet the point in no forwardness, nor in none is likely to be, except by some good means, the onset be given and freshly followed, surely might one generation sip a little of this liquor, and so be induced to long for more, both our countrymen that live obeisant, would ensue with a courage the fruits of peace, whereby good learning is supported, and our unquiet neighbours would find such sweetness in the taste thereof, as it should be a ready way to reclaim them. In mine experience, who have not yet seen much more than forty years, I am able to say that our Realm is at this day a half deal more civil than it was, since noble men and worshipful, with others of ability, have used to send their sons into England to the Law, to Universities, or to Schools. Now when the same Schools shall be brought home to their doors, that all that will may repair unto them, I doubt not, considering the numbers brought up beyond the Seas, and the good already done in those few places, where learning is professed, but this addition discreetly made, will foster a young fry, likely to prove good members of this commonwealth, and desirous to train their children the same way. Neither were it a small help to the assurance of the Crown of England, when Babes from their Cradles should be inured under learned School-masters, with a pure English tongue, habit, fashion, discipline; and in time utterly forget the affinity of their unbroken borderers, who possibly might be won by this example, or at the least wise lose the opportunity, which now they have, to infect others: And seeing our hap is not yet, to plant an University here at home, which attempt can never be remembered without many thanks to your good Lordship for your bountiful offer, me seems it is the more expedient to enter so far forth as our commission reaches and to hope for the rest.

2.12 *A Historie of Ireland*, Edmund Campion, 1571

Of the Irish Tongue and the Name Hibernia, Ireland.

I find it solemnly avouched in some of their pamphlets, that *Gathelus*, and after him *Simon Brecke*, devised their language out of all other tongues then extant in the world. But considering the course of interchanging and blending speeches together, I am rather led to believe (seeing Ireland was inhabited within one year after the division of tongues) that *Bastolenus* a branch of *Japhet* who first seized upon Ireland, brought thither the same kind of Speech, some one of the 72 Languages, that to this family befell at the dissolution of Babel, unto whom succeeded the Scythians, Grecians, Egyptians, Spaniards, Danes: of all which the tongue must needs have borrowed part, but especially retaining the steps of Spanish then spoken in Granada, as from their mightiest ancestors. Since then to *Henry Fitz Empress* the Conqueror, no such invasion happened them, as whereby they might be driven to infect their native language, untouched in manner for the space of 1700 years after the arrival of *Hiberius*. The tongue is sharp and sententious, and offereth great occasion to quick apothegms and proper allusions, wherefore their common Jesters, Bards, and Rhymers, are said to delight passingly those that conceive the grace and propriety of the tongue. But the true Irish indeed differeth so much from that they commonly speak, that scarce among five score, can either write, read, or understand it. Therefore it is prescribed among certain [of] their Poets and other Students of Antiquity.

Touching the name *Ibernia*, the learned are not yet agreed. Some write it *Hibernia*, and suppose that the strangers finding it in an odd end of the world, wet and frosty, took it first for a very cold country, and accordingly named it, as to say, the winter land: Another brings a guess of Irlamal, of whom because I read nothing, I neither build upon that conjecture, nor control it. Thirdly, they fetch it from *Hiberus* the Spaniard. Most credibly it is held that the Spaniards their founders for devotion toward Spain, called the Iberia, and the rather for that themselves had dwelled besides the famous river Iberus, named this land Iberia (for so *John Leland*, and many foreign Chroniclers write it) or Ibernia, adding the letter n. for difference sake, there being a rich City which *Ptolomey* recounts called then Ibernis, & from Ibernia proceeds Iberland or Iverland, from Iverland by contraction Ireland, for so much as in corruption of common talk, we find that v, with its vowel, are easily lost and suppressed. So we say ere for ever, ore for over, ene for even, nere for never, shoole for shovel, dile for devil. At the same time it was also named *Scotia* in reverence of *Scota*, the wife of *Gathelus*, ancient Captain of those Iberians, that flitted from Spain into Ireland. And the said *Scota* was old grandame to *Hiberus* and *Hirimon*, after the Scottish Chronicles, who in any wise will have their Countrymen derived from the Irish, and not from the Britons. . . .

Hitherto the Irish of both sorts, mere and English, are affected much indifferently, saving that in these, by good order, and breaking the same, virtues are far more pregnant. In those others, by licentious and evil custom, the same faults are more extreme and odious, I say, by licentious and evil custom, for that there is daily trial of good natures among them. How soon they be reclaimed, and to what rare gifts of grace and wisdom, they do and have aspired. Again, the very English of birth conversant with the brutish sort of that people, become degenerate in short space, and are quite altered into the worst rank of Irish rogues, such a force has education to make or mar. It is further to be known, that the simple Irish are utterly another people than our English in Ireland, whom they call spitefully *boddai Sassoni's*, and *boddai Ghalt*, that is, English and Saxon churls, because of their English ancestors planted here with the Conquest, and since with descent has lasted now 400 years.

2.13 *Cal.S.P. Ire.*, 1574–85, Sir Henry Sidney, Letter to the Queen, 1576

And now, most dear Mistress and most honoured Sovereign, I solely address to you – as to the only Sovereign Salve-giver to this your sore and sick Realm, the lamentable estate of the most noble and principal limb thereof:- the Church, I mean, as foul, deformed and as cruelly crushed as any other part thereof – by only your gracious and religious order to be cured, or at least mended. I would not have believed, had I not for a great part viewed the same throughout the whole Realm, and was advertised of the particular estate of the Church in the bishopric of Meath (being the best inhabited county of all this Realm) by the honest, zealous, and learned bishop of the same, Mr. Hugh Brady, a godly Minister of the Gospel and a good servant to your Highness, who went from church to church himself and found that there are within his diocese 224 parish churches, out of which 105 are impropriated to sundry possessions now out of your Highness – and all leased out for years in fee farm to several Farmers, and great gain reaped out of them, above the rent which your Majesty receiveth. No Parson or Vicar resident upon any of them, and a very simple or sorry curate, for the most part, appointed to serve therein. Among which number of curates, only eighteen were found able to speak English – the rest Irish priests or rather Irish rogues, having very little Latin, less learning and civility. . . .

If this be the state of the churches of the best peopled diocese, and best governed county of this your Realm, (as in troth it is,) easy it is for your

Majesty to conjecture in what case the rest is, where little or no Reformation, either of Religion or manners, hath yet been planted and continued among them.

In choice of which ministers for the remote places where the English tongue is not understood, it is most necessary that such be chosen as can speak Irish. For which, search would be made, first and speedily, in your own Universities. And any found there, well affected in Religion and well conditioned beside, they would be sent hither animated by your Majesty. Yea, though it were somewhat to your Highness' charge, and on peril of my life, you shall find it returned with gain before three year be expired. If there be no such there, or not enough (for I wish ten or twelve, at the least) to be sent, who might be placed in offices of dignity in the Church in remote places of this Realm, then do I wish, but this most humbly, under your Highness's correction – that you would write unto the Regent of Scotland, where, as I learn, there are many of the reformed Church that are of this language, that he would prefer to your Highness so many as shall seem good to you to demand of honest, zealous and learned men, and that could speak this language. And though for a while your Majesty were at some charge, it were well bestowed, for in short time their own preferments would be able to suffice them, and in the meantime thousands would be gained to Christ, that now are lost, or left at the worst.

2.14 *A Treatise Containing a Plain and Perfect Description of Ireland*, Richard Stanihurst, 1577

Touching the name Ibernia, historiographers are not yet agreed from whence it is deducted. Some write it Hibernia corruptly, and suppose that the strangers finding it in an odd end of the world, foisty and moisty, took it at the first for a very cold country, and thereof named it Hibernia, as to say, the Winter land. But this error being upon short experience reformed, it could not be that the name should have lived long, especially the first impositors surviving the trial, and able to alter the first nomination. Others bring a guess, that it should be named of Irlamale. But because I read nothing of them in any probable history, I purpose not to build upon that conjecture. Most credibly it is held, that the Spaniards (the founders of the Irish) for devotion towards Spain, called then Iberia of Iberius the son of Iuball, and the rather, for that themselues had dwelled beside the famous riuer Iberus, named the land Iberia (for so Leland and many foreign chroniclers write it) or Ibernia, adding the letter (n) for difference sake. And from Ibernia proceedeth Iberland, or Iverland; from Iverland, by contraction Ireland: forsomuch as in corruption of common talk we find that (v) with its vocal is easily lost and suppressed; so we say ere for ever, nere for never, shoole for shovell, ore for over, ene for even, dile for divell. At the same time it was also named Scotia, in reverence of Scotach the wife of

Gathelus, ancient captain of those Iberians that flitted from Hispaine into Ireland: & the said Scotach was old grandame to Hiberus and Hermon after the Scottish chronicles, who in any wise will have their countrymen derived from the Irish, and not from the Britons. The name Scotia is of late years so usually taken for that part of Britain that compriseth Scotland, that diverse ancient Irish authors are held to be born in Scotland, whereas in very deed their native soil is Ireland. As the famous schoolman Iohannes Duns Scotus, otherwise named Doctor subtilis, for his subtle quiddities in scholastic controversies, was an Irish man born, and yet is taken for a Scot. . . .

There is also another division of Ireland, into the English Pale, and the Irishry. For when Ireland was subdued by the English, diverse of the conquerors planted themselues near to Dublin, and the confines thereto adjoining, and so as it were enclosing and impaling themselves within certain lists and territories, they frightened away the Irish; insomuch as that country became mere English, and thereof it was termed the English pale: which in ancient time stretched from Dundalk to Catherlagh or Kilkenny. But now what for the slackness of marchers, and encroaching of the Irish enemy, the scope of the English pale is greatly impaired, & is cramped and caught into an odd corner of the country named Fingall, with a parcel of the king's land, Meath, the countries of Kildare and Louth, which parts are applied chiefly with good husbandry, and taken for the richest and civilest soils in Ireland. But Fingall especially from time to time hath been so addicted to all the points of husbandry, as that they are nicknamed by their neighbours, for their continual drudgery, Colons, of the Latin word Coloni, whereunto the clipped English word clown seemeth to be answerable. The word Fingall countervaileth in English the race or sept of the English or Strangers, for that they were solely siezed of that part of the Island, gripping with their talons so firmly that warm nest, that from the conquest to this day the Irish enemy could never rouse them from thence. The inhabitants of the English pale have been in old times so much addicted to their civility, and so far sequestered from barbarous savageness, as their only mother tongue was English. And truly, so long as these impaled dwellers did sunder themselves as well in land as in language from the Irish: rudeness was day by day in the country supplanted, civility engrafted, good laws established, loyalty observed, rebellion suppressed, and in fine the cornerstone of a young England was like to shoot in Ireland. But when their posterity became not altogether so wary in keeping, as their ancestors were valiant in conquering, the Irish language was free denizened in the English pale: this canker took such deep root, as the body that before was whole and sound, was by little and little festered, and in manner wholy putrified. And not only this parcel of Ireland grew to that civility, but also Ulster and the greater part of Munster, as by the sequel of the Irish history shall plainly appear. But of all other places, Wexford with the territory bayed and perclosed within the river called the Pill, was so quite estranged from Irishry, as if a traveller of the Irish, (which was rare in those days) had pitched his foot within the Pill and spoken Irish, the Wexfordians would command him forthwith to turn the other end of his tongue and speak English, or else bring his trouchman with him. But in our days they have so acquainted themselves with the Irish, as they have made a mingle mangle or gallimaufry of both languages, and have in such medley or checkerwise so crabbedly jumbled them both together, as commonly the inhabitants of the meaner sort speak neither good English nor good Irish. There was of late days one of the peers of England sent to Wexford as commissioner, to decide the controversies of that country; and hearing in affable wise the rude complaints of the country clowns, he conceived here & there some time a word, other whiles a sentence. The noble man being very glad, that upon his first coming to Ireland, he understood so many words, told one of his familiar friends, that he stood in very great hope to become shortly a well spoken man in the Irish, supposing that the blunt people had prattled Irish, all the while they jangled English. Howbeit to this day, the dregs of the old ancient Chaucer English are kept as well there as in Fingall, as they term a spider, an attercrop, a wisp, a wad, a lump of bread, a pocket, or a pucket, a sillybuck, a copprous, a faggot, a blease, or a blaze, for the short burning of it (as I judge) a physician, a leach, a gap, a shard, a base court or quadrangle, a bawn, or rather (as I do suppose) a barton, the household or folks, meany, sharp, keen, strange, uncouth, easy, eeth or eef, a dunghill, a mizen. As for the word bater, that in English purporteth a lane, bearing to a highway, I take it for a mere Irish word that crept unawares into the English, through the daily intercourse of the English and Irish inhabitants. And whereas commonly in all countries the women speak most neatly and pertly, which Tully in his third book *De Oratore*, speaking in the person of Crassus seemed to have observed: yet notwithstanding in Ireland it falleth out contrary. For the women have in their English tongue a harsh and broad kind of pronunciation, with uttering their words so peevishly and faintly, as though they were half sick, and ready to call for a posset. And most commonly in words of two syllables they give the last the accent; as they say, markeat, baskeat, gossoupe, pussoat, Robart Niclase, &c: which doubtless doth disbeautify their English above measure. And if they could be weaned from that corrupt custom, there is none that could dislike of their English.

Here percase some snappish carper will take me at rebound, and suffingly snib me for debasing the Irish language: but truly, whosoever shall be found so overthwartily bent, he takes the matter far awry. For as my skill is very simple therein, so I would be loth to disveil my rashness, in giving light verdict in anything to me unknown: but only my short discourse tendeth to this drift, that it is not expedient that the Irish tongue should be so universally gaggled in the English pale: because by that proof and experience we see, that the Pale was never in more flourishing state than when it was wholly English, and never in worse state than since it hath enfranchised the Irish. . . . First therefore take this with you, that a conquest draweth, or at leastwise ought to draw to it three things, to wit, law, apparel, and language. For where the country is subdued, there the inhabitants ought to be ruled by the same law that the conqueror is governed, to wear the same fashion of attire that wherewith the victor is vested, and speak the same language that the vanquisher parleth. And if any of these three lack, doubtless the conquest limpeth. Now whereas Ireland hath been by lawful conquest been brought under the subjection of England, not only in King Henry the Second's reign, but also as well before as after (as by the discourse of the Irish history shall evidently be deciphered) and the conquest hath been so absolute and perfect, that all Leinster, Meath, Ulster, the more part of Connaught and Munster, all the cities and boroughs in Ireland have been wholly Englished, and with English conquerors inhabited, is it decent (think you) that their own native tongue shall be shrouded in oblivion, and suffer the enemy's language, as it were a tettar or ringworm, to harbour itself within the jaws of English conquerors? No truly. And now that I have fallen unawares into this discourse, it will not be far amiss to stand somewhat roundly upon this point. It is known, and by the history you may in part perceive, how bravely Ulster whilholme flourished. The English families were there implanted, the Irish either utterly expelled or wholly subdued, the laws duly executed, the revenue great, and only English spoken. But what brought it to this present ruin and decay? I doubt not but that you guess before I tell you. They were environed and compassed with evil neighbours. Neighborhood bred acquaintance, acquaintance waffed in the Irish tongue, the Irish hooked with it attire, attire hailed rudeness, rudeness engendered ignorance, ignorance brought contempt of laws, the contempt of laws bred rebellion, rebellion raked there to wars, and so consequently the utter decay and desolation of that worthy country.

If these chinks, when they first began to chap, had been diligently by the dwellers stopped; her Majesty at this day, to her great charges, should not have been occasioned to dam up with many thousand pounds, yea and with the worthy carcasses of valiant soldiers, the gaps of that rebellious northern country. Now put the case that the Irish tongue were as sacred as the Hebrew, as learned as the Greek, as fluent as the Latin, as amorous as the Italian, as courteous as the Spanish, as courtlike as the French; yet truly (I know not which way it falleth out) I see not but it may be very well spared in the English pale. And if reason will not lead you to think it, truly experience must force you to grant it. In old time, when the Romans were first acquainted with the Greek tongue, as it is commonly the nature of man to be delighted with newfangled wares: so he was accounted no gallant among the Romans, that could not prattle and chat Greek. Marcus Cicero father to Tully, being at that time steeped in years, perceiving his countrymen to become changelings, in being bilwise and polmad, and to suck with the Greek the conditions of the Grecians, as to be in words talkative, in behaviour light, in conditions quaint, in manners haughty, in promises unsteadfast, in oaths rash, in bargains wavering (which were reckoned for Greekish properties in those days) the old gentleman not so much respecting the neatness of the language, as the naughty fruit it brought with it; said, that his countrymen the Romans resembled the bond-slaves of Syria; for the more perfect they were in the Greek, the worse they were in their manners and life. If this gentleman had been now living, and had seen what alteration hath happened in Ireland, through the intercourse of languages, he would (I dare say) break patience, and would demand why the English pale is more given to learn the Irish, than the Irishman is willing to learn English: we must embrace their language, and they detest ours. One demanded merrily why O'Neill that last was would not frame himself to speak English? What (quoth the other) in a rage, thinkest thou that it standeth with O'Neill's honour to writhe his mouth in clattering English? and yet forsooth we must gag our jaws in gibbering Irish? But I dwell too long in so apparent a matter. As all the cities and towns in Ireland, with Fingall, the King's land, Meath, the county of Kildare, Louth, Wexford, speak to this day English (whereby the simplicity of some is to be derided, that judge the inhabitants of the English pale, upon their first repair into England, to learn their English in three or four days, as though they had bought at Chester a grote's worth of English, and so packed up the rest to be carried after them to London) even so in all other places their native language is Irish.

I find it solemnly avouched, as well in some of the Irish pamphlets as in Giraldus Cambrensis, that Gathelus, or Gaidelus, and after him Simon Brecke, devised the Irish language out of all other tongues then extant in the world. And thereof (saith Cambrensis) it is called Gaidelach, partly of Gaidelus the first founder, and partly for that it is compounded of all languages. But considering the course of interchanging and blending of speeches together, not by invention of art, but by use of talk, I am rather led to believe (seeing Ireland was inhabited within one year after the division of tongues) that Bastolenus a branch of Japhet, who seized upon Ireland, brought thither the same kind of speech, some of the 72 that to this family befell at the desolation of Babel. Unto whom succeeded the Scythians, Grecians, Egyptians, Spaniards, Danes, of all which the tongue must needs have borrowed part, but especially retaining the steps of Spanish then spoken in Granada, as from their mightiest ancestors. Since then to Henry Fitzempress the conqueror no such invasion happened them, as whereby they might be driven to infect their native language, untouched in manner for the space of seventeen hundred years after the arrival of Iberius. It seemeth to borrow of the Spanish the common phrase, Commestato, that is, How do you? or how fareth it with you? It fetcheth sundry words from the Latin, as arget of *Argentum*, money; salle of *soel*, salt;

cappoulle of *Caballus*, a plough horse, or (according unto the Old English term) a caball or caple; birreat of the old motheaten Latin word *Birretum*, a bonnet. The tongue is sharp and sententious, and offereth great occasion to quick apothegms and proper allusions. Wherefore their common jesters and rhymers, whom they term Bards, are said to delight passingly these that conceive the grace and propriety of the tongue. But the true Irish indeed differeth so much from that they commonly speak, that scarce one in five hundred can either read, write, or understand it. Therefore it is preserved among certain of their poets and antiquaries. And in very deed the language carrieth such difficulty with it, what for the strangeness of the phrase, and the curious features of the pronunciation, that a very few of the country can attend to the perfection thereof, and much less a foreigner or stranger. A gentleman of my acquaintance reported, that he did see a woman in Rome, which was possessed with a babbling spirit, that could have chatted any language saving the Irish: and that it was so difficult, as the very devil was gravelled therewith. A gentleman that stood by answered, that he took the speech to be so sacred and holy, that no damned fiend had the power to speak it; no more than they are able to say (as the report goeth) the verse of Saint John the Evangelist, 'Et verbum caro factum est'. Nay by God mercy man (quoth the other) I stand in doubt (I tell you) whether the apostles in their copious mart of languages at Jerusalem could have spoken Irish, if they were apposed: whereat the company heartily laughed. As fluent as the Irish tongue is, yet it lacks diverse words, and borrows them verbatim from the English. As there is no vulgar Irish word (unless there be some odd term that lurks in any obscure shrouds or other of their storehouse) for a coat, a gown, a doublet, a hat, a drinking cup: but only they use the same words with a little inflection. They use also the contracted English phrase, God morrow, that is to say, God give you a good morning . . . I have apposed sundry times the expertest men that could be had in the country, and all they could never find out an equivalent Irish word for knave. . . .

As the whole realm of Ireland is sundered into four principal parts, as before is said, so each part differs very much in the Irish tongue, every county having its dialect, or peculiar manner in speaking the language; therefore commonly in Ireland they ascribe a property to each of the four counties in this sort. Ulster has the right Irish phrase, but not the true pronunciation; Munster has the true pronunciation, but not the phrase; Leinster is devoid of the right phrase, and true pronunciation; Connaught has both the right phrase and true pronunciation. There is a choleric or disdainful interjection used in the Irish language called Boagh, which is as much in English as twish. The Irish both in ancient times and to this day commonly use it, and therefore the English conquerors called them Irish poghes, or pogh Morice. Which taunting term is at this day very wrongfully ascribed to them of the English pale. The English interjection, Fough, which is used in loathing a rank or strong savour, seems to be sibling to the other.

2.15 *Cal.S.P. Ire.*, 1574–85, 1578

Note of observations on the government of Ireland delivered, to Her Majesty's Commissioners appointed for those causes by the Lord Chancellor Gerrarde, to be considered and resolved on by them. Gerrarde affirms that all English, and the most part with delight, even in Dublin, speak Irish, and are greatly spotted in manners, habit, and conditions with Irish stains.

2.16 *Queen Elizabeth's Primer of the Irish Language.*
Christopher Nugent, *c.*1584–85

Among the manifold actions (most gracious and virtuous Sovereign) that bear testimony to the world of your Majesty's great affection, tending to the reformation of Ireland, there is no one (in my opinion) that more evident showeth the same, than the desire your Highness hath to understand the language of your people there. For as speech is the special means whereby all subjects learn obedience, and their Princes, or Governors, understand their griefs and harms; so the same being delivered by an interpreter, can never carry that grace, or proper intelligence, which the tongue itself being understood expresseth. This defect, found out by your Majesty, bred that gracious desire formerly spoken of, which being an act deserving the praise of all men, so the same made known unto your subjects, no doubt would greatly increase their love and obedience: And for as much as it pleased your Majesty (which I take a special favour) to command me deliver your Highness the Irish characters, with instructions for reading of the language, I thought it not inconvenient to join thereto the original of the nation also; to the end, your Majesty, knowing from whence they came, and their tongue derived, might the sooner attain to the perfection thereof. And albeit that few or none of English nation born and bred in England, ever had that gift; yet the same chanced not through difficulty of the speech, but only for want of taking the right manner of instruction; for commonly men do learn by demanding the signification of the words, not by the letter, as your Majesty hath here set down unto you, which is the speedier, and better way. In proof whereof, men yet living which knew Elizabeth Zouche, daughter to the Lord Zouche, sometime Countess of Kildare, do affirm that in short time she learned to read, write, and perfectly speak the tongue. What then must we think that your Majesty will do, who in depth of wisdom, quickness of conceit, and rare perfection in the languages, exceeding all we ever read or heard of? Truly not out of the tongue, but with all humility render thanks to God, for inspiring your Majesty with so good a thought. Proceed, therefore, proceed, most gracious Sovereign in your holy intent, that as your Majesty hath in exhausting your treasure more than any three of your most noble progenitors, showed how far you exceed them in affection touching the reformation of that country: so in this generous act you shall excell them all. For thereby your subjects shall receive justice, civility planted, their love towards your Majesty increased, leaving to posterity an example of virtue to follow your most glorious acts and deeds.

2.17 *Cal. Carew MSS.*, A Discourse for the Reformation of Ireland, Sir Henry Sidney, 1585

The Charge your Majesty committed unto me for the setting down of my opinion how your realm of Ireland might with the least charge be reclaimed from barbarism to a godly government is somewhat difficult. There is a want of religion and law; St. Patrick is of better credit than Christ Jesus; and they fly from the laws as from a yoke of bondage. God's will and word must first be duly planted and idolatry extirped; next law must be established, and licentious customs abrogated. . . .

The [Desmond] rebellion being suppressed, it will be necessary to call a parliament to enact new statutes for establishing the articles ensuing:

(1) Two new universities to be established at Limerick and Armagh. . . .
(7) All brehons, carraghes, bards rhymers, friars, monks, Jesuits, pardoners, nuns, and such like, to be executed by martial law. . . .
(12) Honest and skilful men to be taken out of every Court of record here, and established there.
(13) Irish habits for men and women to be abolished, and the English tongue to be extended. . . .

Here, now, lastly, doth the common objection oppose itself, requiring an answer, whether it be safety or danger, good or evil, for England to have Ireland reformed, lest, growing to civility, government, and strength, it should cast off the yoke, and be more noisesome and dangerous neighbours to England. This objection is of no force. The Kings of Spain have now of long time governed other countries, being civil and lying further off.

2.18 *Cal.S.P. Ire.*, 1586–88, 1587

Sir William Herbert to Lord Burghley. – I came hither to the Castle of the Island the 26th April, having arrived at Cork the 22nd of the same, after ten days being at sea, beaten back by contrary winds first to Milford, then to Tenby, where for my own safety I was forced to surprise a pirate that lay at road hard by me. Touching this place and seignory I find here divers inhabitants, some upon title, some upon sufferance; much heath ground, much barren ground, and much bog, and interlaced with them reasonable fruitful land. . . . Touching the estate of religion in these parts, here is neither public prayers in any church nor private prayers that any of them doth understand, whereby it seemeth God is altogether unserved. I have taken order that public prayers shall be said in their own tongue and that they shall assemble themselves at their churches on the Sundays. I have caused the Lord's Prayer and the Ten Commandments, and the Articles of the Belief, to be translated into Irish, and this day the ministers of these parts repair unto me to have it in writing. I find them very tractable and willing to learn the truth. I hope to do some good therein with them. As for matters of justice I find here sundry complaints against some officers, whose corrupt courses I trust to repress and redress to the great contentment of the country, for the people, generally the richer sort, are very subtle and fraudulent; the poor are very filthy and barbarous. I know not which will be the more difficult unto me, to bring the subtler unto sincerity, or the simpler to civility. I will by God's grace endeavour both.

2.19 *Cal.S.P. Ire.*, 1586–88, 1587

Answer of Donnell O'Sullivan to the false accusations and surmises of Sir Owen O'Sullivan.

And where my adversary setteth down for reasons to avoid the course of common law touching descents from father to the son that the said lands is barbarous and uncivil, and the people unacquainted with civil government till his time, and that the other lands adjoining to his county did always follow the said Irish custom; for answer thereunto, I say that the county was not so barbarous, but that the heirs thereof were always brought up in learning and civility, and could speak the English and Latin tongues; but to excuse his own ignorance and want of bringing up, being not able to speak the English language, he would gladly discredit the country and all his ancestors, who were ever better disposed people, to good government, learning and civility, than the said Sir Owen, as hereunder written shall appear.

2.20 *Cal.S.P. Ire.*, 1586–88, 1587

Considerations touching the state of Munster. To repress kerne and exalt the churl. To have the Lord's Prayer and the Belief taught in English where the incumbent can, and in Irish where he may not have so much learning. To erect free schools. To divide the great territories between Sir Own McCarthy and Donnel na Pipi McCarthy.

2.21 *Cal.S.P. Ire.*, 1586–88, 1588

Touching the inhabitation of these waste and desolate parts (through the attainder of sundry accrued unto Her Majesty) and by reason of the calamities of the late wars void of people to manure and occupy the same, as it hath with great reason been thought meet to be performed by gentlemen of good ability and disposition out of England, that by their good example, direction, and industry, both true religion, sincere justice, and perfect civility, might here be planted, and hence derived and propagated into the other parts of this realm, so the placing amongst this forward and undisciplined people inhabitants so much differing both in manners, language and country from them, shall be unto them at the first, (without doubt) and ever without care had, unpleasant and odious, which will easily be acknowledged by any that weigheth the nature of the action together with the disposition of this nation.

The inconveniences that of this in time may grow when they increase both in dislike, number and ability, may probably be conjectured but hardly measured, unless it be prevented. The prevention of it consisteth in two points whereof neither may be neglected, the bettering and reforming of their wills and dispositions, and the weakening and lessening of their powers and forces. Their minds and wills are to be bettered principally by instructing them in true religion, the firm foundation of the fear of God, of their loyalty to Her Majesty, and of their love and charity to one another. Secondly, by the sincere and impartial administration of justice, whereby they may repose the safety of their lives, lands and goods in her Highness' laws and government. Thirdly, in a courteous demeanour, affability of speech, and care of their well doing, ever expressed towards them by such English gentlemen as shall inhabit and govern amongst them. For the first I have been careful those parts wherein I am, to have them taught the truth in their natural tongue, to have the Lord's prayer, the Articles of the Creed, the Ten Commandments, translated into the Irish tongue; public prayers in that language, with the administration of the sacraments and other ecclesiastical rites, which in a strange tongue could be to them but altogether unprofitable, and in these things I have hitherunto found very great want of a good and godly bishop, but now Mr. Keenam being here placed, a man both learned, godly, and of this country birth, I am in assured hope that by his good example and travail these parts will easily be reformed.

2.22 *Cal.S.P. Ire.*, 1586–88, 1588

The Laws of Kilkenny to be put in execution against Irish manners and habit. The Lord Deputy and Council weighing and considering of the cause, how those of the English race as well within that province as universally throughout this land, are grown to such barbarous, disordered manner and trade of life, as heretofore hath been and at this day is used amongst the very Irish in speech, habit, feeding, trade of housekeeping, manners, conditions and conversations in trade of life, are fully resolved that the want of execution of such laws as from age to age have been set down by Parliament, restraining all those of the English race from the using and trading any of these 'forecited' Irish disorders and customs. Therefore the said Lord Deputy and Council do will and require, and in Her Majesty's name straightly charge and command the said Chief Commissioner and Council that [at] all these said Sessions, or Oyer or Terminer, by charge and inquiry and in all other their Sitting Terms by way of information they principally and specially put these several laws, namely the laws made at Kilkenny with all the severity in due execution, the brief of which several laws they shall receive in a book lately put in print.

2.23 *A View of the Present State of Ireland*, Edmund Spenser, 1596

Irenius: Here it shall only suffice to touch customs of the Irish as seem offensive and repugnant to the good government of that realm. . . . Before we enter into the treatise of their customs it is first needful to consider from whence they first sprung, from the sundry manners of the nations from whence that people which are now called Irish are derived, some of the customs which now remain amongst them have been fetched, and since when they have been continued amongst them. For not of one nation was it peopled as it is, but of sundry people of different conditions and manners, but the chiefest which have first possessed and inhabited it, I suppose to be Scythians, which at such time as the Northern nations overflowed all Christendom, came down to the sea coast, where inquiring for other countries abroad and getting intelligence of this country of Ireland, finding shipping convenient, passed over thither and arrived in the North part thereof, which is now called Ulster, which first inhabiting, and afterwards stretching themselves forth into the land as their numbers increased, named it all of themselves Scuttenland – which more briefly is called Scuteland or Scotland.

Eudoxus: I wonder, Irenius, whither you run so far astray, for whilst we talk of Ireland, me thinks you rip up the original of Scotland; but what is that to this?

Irenius: Surely very much, for Scotland and Ireland are all one and the same.

41

Eudoxus: That seemeth more strange, for we all know right well, that they are distinguished, with a great sea running between them, or else there are two Scotlands.

Irenius: Neverthemore are there two Scotlands, but two kinds of Scots there were indeed, as you may gather out of Buchanan, the one Irine or Irish Scots, the other Albyn Scots; for those Scots or Scythians arrived (as I suppose) in the north parts of the island, where some of them afterwards passed into the next coast of Albyn, now called Scotland, which after much trouble they possessed and of themselves renamed it Scotland. But in the process of time, as is commonly seen, the denomination of the part prevailed in the whole; for the Irish Scots putting away the name of Scots were called only Irish, and the Albyn Scots, leaving the name of Albyn, were called only Scots. Thereof it cometh that of some writers Ireland is called Scotland major, and that which is now named Scotland is called Scotia minor.

Eudoxus: I do now well understand your distinguishing the two sorts of Scots and two Scotlands, how that this which is now called Ireland was anciently called Irine and afterwards of some written Scotland, and that which is now called Scotland, was formerly called Albyne, before the coming of the Scots thither, but what other nations inhabited the other parts of Ireland?

Irenius: After this people thus planted in the north or before, (for the certainty of times in things so far from all knowledge cannot be justly avouched) another nation coming out of Spain arrived in the west part of Ireland, and finding it waste or weakly inhabited, possessed it, who whether they were native Spaniards or Gauls or Africans or Goths, or some other of those northern nations which did overspread over all Christendom, it is impossible to affirm. Only some naked conjectures may be gathered; but that out of Spain certainly they came, that do all the Irish chronicles agree.

Eudoxus: You do very boldly, Irenius, venture upon the histories of ancient times and lead too confidently unto those Irish chronicles, which are most fabulous and forged, in that out of them ye dare take in hand to lay open the original of a nation so antique, as that no monument remaineth of her beginning and inhabiting there; specially having been always without letters, but only bare traditions of times and remembrances of bards, which use to forge and falsify everything as they list to please or displease any man.

Irenius: Truly, I must confess I do so, but not yet so absolutely as ye suppose. I do herein rely upon those bards or Irish chronicles, though the Irish themselves, through their ignorance in matters of learning, and deep judgement, do most constantly believe and avouch them, but unto them besides I add my own reading and out of them both together with comparison of times, likenesses of manners and customs, affinity of words and names, properties of natures and uses, resemblances of rites and ceremonies, monuments of churches and tombs, and many other like circumstances, I do gather a likelihood of truth; not certainly affirming anything, but by conferring of times, languages, monuments and such like, I do hunt out a probability of things which I leave unto your judgement to believe or refuse. Nevertheless, there be some very ancient authors which make mention of those things, and some modern, which by comparing of them with the present time's experience and their own reason, do open a window of great light unto the rest that is yet unseen as namely of the older: Caesar, Strabo, Tacitus, Ptolomy, Pliny, Solinus, Pompeus Mela, and Berosus; of the latter Vincentius, Aeneas Silvius, Luddus, and Buchanan, of all which I do give most credit unto Buchanan, for that he himself being an Irish Scot, or Pict by nation, and being very excellently learned and industrious to seek the truth of these things concerning the original of his own people, hath both set down the testimonies of the ancients truly, and his own opinion withal very reasonably, though in some things he doth somewhat flatter. Besides the bards and Irish chronicles themselves, though, through desire of pleasing perhaps too much and ignorance of art and pure learning, they have clouded the truth of those times, yet there appeareth amongst them some relics of the true antiquity, though disguised, which a well-eyed man may happily discover and find out.

Eudoxus: How can there be any truth in them at all, since the ancient nations which first inhabited Ireland were altogether destitute of letters, much more of learning, by which they might leave the verity of things written, and those bards coming also so many hundred years after, nor deliver any certainty of anything but what they feigned out of their own unlearned heads?

Irenius: Those bards, indeed, Caesar writeth, deliver no certain truth of anything, neither is there any certain hold to be taken of any antiquity which is received by tradition, since all men be liars and may lie when they will; but yet for the ancientness of the written chronicles of Ireland, give me leave to say something, not to justify them, but to show that some of them may say truth, for where ye say that the Irish have always been without letters, ye are therein much deceived, for it is certain that Ireland hath had the use of letters very anciently, and long before England. . . .

Eudoxus: Surely you have showed a great probability of that which I had thought possible to have been proved, but that which you now say that Ireland should have been peopled with the Gauls seemeth

43

much more strange, for all their chronicles do say that the west and south was possessed and inhabited of Spaniards, and Cornelius Tacitus also doth strongly affirm the same, all which ye must either overthrow and falsify or renounce your opinion.

Irenius: Neither so nor so, for the Irish chronicles, as I said unto you, being made by unlearned man, and writing things according to the appearance of the truth which they conceived, do err in the circumstances, not in the matter; for all that came out of Spain they (being no diligent searchers into the differences of nations) supposed to be Spaniards, and so called them. But the ground-work thereof is nevertheless (as I said) true and certain, however they through ignorance maintain the same, or through their own vanity whilst they would not seem to be ignorant, do thereupon build and enlarge many forged histories of their own antiquity, which they deliver to fools and make them believe them for true, as for example, that first of all one Gathelus, the son of Cecropes, or Argos, who having married the King of Spain's daughter, thence sailed with her into Spain and there inhabited, then that of Nemed, and his four sons who coming out of Scythia peopled Ireland and inhabited with his sons two hundred and fifty years, till he was overcome of the Giants dwelling then in Ireland, and at last quite banished and rooted out; after whom two hundred years the sons of one Dela, being Scythians, arrived there again and possessed the whole land, of which the youngest called Slaynius in the end made himself monarch; lastly of the four sons of Milesius, King of Spain, which conquered that land from the Scythians, and inhabiting it with Spaniards, called it of the youngest, Hiberus, Hibernia, all which are in truth mere fables, and very Milesian lies (as the Latin proverb is): for was there never such a King of Spain, called Milesius, nor any such colony seated with his sons as they feign, that can ever be proved. But yet under these tales ye may in a manner see the truth lurk. For Scythians here inhabiting, they name and do speak of Spaniards, whereby appeareth, that both these nations here inhabited, but whether very Spaniards is no ways to be proved.

Eudoxus: Whence cometh it then that the Irish do so greatly covet to fetch themselves from the Spaniards, since the old Gauls are a more ancient, and much more honourable nation?

Irenius: Even of a very desire of newfangledness and vanity for being, as they are now accounted the most barbarous nation in Christendom, they to avoid that reproach would derive themselves from the Spaniard, whom they now see to be a very honourable people, and next bordering unto them. But all that is most vain, for from the Spaniard that now is, or the people that now inhabits

| | Spain, they no way can prove themselves to descend, neither indeed should it be greatly glorious unto them, for the Spaniard that now is, is come from as rude and savage nations as they. . . . |

Eudoxus: You speak very sharply, Irenius, in dishonour of the Spaniard, whom some other boast to be the only brave soldier under the sky.

Irenius: So surely he is a very brave man, neither is that which I speak anything to his derogation. For in that I said he is a mingled people it is no dispraise, for I think that there is no nation now in Christendom, nor much further, but is mingled and compounded with others. For it was a singular providence of God, and a most admirable purpose of his own wisdom, to draw those northern heathen nations down into these Christian parts where they might revive Christianity, and to mingle nations so remote, so miraculously, to make as it were one kindred and blood of all people, and each to have knowledge of him.

Eudoxus: Neither have you sure any more dishonoured the Irish, for you have brought them from very great and noble nations as anywhere in the world, however fondly they affect the Spaniard. For both the Scythians and the Gauls were two as mighty nations as ever the world brought forth. But is there any token, denomination or monument of the Gauls yet remaining in Ireland as there is of the Scythians?

Irenius: Yea, surely very many, for there is first in the Irish language many words of Gauls remaining and yet daily used in common speech.

Eudoxus: Why, what was Gallish speech? Is there any part of it still used amongst any nation?

Irenius: The Gallish speech is the very British, the which was generally used here in all Britain before the coming in of the Saxons, and yet it is retained of the Welshmen, the Cornishmen, and the Britons of France . . . there be many places, as havens, hills, towns and castles which yet bear the name from the galles of which Buchanan rehearseth above three hundred in Scotland, and I can, I think, recount nearly as many in Ireland. Moreover, there be of the old Gauls certain nations yet remaining in Ireland, which detain the old denominations of the Gauls, as the Manapii, the Cauci, the Venti, and others; by all which and many other reasonable probabilities, which this short course will not suffer to be laid forth, it appeareth that the first inhabitants in Ireland were Gauls coming thither first from Spain and afterwards from beside Tannis, where the Goths, the Huns, and the Getes were set down, the all so being (as it is said) of some ancient Gauls; and lastly passing out of Gallia itself from all the seacoasts of Belgium and Celtica into all the Southern coasts of Ireland

45

which they possessed and inhabited, whereupon it is at this day amongst all the Irish a common use to call any strange inhabitant there amongst them Gald, that is descended from the Gauls. . . .

Eudoxus: This ripping up of ancestries is very pleasing unto me, and indeed savoureth of good conceit and some reading withall, I see hereby how profitable travel and experience of foreign nations is to him that will apply them to good purpose. Neither indeed would I have thought that any such antiquities could have been avouched for the Irish. That maketh me the more to long to see some other of your observations, which ye have gathered out of that country, and have erst half promised to put forth; and sure in this mingling of nations appeareth (as you erst well noted) a wonderful providence and purpose of Almighty God that stirred up the people in the farthest part of the world to seek out these regions, so remote from them, and by that means both to restore their decayed habitations, and to make himself known to the heathen. But was there, I pray you, no more general impeopling of that island than first by the Scythians, which ye say were the Scots, and afterwards by the Africans, besides the Gauls, Britons, and Saxons?

Irenius: Yes, there was another, and that the last and the greatest, which was by the English, when the Earl Strongbow, having conquered that land, delivered up the same unto the hands of Henry the Second, then King, who sent over thither great store of gentlemen and other warlike people amongst whom he distributed the land and settled such a colony therein as never since could with all the subtle practices of the Irish be routed out but abide still a mighty people of so many as remain English of them.

Eudoxus: What is this that ye say of so many as remain English of them? Why are not they that were once English abiding English still?

Irenius: No, for the most part of them are degenerated and grown almost mere Irish, yea and more malicious to the English than the very Irish themselves. . . .

Eudoxus: It now remaineth that you take in hand the customs of the old English which are amongst the Irish, of which I do not think that ye shall have much to find fault with any, considering that by the English most of the old bad Irish customs were abolished, and more civil fashions brought up in their stead.

Irenius: You think otherwise, Eudoxus, than I do, for the chiefest abuses which are now in that realm are grown from the English, and the English that were are now much more lawless and licentious than the very wild Irish, so that as much care as was then by them had to reform the Irish, so much and more must now be used to reform them so much time doth alter the manners of men.

Eudoxus: That seemeth very strange which you say, that men should so much degenerate from their first natures as to grow wild.

Irenius: So much can liberty and ill example do. . . . This ye may read plainly discovered by a letter written by the citizens of Cork out of Ireland to the Earl of Shrewsbury then in England and remaining yet upon record both in the Tower of England, also among the chronicles of Ireland, wherein it is by them complained that the English lords and gentlemen who then had great possessions in Ireland began through pride and insolence, to make private wars one against another . . . I mean of such English as were planted above towards the west, for the English pale hath preserved itself through nearness of their state in reasonable civility, but the rest which dwell above in Connaught and Munster, which is the sweetest soil of Ireland, and some in Leinster and Ulster, are degenerate and grown to be as very patchocks as the wild Irish, yea and some of them have quite shaken off their English names and put on Irish, that they might be altogether Irish.

Eudoxus: Is it possible that they should so far grow out of frame that they should in so short space quite forget their country and their own names? That is a most dangerous lethargy, much worse than that of Messala Corvinus, who being a most learned man, through sickness forgot his own name. But can you count us any of this kind?

Irenius: I cannot speak but by report of the Irish themselves, who report that in the north were anciently English, to wit, were descended from the Fitz-Ursulas, which was a noble family in England, and that the same appeareth by the signification of their Irish names. Likewise that the Macswineys now in Ulster were anciently of the Veres of England, but that they themselves for hatred of the English so disguised their names.

Eudoxus: Could they ever conceive such devilish dislike of their own natural country as that they would be ashamed of her name, and bite off her dug from which they sucked life?. . .

Irenius: Other great houses there be of the old English in Ireland, which through licentious conversing with the Irish, or marrying and fostering with them, or lack of meet nurture, or other such unhappy occasions, have degenerated from their ancient dignities and are now grown as Irish as O'Hanlon's breech, (as the proverb there is) of which sort there are two most pitiful examples above the rest, to wit the Lord Bremingham, who being the most ancient Baron I think in England, is now waxen the most savage Irish, naming himself, Irish-like, Maccorish; and the other is the great Mortimer, who forgetting how great he was once in

47

England, or English at all, is now become the most barbarous of them all, and is called Macnemarra; and not much better is he than the old Lord Courcie, who having lewdly wasted all the lands and signories that he had and aliened them unto the Irish is himself also now grown quite Irish.

Eudoxus: In truth, this which you tell is a most shameful hearing and to be reformed with most sharp censures in so great personages to the terror of the meaner. For where the lords and chief men wax so barbarous and bastardlike, what shall be hoped of the peasants and base people? And hereby sure you have made a fair way unto yourself to lay open the abuses of their evil customs which ye have now next to declare, the which no doubt but are very bad and barbarous, being borrowed from the Irish: as their apparel, their language, their riding, and many other the like.

Irenius: Ye cannot but think them sure to be very brute and uncivil, for they were at the best, that they were of old when they were brought in, they should in so long an alteration of time seem so very strange and uncouth: for it is to be thought that the use of all England was, in the reign of Henry the Second when Ireland was first planted with English, very rude and barbarous, so as if the same should be now used in England by any it would seem worthy of sharp correction, and of new laws for reformation; but it is even the other day since England grew civil. Therefore in counting the evil customs of the English there I will not have regard whether the beginning thereof were English or Irish, but will have respect only to the inconvenience thereof, and first I have to find fault with the abuse of language, that is for the speaking of Irish amongst the English, which, as it is unnatural that any people should love another's language more than their own, so it is very inconvenient and the cause of many other evils.

Eudoxus: It seemeth strange to me that the English should take more delight to speak that language than their own, whereas they should (methinks) rather take scorn to acquaint their tongues thereto, for it hath ever been the use of the conqueror to despise the language of the conquered, and to force him by all means to learn his. So did the Romans always use, insomuch that there is almost no nation in the world but is sprinkled with their language. It were good, therefore (methinks) to search out the original cause of this evil, for the same being discovered a redress thereof will be the more easily provided; for I think it strange that the English being so many and the Irish so few, as they then were left, the fewer should draw the more unto their use.

Irenius: I suppose that the chief cause of bringing in the Irish language amongst them was specially their fostering and marrying with the Irish, which are two most dangerous infections, for first the child that sucketh the milk of the nurse must of necessity learn his first speech of her, the which being the first that is inured to his tongue is ever after most pleasing to him, insomuch as though he afterwards be taught English, yet the smack of the first will always abide with him, and not only of the speech, but of the manners and conditions. For besides the young children be like apes, which will affect and imitate what they see done before them, specially by their nurses whom they love so well. They moreover draw into themselves together with their suck, even the nature and disposition of their nurses, for the mind followeth much the temperature of their body; and also the words are the image of the mind, so as they proceeding from the mind, the mind must needs be affected with the words; so that the speech being Irish, the heart must needs be Irish, for out of the abundance of the heart the tongue speaketh. The next is the marrying with the Irish, which how dangerous a thing it is in all commonwealths appeareth to every simple sense, and though some great ones have used such matches with their vassals, and have of themselves nevertheless raised worthy issue, as Telamon did with Tocmissa, Alexander the Great with Roxan, and Julius Caesar with Cleopatra, yet the example is so perilous as it is not to be adventured, for instead of these few good, I could count unto them infinite many evil; and indeed how can such matching but bring forth an evil race, seeing that commonly the child taketh most of his nature from the mother, besides, speech, manners, inclination, which are for the most part agreeable to the conditions of their mothers, for by them they are first framed and fashioned, so as they receive anything from them, they will hardly ever after forego. Therefore are these two evil customs, of fostering and marrying with the Irish most carefully to be restrained, for of them two, the third, that is the evil custom of language which I spake of, chiefly proceedeth.

2.24 *Henry the Fifth*, William Shakespeare, 1599

Gower.　The Duke of Gloucester, to whom the order of the siege is given, is altogether directed by an Irishman, a very valiant gentleman yfaith.

Welch.　It is Captaine *Makmorrice*, is it not?

Gower.　I thinke it be.

Welch.　By *Chesu* he is an Asse, as in the World, I will verify as much in his Beard: he ha's no more directions in the true disciplines of the Warres, looke you, of the Roman disciplines, then is a Puppy-dog

Enter Makmorrice, *and Captaine* Iamy.

Gower.	Here a comes, and the Scots Captaine, Captaine *Iamy*, with him.
Welch.	Captaine *Iamy* is a marvellous falorous Gentleman, that is certain, and of great expedition and knowledge in the aunchiant Warres, vpon my particular knowledge of his directions: by *Chesu* he will maintaine his Argument as well as any Militarie man in the World, in the disciplines of the Pristine Warres of the Romans.
Scot.	I say gudday, Captaine *Fluellen*.
Welch.	Godden to your Worship, good Captaine *Iames*.
Gower.	How now Captaine *Mackmorrice*, haue you quit the Mynes? haue the Pioners giuen o're?
Irish.	By Chrish Law tish ill done: the Worke is giue ouer, the Trompet sound the Retreat. By my Hand I sweare, and my fathers Soule, the Worke ish ill done: it ish giue ouer: I would haue blowed vp the Towne, so Chrish saue me law, in an houre. O tish ill done, tish ill done: by my Hand tish ill done.
Welch.	Captaine *Mackmorrice*, I beseech you now, will you voutsafe me, looke you, a few disputations with you, as partly touching or concerning the disciplines of the Warre, the Roman Warres, in the way of Argument, looke you, and friendly communication: partly to satisfie my Opinion, and partly for the satisfaction, looke you, of my Mind: as touching the direction of the Militarie discipline, that is the Point.
Scot.	It sall be very gud, gud feith, gud Captens bath, and I sall quit you with gud leue, as I may pick occasion: that sall I mary.
Irish.	It is no time to discourse, so Chrish saue me: the day is hot, and the Weather, and the Warres, and the King, and the Dukes: it is no time to discourse, the Town is beseech'd: and the Trompet call vs to the breech, and we talke, and be Chrish do nothing, tis shame for vs all: so God sa'me tis shame to stand still, it is shame by my hand: and there is Throats to be cut, and Workes to be done, and there ish nothing done, so Chrish sa'me law.
Scot.	By the Mes, ere theise eyes of mine take themselues to slomber, ayle de gud seruice, or Ile ligge i'th'grund for it: ay, or goe to death: and Ile pay't as valorously as I may, that sal I suerly do, that is the breff and the long: mary, I wad full faine heard some question tween you tway.
Welch.	Captaine *Mackmorrice*, I thinke, looke you, vnder your correction, there is not many of your Nation—
Irish.	Of my Nation? What ish my Nation? Ish a Villaine and a Basterd, and a Knaue, and a Rascall. What ish my Nation? Who talkes of my Nation?

Welch.	Looke you, if you take the matter otherwise than is meant, Captaine *Mackmorrice*, peraduenture I shall thinke you doe not vse me with that affibilitie, as in good discretion you ought to vse me looke you, being a good man as yourselfe, both in the disciplines of Warre, and in the deriuation of my Birth, and in other particularities.
Irish.	I doe not know you so good a man as my selfe: so Chrish saue me, I will cut off your head.
Gower.	Gentlemen both, you will mistake each other.
Scot.	A, that's a foule fault. [*A Parley.*]
Welch.	Captaine *Mackmorrice*, when there is more better opportunitie to be required, looke you, I will be so bold as to tell you, I know the disciplines of Warre: and there is an end.

[Exit.]

2.25 *Tiomna Nuadh (New Testament)*, Uilliam Ó Domhnaill (William Daniel) 1602

The quietness and peace of Kingdoms (most gracious Sovereign) consisteth chiefly in the planting of true Religion, and in the utter extirpation of idolatry and superstition, as both the examples of the Word and of the World do prove abundantly, where upon Satan by his wicked instruments, hath laboured in all ages, to uphold his Kingdom of darkness, with rotten pillars of falsehood and ignorance; so hath the Lord Jesus by the Ministry of his servants, plainly discovered Satan's sleights, and mightily battered his Kingdom, with the Canon of his Word and Gospel. And as in his heavenly wisdom he hath sanctified the preaching thereof to beget faith and repentance unto salvation: so hath he in mercy given excellent blessings unto the godly labours of such, as with judgement, care and conscience have travailed in deriving of the saving light from the pure fountain of the original unto the vulgar tongue (as all the Churches of God do confess unto his glory, and their exceeding comfort, whose translations are extant, to the condemnation of Antichrist and his synagogue, who hate the light because their works are evil). The mere Irish of your Majesty's Kingdom of Ireland (a people that of long time have sat in darkness and in the shadow of death, without hope, without Christ, without God in the world) have been hitherto deprived of this heavenly comfort and means of their salvation: to the great dishonour of God, the heavy loss of many thousand souls, the everlasting shame of their spiritual Pastors and governors, and the great disquieting of your Majesty's noble predecessors, and your loyal subjects of England. And notwithstanding that our late dread Sovereign Elizabeth of famous memory, (as God had richly furnished her with all the Princely and Christian virtues) had in conscience of her duty, and in Christian pity and compassion of the misery of her subjects, afforded many good means of

51

reformation, by establishing good and wholesome laws and statutes, and by sending over many choice and wholesome persons, for the administration of justice, and maintenance of the truth: and even in the beginning of her most happy reign (out of her motherly care, and Princely bounty) provided the Irish Characters and other Instruments for the Press, in the hope that God in mercy would raise up some to translate the New Testament into their mother tongue: yet hath Satan hitherto prevailed, and still they remain *Lo – ruchama*, *Lo – ammi*, through the ignorance of our ministers, the carelessness of our Magistrates, and the subtlety of AntiChrist and his vassals, the filthy fry of Romish seducers, the hellish firebrands of all our troubles.

2.26 *The Life and Death of Captain Thomas Stukeley,* anon. [G.Peele?], 1605

Enter Shane O'Neale, O'Hanlon, Neale Mackener *softly as by night.*

O'Neale	O'Hanlon.
Hanlon.	Owe.
O'Neale.	Fate is the token? fate siegne that Brian Mack Phelem said he would hang oot?
Han.	I'feate, I kno not; ask the Shecretary.
O'Neale.	Neale Mackener.
Mack.	Hest, O'Neale, Hest, pease! too art at the vater seed.
O'Neale.	Fate is the token bodeaugh breene? that I shall see Ovare the valles of this toone of Dundalke?
Mack.	I'feat O'Neale thoo art Saint Patrick his cushin and a great Lord, but thou art not weeze. The siegne is a paire
	Of feet trouzes, or a feet shurt, or some feete blankead
	To be hang oote over the valles, fan we sall be let in at the lettle Booygh dore by the abbay.
O'Neale.	Esta clamper, thoo talkest too much, the English
	Upon the vall will heare thee, lake, feagh, bodeaugh
	Dost thou see any feet.
Mack.	No by this hand, Shan O'Neale, we see no feat thing.
	[*One coughs within.*]
Han.	Cresh blesh us, fo ish tat ishe coughes?
Mack.	Saint Patrick blesh us we be not betraid.
O'Neale.	Mackener, Mac Deawle, marasfot art thou a feete liverd kana: Tish some English churl in the toone
	That coughes, that is dree, some prood English soudiour hees a dree cough, can drinke no vater. The English churle dees
	If he get not bread and porrage and a hose to lee in: but looke is

the sieegne oote? zeele cut his troate and help him of his cough
fan I get into Dundalk.

Mack.   Bee this hand O'Neale der is no siegne, zee am afraid
Brian Mack Phelemy is wid his streepo, and forgeats To hang a
siegne or let us in.

O'Neale.   No matter; come, no noyse, 'tis almost day
Softly, let us creepe aboote by the valles seed, ana awan sone at
night
Even at shuttene of the gates fan O'Con and Magennis
Come from Carlingford, we will enter lustily the town
Mackener, O'Hanlon, zee will give you tree captaines to ransom.

Han.   Zee will take tree prishoners, and give thee too, and take de turd
myself.

O'Neale.   Speake softly O'Hanlon, and gow, make ready oore kerne and
gallinglasse against night, and bid my bagpiper be ready to peep
Ballootherie soon, for I will sleep in Dundalke at night. Come,
go back into the Fewes again.

Han.   Slave haggat Bryan Mac Phelemy.

Mack.   Slave, let's Rorie beg.

[*Exit.*]

3

1607–1690

INTRODUCTION

Ireland was a turbulent and divided society in the seventeenth century; it witnessed the realisation of the worst fears of both the English Crown and its Planters and the Gaelic Catholic populace. In terms of colonial policy there were clear continuities with the practice of the past. Stress was again laid upon education as a way of reforming Catholics (a Catholic account of this policy is given below). In the mid-seventeenth century concern was once more expressed that the Irish language was still being used even in the securely English capital. The other link with the previous period was the pattern of rebellion against the English Crown, followed by banishment and Plantation. This occurred three times during the century and the political and cultural effects were far-reaching.

The defeat of the Irish forces at Kinsale in 1601 brought the Nine Years' War to an end, though Hugh O'Neill, the English Crown's main opponent, did not submit until 1603. O'Neill's use of the Roman concept of *patria*, the sense of a homeland demanding allegiance, though it did not stir the Old English at this point, prefigured the later development of Irish nationalism and was perceived by the Crown as a threat serious enough to call for a decisive response. Victory at Kinsale gave the English Crown complete military control over Ireland in effect for the first time. This, together with the Flight of the Earls in 1607 (the departure of the Gaelic chieftains to the haven of Catholic Europe) and the Plantation of Ulster, is usually taken to signal an important step towards the end of Gaelic Ireland.

The second significant event occurred in the mid-seventeenth century in the form of the Confederate War. The long-standing fear of the Crown and its loyal Protestant Planters – the political unification of the Gaelic Catholics with their Old English co-religionists – was realised as a result of increasing hostility on both sides of the divide. Specific issues included religious freedom and, of course, the sequestration of land for Plantation. The rising of 1641 and the subsequent convocation of an assembly and executive body, taking place as it did during the English Civil War, placed colonial order in danger. The revolt was finally crushed by a combination of internal division, poor leadership, economic weakness and the onslaught of Cromwell's New Model Army between 1649 and 1651. The Cromwellian land settlement which followed was executed with a level of severity proportionate to the estimation of the threat which had been countered. Catholic landowners were removed in Leinster, Munster and Ulster and replaced by a new generation of Planters.

The final conflict of the period directly affected social and cultural life in Ireland for a hundred years or more. If the Catholic Confederation had been traumatic for the Protestant community, defeat in the Williamite Wars, and the land seizures and legal constraints which followed, was the realisation of the nightmare for Irish Catholics. It put the seal on an era which had seen Catholic Gaelic Ireland utterly defeated, and ushered in a century of repression. The practical implications of defeat in the wars of 1689 and 1691 will be explored in Chapter 4; here it will serve as the end-point of a process which had developed throughout the seventeenth century: the gradual and bitterly gained emergence of Protestant colonial rule based on the elimination of Catholicism and the Gaelic order.

As noted earlier, the continuing use of Irish remained a problem to which a solution had yet to be found, demonstrated here in the extra payment to a colonial servant made on the grounds that he was loyal, efficient and spoke Irish, the latter quality adding to his usefulness. The legislation on the matter of place-names introduces a theme which was to be a repeated concern and which culminated, indirectly, in the achievement of the Ordnance Survey in the nineteenth century. Yet colonial policy and thinking at this time evinced more sophistication (if not always veracity) than earlier, as shown in the writings of observers such as Davies, Moryson and Petty. Davies, for example, reiterates that grand theme of the Chroniclers, the cultural 'degeneration' of the English. Yet he also raised the pertinent questions of why and how the English had been allowed to 'degenerate' to the point at which they were worse enemies to the King than the 'mere' (unmixed or pure) Irish. He also posed the important if uncomfortable question of why it was that after more than four hundred years of conflict Ireland had not yet become a loyal subject kingdom. It was a politically astute question, which necessarily, if implicitly, contained a criticism of the faults of colonial government rather than a simple citation of the rebellious nature of the Irish. The intelligence evident in this point is also notable in the general observations of one of the period's travel-writers, Fynes Moryson. His comment that languages create communities was both perceptive and prescient: it was to become one of the central tenets of European cultural nationalism.

The response of Catholic Gaeldom to its unprecedented wholescale defeat took two forms: allegiance to the European Counter-Reformation, and cultural attacks on the new order, coupled to the lament for the lost cultural formation of Gaelic Ireland. The establishment of Irish colleges in Europe (the first, at Salamanca, was founded in the same year as Trinity College) was part of a strategy to rebut the progress of Protestantism. It was given particular impetus by the publication of the *New Testament* by the established Church, which prompted in turn the appearance of a number of devotional works in Irish. Early examples include Ó hEódhasa's *An Teagasg Críosdaidhe* (Antwerp, 1611), Ó Maoilchonaire's *Sgáthán an Chrábhaidh* (Louvain, 1616) and Mac Aingil's *Sgáthán Shacramuinte na hAithridhe* (Louvain, 1618). The *Catechismus* by Teabóid Gallduf (Theobald Stapleton), published in Brussels in 1639, is important for two reasons: it was printed in Roman rather than Gaelic type, and it altered traditional orthography in order to make the text more easily comprehensible. Also worthy of notice is his defence of, and expression of love for, the native language *per se*. His rebuke to those who were meant to protect Gaelic culture, here the Gaelic aristocracy and the bards, for their neglect and corruption of the language was a charge which was to be heard again.

Other responses to the wrecking of Gaelic culture were made in the forms of histories and poetry. The work of Giraldus and the Chroniclers had set the agenda in historiography and the seventeenth century saw the native riposte. Foremost amongst the historians were Seathrún Céitinn and Mícheúl Ó Cléirigh. Céitinn's *Foras Feasa ar Éirinn* [*Basis of Knowledge about Ireland*], written *c*.1618–34, is a monumental work written in an accessible style. Ó Cléirigh was the principal compiler of *Annala Ríoghachta Éireann* [*Annals of the Kingdom of Ireland*], usually known as the *Annals of the Four Masters*, written 1632–36, which is the gathering of the Annals of Irish history from the earliest times to 1616. His *Foclóir na Sanasán Nua* [*A New Vocabulary or Glossary*] (1643) is a continuation of the native practice of lexicography dating back to the Old Irish period, and the forerunner of the dictionaries of the eighteenth century. Lynch, another defender of Gaelic history and culture against Giraldus, like Céitinn, pays particular attention to the origin and qualities of Irish.

The Gaelic bards, whose economic livelihood and social status were fatally damaged by the destruction of the Gaelic order, gave vent to savage attacks on the new situation and keened their grievous loss. The bitter denunciation is captured in the anonymous prose work *Pairlement Chloine Tomáis*, a harsh satire on the social pretensions of those of the Gaelic Irish who had benefited from the overturning of the old regime. The mockery centres in the extract given here on the speaking of a half-acquired mongrel form of English. The use of English, with all that it signifies, is also one of the themes of desolation and despair in the work of seventeeth-century poets, including that of the most accomplished, Dháibhidh Ó Bruadair.

3.1 *Leabhar na nUrnaightheadh gComhchoidchiond [The Book of Common Prayer]*, Uilliam Ó Domhnaill (William Daniel) 1608

Right Honourable [Lieutenant Deputy General], if learning and religion were hereditary to any Nation (as they are not, witness Jews and Grecians) this noble Island, (noble in respect of the quantity, and quality of the soil) might compare with any other whatsoever. . . . And notwithstanding that since the time that Satan was set at liberty, the smoke of the bottomless pit hath darkened the Sun and Air, as well in this Kingdom, as in all other Christian Kingdoms of the World: yet there is great hope that (Satan being now tied, the short time of his tyranny for deceiving universally being expired) this Kingdom may flourish in the same mercy that the neighbour Kingdoms do, and may see greater glory then ever it hath seen heretofore. . . . What though Satan do now rage more among us than ever heretofore? His rage argues his desperate estate, and the utter ruin of his Kingdom. The blessed Trinity hath already founded a College upon our Eastern shore, wherein learning and Religion begins to flourish and (rising with the Sun) to spread the beams thereof already to some parts, with much comfort and joy: And I nothing doubt, but that in God's good time, by the means thereof, and of the like Schools of good learning, (the chiefest means of reformation) the country that doth now generally sit in darkness, shall in time see great light . . . I see nothing wanting but zealous hearts and hands to build the Temple of the Lord, our gracious God having made the way plain, by causing our wars to cease, the Lord having partly swallowed up in displeasure the disturbers of our peace, and partly spewed them out into Strange Countries, craving better Inhabitants to enjoy her blessings. . . . And having out of an understanding heart wisely considered, that the liturgy of the Church coming in the cloud of an unknown tongue, can leave no blessing behind it, (as both the Apostle teacheth, and this poor Church can testify by woeful experience) it pleased your Lordship to impose upon myself, the burden of translating the Book of Common Prayer, (the liturgy of the Famous Church of England) into the mother tongue (for the comfort of the mere Irish Churches) to the end that the ignorant may understand, how grossly they are abused by their blind malicious guides, which bear them in hand that without divine is nothing else, but the service of the Devil . . . I humbly pray your Lordship to send it abroad into the Country Churches, together with the elder brother the new Testament, to be fostered and fomented; God's blessing and mine be with them.

3.2 *Cal.S.P. Ire.*, 1608–10, 1609

Certain Considerations touching the Plantation of the Escheated Lands in Ulster.

It is worthy of consideration how the English language and customs may be preserved, neat and pure, unto posterity, without which he accounts it no good plantation nor any great honour and security to them to induce people thither.

The way to perform that is to separate the Irish by themselves, to forebear marrying and fostering, and if possible to exceed them in multitude; for all other effectual courses are either too severe or too difficult to attempt.

Consider how the old English language was first brought in and continued to this day, both in the English Pale and in some baronies in the County of Wexford, and also in some places in South Wales, and whether the same happened by laws, or extirpation of the ancient inhabitants.

3.3 *A Discovery of the True Causes Why Ireland Was Never Entirely Subdued*, Sir John Davies, 1612

During the time of my service in Ireland, which began in the first year of His Majesty's reign, I have visited all the provinces of that kingdom in sundry journeys and circuits. . . . The observation thereof hath bred in me some curiosity to consider what were the true causes why this kingdom, whereof our kings of England have borne the title of sovereign lords for the space of four hundred and odd years, a period of time wherein divers great monarchies have risen from barbarism to civility, and fallen again to ruin, was not in all that space of time thoroughly subdued and reduced to obedience of the Crown of England, although there hath been almost a continual war between the English and the Irish; and why the manners of the mere Irish are so little altered since the days of King Henry the Second, as appeareth by the description made by Giraldus Cambrensis, who wrote and lived in that time, albeit there have been since that time so many English colonies planted in Ireland as that, if the people were numbered at this day by the poll, such as are descended of English race would be found more in number than the ancient natives. . . . The defects which hindered the perfection of the conquest of Ireland were of two kinds, and consisted, first, in the faint prosecution of the war, and next in the looseness of the civil government. For the husbandman must first break the land before it be made capable of good seed; and when it is thoroughly broken and manured, if he do not forthwith cast good seed into it, it will grow wild again and bear nothing but weeds. So a barbarous country must first be broken by a war before it will be capable of good government; and when it is fully subdued and conquered, if it be not well planted and governed after the conquest, it will eftsoons return to the former barbarism. . . . For that I call a perfect conquest of a country which doth reduce all people thereof to the condition of subjects; and those I call subjects which are governed by the ordinary laws and magistrates of the sovereign. . . .

It now remaineth that we show the defects of the civil policy and government which gave no less impediment to the perfection of this conquest . . . : First, that the Kings of England, which in former ages attempted the conquest of Ireland, being ill advised and counselled by the great men here, did not, upon the submissions of the Irish, communicate their laws unto them, nor admit them to the state and condition of free subjects. Secondly, that for the space of two hundred years at least after the arrival of Henry the Second in Ireland the Irish would gladly have embraced the laws of

England, and did earnestly desire the benefit and protection thereof, which being denied them, did of necessity cause a continual bordering war between the English and the Irish. And lastly, if, according to the examples before recited, they had reduced as well the Irish counties as the English colonies under one form of civil government, as now they are, the meres and bounds of the marches and borders had been long since worn out and forgotten – for it is not fit, as Cambrensis writeth, that a King of an island should have any borders but the four seas – both nations had been incorporated and united, Ireland had been entirely conquered, planted, and improved, and returned a rich revenue to the Crown of England. . . .

[On the adoption of Irish customs by the colonisers]: These were the Irish customs which the English colonies did embrace and use after they had rejected the civil and honourable laws and customs of England, whereby they became degenerate . . . insomuch as within less time than the age of a man they had no marks or differences left amongst them of that noble nation from which they were descended. For, as they did not only forget the English language and scorn the use thereof, but grew to be ashamed of their very English names, though they were noble and of great antiquity, and took Irish surnames and nicknames. Namely, the two most potent families of the Bourkes in Connaught, after the House of the Red Earl failed of heirs-males, called their chiefs MacWilliam Eighter and MacWilliam Oughter. In the same province, Bremingham, Baron of Athenrie, called himself MacYoris; Dexecester, or De'exon, was called Mac-Jordan; Dangle, or De Angulo, took the name of MacCostelo. Of the inferior families of the Bourkes, one was called MacHubbard, another MacDavid. In Munster, of the great families of the Geraldines planted there, one was called MacMorice, chief of the House of Lixnaw; and another MacGibbon, who was also called the White Knight. The chief of the Baron of Dunboyne's house, who is a branch of the House of Ormond, took the surname of MacFeris. Condon, of the county of Waterford, was called MacMaoige; and the Arch-deacon of the county of Kilkenny, MacOdo. And this they did in contempt and hatred of the English name and nation, whereof these degenerate families became more mortal enemies than the mere Irish. And whereas the State and Government, being grown weak by their defection, did, to reduce them to obedience, grant them many protections and pardons, the cheapness whereof in all ages hath brought great dishonour and damage to this commonweal, they grew so ungrateful and unnatural as in the end they scorned that grace and favour, because the acceptance thereof did argue them to be subjects, and they desired rather to be accounted enemies to the Crown of England. . . .

And now I am come to the happy reign of my Most Gracious Lord and Master King James, in whose time, as there hath been a concurrence of many great felicities, so this, among others, may be numbered in the first rank, that all the defects in the government of Ireland spoken of before have been fully supplied in the first nine years of his reign, in which time there hath been more done in the work and reformation of this kingdom than in the 440 years which are past since the conquest was first attempted. . . .

Civil assemblies at assizes and sessions have reclaimed the Irish from their wildness, caused them to cut off their glibs and long hair, to convert their mantles into cloaks, to conform themselves to the manner of England in all their behaviour and outward forms. And because they find a great inconvenience in moving their suits by an interpreter, they do for the most part send their children to schools, especially to learn the English language; so as we may conceive an hope that the next generation will in tongue and heart and every way else become English, so as there will be no difference or distinction but the Irish sea betwixt us. And thus we see a good conversion and the Irish game turned again.

For heretofore the neglect of the law made the English degenerate and become Irish; and now, on the other side, the execution of the law doth make the Irish grow civil and become English.

3.4 *An Account of the Decrees and Acts . . . in the year 1611 in Dublin*, Richard Conway, S.J., 1612

The greatest injury they have done, and one of the most serious consequences, was the prohibition of all Catholic schools in our nation (naturally so inclined to learning) except an odd infant school in the principal cities and towns, where only reading, writing, and a little grammar are taught; with the object of sinking our people to degradation, or filling the Universities of England with the children of those who had any means to educate them, where they might become more dependent on heretics, and contaminated with their errors. They have also taken singular care that all children be taught English, and they chastise them if they hear them speak their own native tongue. But as these . . . efforts did not have the desired effect, and the natives did not only not go to England, but rather preferred to remain in ignorance, than run the risk of their faith and religion by doing so, or went secretly and quietly to many foreign parts, but particularly to Spain, where his Catholic Majesty assisted them, and gave them some Colleges . . . they determined, in order to stop the ravages these colleges were committing . . . to found a University in the capital of the Kingdom, in which they put heretical masters to teach . . . and uproot the desire of Catholics to cross the sea.

3.5 *The Irish Masque at Court*, Ben Jonson, 1613

The King being set in expectation, out ran a fellow attired like a citizen: after him, three or four foot-men.

Dennise. Donnell. Dermock. Patrick.

For chreeshes sayk, phair ish te king? Phich ish hee, an't be? show me te shweet faish, quickly. By got, o' my conshence, tish ish he! Ant tou bee king YAMISH, me name is DENNISH, I sherve ti mayesties owne cashter-monger, bee mee trote: ant cry peep'sh, ant pomwater'sh i' ty mayesties shervice, 'tis five yeere now. An't tou vilt not trush me now, cal up to clarke o' ti kitchin, be ant be, shall give hish wort, upon hish booke, ish true.

DON.	Ish it te fashion, to beate te Imbasheters, here? ant knoke 'hem o' te heads, phit te phoit stick?
DER.	Ant make ter meshage runne out at ter mouthsh, before tey shpeake vit te King?
DENNISE.	Peash DERMOCK, here ish te King.
DER.	Phair ish te King?
DON.	Phich ish te King?
DEN.	Tat ish te King.
DER.	Ish tat te King? got blesh him.
DEN.	Peash, ant take heet, vat tou saysht, man.
DER.	Creesh blesh him, I shay. Phat reason I tayk heet, for tat?
DON.	Creesh blesh ti shweet faish, King YAMISH; ant my mistresh faish too: Pre tee, heare me now. I am come a great vay of miles to shee tee now, by my fayt and trote, and grasih o' got.
DEN.	Phat ish ti meaning o' tish, DONNELL? Didsh tou not shay a gotsh name, I should tell ti tayle for tee? ant entrayt me com to te court, ant leave me vare at shixe, ant seven? By got, ish true now.
DON.	Yesh. But I tanke got I can tell my tayle my shelfe, now I be here, I varrant tee: Pre dee heare me, King YAMISH.
DEN.	Pre dee heare me, King YAMISH. I can tell tee better ten he.
PAT.	Pre deee heare neder noder on 'hem.: Here'sh DERMOCK vill shpeake better ten eder oder on 'hem.
DER.	No fayt, shweet hart, tow lyesht. PHATRICK here ish te vesht man of hish tongue, of all de foure; pre tee now heare him.
PAT.	By chreesh shave me, tow lyesht. I have te vorsht tongue in te company at ty shervish. Vill shome body shpeake?
DON.	By my fayt, I vill not.
PAT.	Shpeake DENNISH ten.
DEN.	If I speake, te divell tayke me. I vill give tee leave to cram my mout phit shamrokes ant butter, ant vayter creshes, in stead of pearsh and peepsh.
PAT.	If no body vill shpeake, I vill shpeake. Please ty shweet faish, vee come from Ireland.
DER.	Vee be Irish men, and't please tee.

DON.	Ty good shubsects of Ireland, an't pleash ty mayesty.
DEN.	Fo Connough, Leymster, Ulster, Munster. I mine one shelfe vash borne in te English payle, an't pleash ty Mayesty . . .
DER.	Tou hasht very goot shubsects in Ireland.
DEN.	A great goot many, o' great goot shubshects.
DON.	Tat love ty mayesty heartily.
DEN.	Ant vil runne t'rough fire, ant vater for tee, over te bog, ant te Banncke, be te graish o' got, and graish o' king.
DER.	By got, tey vil fight for tee, king YAMISH, ant for my mistresh tere.
DEN.	Ant my little mayshter.
PAT.	Ant te vfrow, ty daughter, tat is in Tuchland.
DON.	Tey vill spend ter heart, in ter belly for tee, as vell as ter legs, in ter heelsh.
DER.	By creesh, tey vill shpend all teyr cowesh for tee.
DEN.	Pretee make mush on 'tem.
PAT.	Pretee, sweet faysh doe.
DON.	Be not angry vit te honesh men, for te few rebelsh, and knavesh.
PAT.	Nor beleeve no tayles, king YAMISH.
DER.	For, by got, tey love tee in Ireland.

3.6 *Pairlement Chloinne Tomáis [The Parliament of Clan Thomas]*, anon., 1615

'And as for us having noble surnames', said one of them, 'let each man invent a surname to suit himself'. 'That's all the more fitting', said Tomás an Trumpa, 'because I know many people who say they are of the Kindred of Brian, though they are of ignoble and uncouth families'. 'I'll be of the Kindred of Brian from now on', said Little Brian. 'That is fitting', said Diarmuid Ó Clúmháin; and Diarmuid composed a quatrain on that subject:

'Ó Clúmháin, seemly Ó Céirín,
 Ó Curnáin, Ó Feoir, Ó Bruic
we shall be now of the sons of Cian
of the Kindred of Niall and the Kindred of Blod'.

'Blessing and prosperity to you', said Tomás an Trumpa, 'it is not more fitting for many others these days, now that Ó Briain is powerful, to call themselves Ó Briain, than it is for us; and do you think we'll get honour and equality before the law, as many people I know do? Now, Diarmuid, my boy, what is your surname?' 'I am of the family of Caimidil', said Diarmuid, 'that is, Caimidil Ó Briain'. 'Prosperity and blessing to you', said Tomás an Trumpa, 'and let us now discuss our statutes', he said.

'I maintain myself', said Mathghamhuin Ó Clúmháin, 'that it is not right for us to have townlands of our own from now on, since we have become reduced, and we shouldn't be burdened with rent, but we should have to yield one sheaf in every four each year, and to provide hay every quarter'. And that statute was promulgated by them like every other. 'And as far as all the unemployed serfs who are going to France are concerned', they said, 'we are eternally better off for it, for they were only plunderers of many, who used to consume the provisions of the true busy-bees, namely the labourers. They will die over there and their property here will fall to people who are much worthier than they'.

They were not long then until they saw a young Englishman coming towards them. 'Who is yonder Englishman coming this way?' asked one of them. 'I know him', said another, 'it's Roibín an Tobaca, and the tobacco he brings with him is usually of good quality'. 'We'll buy some of it', said Bernard Ó Bruic, 'and who of us will speak English to him?' 'I myself', said Tomás. The young Englishman arrived and greeted them politely and said: *'God bless you, Thomas, and all your company'*. Tomás answered him in no uncivilised fashion and said: *'Pleshy for you, pleshy, goodman Robin'*. 'By my mother's soul', said Bernard Ó Bruic, 'you have swallowed the best of English'. Everybody gathered round him marvelling at Tomás's English. 'Ask him the price of the tobacco', said Bernard. Tomás spoke and said: *'What the bigg greate órdlach for the what so penny for is the la yourselfe for me?'* Roibín said: *'I know, Thomas, you aske how many enches is worth the penny'*, and he raised his two fingers as a sign, and said: *'Two penny an ench'*. 'By my godfather's hand, it's a good bargain', said Tomás. 'What is it?' asked Dour Diarmuid. 'Two pence an inch, said Tomás. 'Act on our behalf', they all said. 'I will', replied Tomás, and he said: *'Is ta for meselfe the mony for fart you all my brothers here'*. Roibín said: *'I thanke you, honest Thomas, you shall command all my tobacco'*. 'Begog, I thanke you', said Tomás. Tomás got the tobacco at his word and gave it to everyone.

Then every man among them brought out his dirty, broken clay-pipe from the bottom of his jerkin or from the ear-piece of his cap, and they set to expelling smoke through their nostrils and the next moment to inhaling it deep into their gullets for a long time. 'This is good tobacco', said Bernard Ó Bruic. 'I reckon you're right', said Tomás, 'since we heard it having a remarkable effect on some of the worthies of the committee'. 'Are you referring to me?' asked Bernard. 'I neither condemn nor acquit anyone', said Tomás. 'It was often your habit', said Bernard, 'to be a stirrer-up, a twister and a malicious jabbering slanderer in excess of many others'. And Tomás recited this quatrain:

'Let Bernard stop his equivocation,
   whether he farted or not;

      great the noise of the oaf's fart
        that blew out from behind his balls.'

'May we lack life and health', said everyone else, 'if we ever heard a wittier or wiser quatrain than that, since the death of Brian Ó Bloingidhe, for he was the best man at rhyming of his contemporaries'.

Then a shout of ridicule and mockery of Bernard went up. Bernard took off his cap and set off northwards, and he cursed everyone from whom he had received that insult; and he besought God not to allow that parliament peace, prosperity nor a successful outcome ever until the end of the world. And he obtained that request as was only right.

3.7 *An Itinerary*, Fynes Moryson, 1617

Touching the English Irish namely such as descend of the first English conquering that Country, or since in diverse ages, and times to this day transplanted out of England, into Ireland. It is wonderful yet most true, that for some later ages they have been (some in high some in less measure,) infected with the barbarous Customs of the mere Irish and with the Roman Religion so as they grew not only adverse to the Reformation of civil policy and religion, as the mere Irish but even combined with them, and showed such malice to the English nation, as if they were ashamed to have any Community with it, of Country, blood, religion, language, apparel, or any such general bond of amity. . . .

Again Contrary to the said laws, the Irish English altogether used the Irish tongue, forgetting or never learning the English. And this communion or difference of language, hath always been observed, a special motive to unite or alienate the minds of all nations, so as the wise Romans as they enlarged their Conquests, so they did spread their language with their laws, and the divine service in the latin tongue, and by rewards and preferments invited men to speak it, as also the Normans in England brought in the use of the French tongue, in our Common law, and all words of art in hawking, hunting, and like pastimes. And in general all nations have thought nothing more powerful to unite minds than the Community of language. But the law to spread the English tongue in Ireland, was ever interrupted by Rebellions, and much more by ill affected subjects, as at this time whereof I write, the mere Irish disdained to learn or speak the English tongue, yea the very English Irish and the very Citizens (excepting those of Dublin where the lord Deputy resides) though they could speak English as well as we, yet Commonly speak Irish among themselves, and were hardly induced by our familiar Conversation to speak English with us, yea Common experience showed, and myself and others often observed, the Citizens of Waterford and Cork having wives that could speak English as well as we, bitterly to chide them when they speak English with us, insomuch as after the Rebellion ended, when the Itinerant Judges went their Circuits through the kingdom each half year to keep assizes, few of the people no not the Jurymen could speak English, and at like Sessions in Ulster, all the gentlemen and common people (excepting only the Judge's train) and the very Jurymen put upon life and death and all trials in law, commonly spoke Irish, many Spanish, and few or none could or would speak English. These outward signs being the outward touchstones of the inward affection, manifestly showed that the English Irish held it a reproach among themselves, to apply themselves any way to the English, or not to follow the Irish in all things.

3.8 *Cal.pat.rolls Ire., James I*, King James to Oliver St John, Deputy, 1620

Right trusty and well beloved We greet you well. . . . And because We understand that the simple natives of that our kingdom, who by experience we hear are found to be far more tractable amongst the rude Irish than amongst the unconformable English, are still kept in darkness and apt and ready thereby to be led into error superstition and disobedience by the popish priests who abuse their simplicity and ignorance, which proceeds through want of ministers who could speak their own language, whom they may understand: Because our college of Dublin was founded by our late sister of happy memory Queen Elizabeth, and has been since plentifully endowed by us, principally for breeding up the natives of that kingdom in civility, learning and religion: We have reason to expect that, in all this long time of our peaceable government, some good numbers of the natives should have been trained up in that college, and might have been employed in teaching and reducing those which are ignorant among that people: And to think that the governors of that house have not performed the trust reposed in them, if the revenues thereof have been otherwise employed; And therefore We do require that henceforth special care be had, and that the visitors of that University be required particularly to look into and take care of this point; And for the supplying of the present want, that choice be made of some competent number of towardly young men already fitted with the knowledge of the Irish tongue, and be placed in the university, and maintained there for two or three years, till they have learned the grounds of religion, and be able to catechise the natives, and deliver unto them so much as themselves have learned, and when any livings that are not of any great value fall void among the mere Irish, these men be thought upon before others, to be placed with other able ministers that possess livings amongst the mere Irish (where for defect of the language they are able to do little good) to be interpreters unto them.

3.9 *Cal.S.P. Ire.*, 1625–32, 1627

The King to the Vice-treasurer and Receiver General in Ireland to the Chancellor and the Barons of the Exchequer there, now being or hereafter to be made.

Edward Keating, Comptroller of the Pipe, and second engrosser of the Great Roll of the Court of Chancery there, complains that his duties increase, and he only gets 120l a year. He wishes for fees and salary similar to those paid in England. He is a loyal and efficient servant and knows Irish, which makes him more useful. We therefore order you to grant him £E8 a year over and above his ancient fee, to be taken out of fines, and forfeited recognizances.

3.10 *Foras Feasa Ar Éirinn [A Basis of Knowledge about Ireland]*, Seathrún Céitinn (Geoffrey Keating), 1634

From the worthlessness of the testimony Stanihurst gives concerning the Irish, I consider that he should be rejected as a witness, because it was purposely at the instigation of a party who were hostile to the Irish that he wrote contemptuously of them; and, I think, that hatred of the Irish must have been the first dug he drew after his first going into England to study, and that it lay as a weight on his stomach till, having returned to Ireland, he rejected it by his writing. I deem it no small token of the aversion he had for the Irish, that he finds fault with the colonists of the English province for that they did not banish the Gaelic from the country at the time when they routed the people who were dwelling in the land before them. He also says, however excellent the Gaelic language may be, that whoever smacks thereof, would likewise savour of the ill manners of the folk whose language it is. What is to be understood from this, but that Stanihurst had so great an hatred for the Irish, that he deemed it an evil that it was a Christian-like conquest the Gaill achieved over Ireland and the Gael, and not a pagan conquest. For, indeed, he who makes a Christian conquest thinks it sufficient to obtain submission and fidelity from the people who have been subdued by him, and to send from himself other new people to inhabit the land over which his power has prevailed, together with the people of that country. Moreover, it is the manner of him who makes a pagan conquest, to bring destruction on the people who are subdued by him, and to send new people from himself to inhabit the country which he has taken by force. But he who makes a Christian conquest extinguishes not the language which was before him in any country which he brings under control: and it is thus William the Conqueror did as regards the Saxons. He did not extinguish the language of the Saxons, seeing that he suffered the people who used that language to remain in the country, so that it resulted therefrom that the language has been preserved from that time down among the Saxons. Howbeit, it is a pagan conquest which Hengist, the chief of the Saxons made over the Britons, since he swept them from the soil of Britain, and sent people from himself in their places; and having altogether banished everyone, he banished their language with them. And it is the same way Stanihurst would desire to act by the Irish; for it is not possible to banish the language without banishing the folk whose language it is: and, inasmuch as he had the desire of banishing the language, he has, likewise, the desire of banishing the people whose language it was, and, accordingly, he was hostile to the Irish; and so his testimony concerning the Irish ought not to be received. . . .

The refutation of these new foreign writers need not be pursued by us any further, although there are many things they insert in their histories, which it would be possible to confute; because, as to the most part of what they write disparagingly of Ireland, they have no authority for writing it but repeating the tales of false witnesses who were hostile to Ireland, and ignorant of her history. . . . If indeed it be that the soil is commended by every historian who writes on Ireland, the race is dispraised by every new foreign historian who writes about it, and it is by that I was incited to write this history concerning the Irish, owing to the extent of the pity I felt at the manifest injustice which is done to them by those writers. . . .

When Feinius Farsaidh became king of Scythia, he determined to become acquainted with the various languages which had sprung up after the confusion of tongues that had taken place long before at the tower of Babel, which was being erected through pride for the space of forty years by Nimrod and his followers. For before that confusion of tongues took place at the tower, the entire human race had but one common language which had existed amongst them from the time of Adam. And the name the Book of Invasions gives this language is Gortighern, as the poet says:

> Gortighern the name of the language
> Used by the son of God of goodly science,
> And by the race of Adam erst
> Ere the building of Nimrod's tower.

And Latin authors call it *lingua humana*, that is, the human language. But when Nimrod and his kinsfolk were building the tower, as the confusion of languages set in and prevented them from finishing a structure they had begun through pride, the human language they derived from Adam was taken from them, as many were engaged in building the tower. However, it remained with Eibhear son of Saile, and with his tribe, so that it was named from him; for they called it Hebrew from Eibhear. Now when Eibhear had learned the cause of their erecting the tower, that it was with a view to protecting themselves against the second flood which it was foretold would come upon the people – they imagined that the second flood

67

would not be higher than the first, and proposed to make the tower so high that the flood would not reach its upper stories, and that accordingly their nobles could be securely situated in these without fear of the flood – and when Eibhear learned that was the cause of their buidling the tower, he declared that he would not help them, and that it was sheer idleness on their part to have to recourse to ingenuity for the purpose of resisting the fulfilment of God's will. Thereupon he separated from them without taking any part with them whatever in the building of the tower. Moreover, when the confusion came on all, God left to Eibhear alone and to his tribe after him, as a mark of good will, that human language of our ancestors.

The principal reason why Feinius Farsaidh went to the plain of Seanair, together with his school, was that he might be with the people whose native language was Hebrew, and that it might thus come about that he and his school would acquire a full and perfect knowledge of that language.

Now, when Feinius, as we have said, had resolved to acquire the various languages, he sent, at his own expense, seventy-two disciples into the various countries of the three continents of the world that were then inhabited, and charged them to remain abroad seven years, so that each of them might learn the language of the country in which he stayed during that time. And at the end of seven years they returned to Feinius to Scythia; and Feinius went with them to the Plain of Seanair, together with a large number of the youths of Scythia, leaving his eldest son Neanual to rule Scythia in his stead, as a certain poet says, in the poem which begins, 'Let us relate the origin of the Gaels':

> Feinius went from Scythia
>   On the expedition,
> A man renowned, wise, learned,
>   Ardent, triumphant;
>
> There was but one tongue in the world
>   When they set out;
> There were seventy-two tongues
>   When they parted;
>
> Feinius had a great school of learning
>   Each science,
> A man renowned, wise, learned
>   In each language.

And some seanchas assert that there was a space of sixty years from the building of the tower until Feinius and his school came southwards from Scythia to the Plain of Seanair, as a certain poet says in this stanza:

Thrice twenty years of renown,
So every seancha says,
Till Feinius came southwards,
From the building of Nimrod's tower.

Feinius established schools for the teaching of the various languages on
the Plain of Seanair in the city which Cin Droma Sneachta calls Eathena, as
the poet says in the following stanza:

In the Plain of Seanair after the tower,
The first school was assembled,
In the city of Eathena,
To learn the various tongues.

And they assembled the youths of the countries next them to learn the
various tongues from them; and the three sages who presided over this
school were Feinius Farsaidh himself from Scythia, and Gaedheal son of
Eathor of the race of Gomer from Greece, and Caoi Caoinbhreathach from
Judea, or Iar son of Neama, as the poet says:

Here are the names of the sages –
I shall reveal them to you speedily –
Gaedheal son of Eathor of wisdom,
Iar son of Neama and Feinius.

Another poet speaks thus:

Feinius the eloquent sage,
Gaedheal and Caoi Caoinbhreathach,
Three of the writers of the schools
Who followed in the true track of the authors.

It was this trio who wrote on wooden tablets the alphabets of the three chief
languages, namely, Hebrew, Greek, and Latin, as Ceannfaolaidh the Learned
asserts in the Accidence which he wrote in the time of Columcille. The same
author states that Nion son of Beil, son of Nimrod, was monarch of the
world at that time. He also states that it was about this time that Niul,
the tanist son of Feinius Farsaidh, was born, and that the same Feinius
continued in charge of the school for twenty years in order that this son
who was born to him might be acquainted with the several languages.

As some seanchas assert that it was when Nion son of Beil had reigned
forty-two years that Feinius Farsaidh established a school in the Plain of
Seanair, I am of opinion that he passed ten years of the reign of Nion son
of Beil, and ten years thereafter, in the Plain of Seanair before he returned
from the school to Scythia. I am also of opinion that it was two hundred

and forty-two years after the Deluge that Feinius established the school in the Plain of Seanair, according to the computation Bellarminus makes in his chronicle, where he says that the age of the world was one thousand eight hundred and fifty-six years when Nion son of Beil began his sovereignty. . . .

Now after twenty years Feinius returned to Scythia, and established schools there, and appointed Gaedheal son of Eathor to take charge of them. Then did Feinius command Gaedheal to arrange and regulate the Gaelic language as it is into five divisions, that is, Bearla na Feine, Bearla na bhFileadh, Bearla an Eaderscartha, Bearla Teibidhe, and Gnaithbhearla, and to name it precisely from himself; hence it is from Gaedheal son of Eathor it is called Gaelic, and not from Gaedheal Glas, as others assert. Moreover, it was through friendship for Gaedheal son of Eathor that Niul son of Feinius Farsaidh gave the name Geadheal to the son whom Scota daughter of Pharoa Cincris bore him, as Ceannfaolaidh the learned says in the Uraicheapt.

Now, it is disputed among authors whence is this word 'Gaedheal'. Becanus says that it is from the word *goedin*, that is, *goethin*, 'noble,' and from the word 'all,' that is *uile*, that Gaedheal is named, that is, 'all noble'; or from the Hebrew word *gadhal*, meaning 'great,' because Gaedheal son of Eathor, the first who was called Gaedheal, was great in learning, in wisdom, and in the languages. However, the seanchas say that he is called Gaedheal from the two words *gaoith dhil*, that is, 'lover of wisdom'; for *gaoith* means 'wise' and *dil* 'loving,' as the Greeks call a sage *philosophos*, that is, 'a lover of wisdom'. . . .

When the race of Breoghan son of Bratha had increased, they were strong and numerous in Spain; and because of the greatness of their exploits, they resolved to extend their sway in other directions. They had another motive also. For, at that time, there was a scarcity of food in Spain for the space of twenty-six years, on account of the great drought that existed during that period, and also because of the many conflicts that took place between them and the Goths, and the other foreign races, with whom they were contending for the mastery of Spain. They accordingly took counsel together as to what country they should explore, and who should be sent to explore it. What they resolved on was, to elect Ioth, son of Breoghan, son of Bratha, who was a valiant man, and also wise and learned in the sciences, for the purpose of exploring the island of Ireland. And the place where they adopted this counsel was at the tower of Breoghan in Galicia.

It was in this manner that they sent Ioth to Ireland, and not, as others assert, that he had seen it in the clouds of heaven on a winter's night from the summit of the tower of Breoghan. For there had been familiarity and intercourse before then between Ireland and Spain since the time when Eochaidh son of Earc, the last king of the Fir Bolg, took Taillte daughter of Maghmhor, king of Spain, to wife. They thus had been in the habit of trading with one another, and of exchanging their wares and valuables, so that the Spaniards were familiar with Ireland, and the Irish had a knowledge of Spain before Ioth son of Breoghan was born. Hence it was not from a view obtained in a single night from the summit of the tower of Breoghan that Ioth, or the children of Breoghan, acquired a knowledge of Ireland, but from there having been intercourse for a long time previously between Spain and Ireland.

Now, Ioth equipped a ship and manned it with thrice fifty chosen warriors, and put out to sea until they reached the northern part of Ireland, and put into port at Breantracht Mhaighe Iotha. And when Ioth landed there, he sacrificed to Neptune, the god of the sea, and the demons gave him bad omens. Thereupon, a company of the natives came and spoke with him in Scoitbhearla, that is, in Gaelic; and he replied to them in the same tongue, and said that it was from Magog he himself was descended, as they were, and that Scoitbhearla was his native language as it was theirs. Taking their cue from this passage in the Book of Invasions, the seanchas state that Scoitbhearla, which is called Gaelic, was the mother tongue of Neimhidh and his tribe, and therefore also of the Fir Bolg and the Tuatha De Danann. For this may be believed from what we have stated above, that it was Gaedheal son of Eathor, at the command of Feinius Farsaidh, King of Scythia, who regulated and set in order the Scoitbhearla; and it is from this Gaedheal that it was called Gaelic as we have said above.

Now, this Gaedheal had been teaching the public schools in Scythia before Neimhidh proceeded from Scythia on an expedition to Ireland; and since Scoitbhearla was the common tongue of Scythia when Neimhidh set out from that country, according to the seanchas, the Scoitbhearla must have been the mother tongue of Neimhidh and of his followers when they came to Ireland, and accordingly of every colony sprung from him or from his descendants who came to Ireland, not to mention the descendants of Milidh, whose native language was the Scoitbhearla from the time that Niul left Scythia to the present time. Richard Creagh, primate of Ireland, supports this view in the book he has written on the origin of Gaelic and of the race of Gaedheal. He speaks as follows: 'The Gaelic speech,' he says, 'has been in common use in Ireland from the coming of Neimhidh, six hundred and thirty years after the Deluge, to this day.' From what we have said, it is not improbable that it was in Scoitbhearla that Ioth and the Tuatha De Danann conversed with one another.

3.11 *Cathecismus seu Doctrina Christina Latino-Hibernica [Catechism, or Christian Doctrine in Latin and Irish]*, Teabóid Gallduf (Theobald Stapleton), 1639

For that reason, it is right and very fitting for us Irishmen to esteem, love and honour our own natural native language, Irish, which is so concealed and so suppressed that it has almost passed out of people's minds; the blame for this can be put on the poets who are authorities on the language, who have put it under great darkness and difficulty of words, writing it in contractions and mysterious words which are obscure and difficult to understand; and many of our nobles are not free [from blame] who bring the native natural tongue (which is efficient, complete, dignified, cultured and acute in itself) into contempt and disregard, and who spend their time developing and learning other foreign tongues.

3.12 *Foclóir Na Sanasán Nua [A New Vocabulary or Glossary]* Michéul Ó Cléirigh (Michael O'Clery), 1643

Here my Lord, is a small gleaning of hard words of our native tongue, collected from many of the old books of our country, and explained according to the knowledge and interpretation of the chief authors who have been in our country of late, who have devoted themselves to the interpretation of the old Gaelic. . . .

Accept then kindly this little offering, for our desire is only to give a little knowledge to those who are ignorant of their ancient mother-tongue, and also to incite the learned to make another such work, better and fuller.

Louvain, 28 October, 1643.

To the Reader.

The reader who wishes to read this book must know four things. First, we have not put down any word of interpretation or gloss on the difficult words of the mother tongue, except such words as we have ourselves heard interpreted, or have found explained by the ablest and most learned masters of the knowledge of the difficulty of the Gaelic in our own days. Of these especially are Baothghalacha Ruadh Mac Egan, Torna O'Mulconry, Malachy Modardha O'Mulconry, and Lughaidh O'Clery. Although each of these was a distinguished scholar, it is Baothghalach whom we have chiefly followed, because it is from him that we have ourselves received and found with all others the interpretation of the words of which we treat, and also because he was a distinguished and remarkable scholar in the profession. . . .

There are known to us good scholars in this art and even in the later time, as John Mulconry, the chief historian of those whom we have mentioned, and of the men of Ireland, in his own time, and Flann, son of Caibre Mac Egan, who still lives, and others whom I do not mention; but because we are on this side of the sea where we are in exile and have only a few of the books on which they made interpretation, we have been able to follow them but little.

Secondly, you must know that the following are the difficult books which the old authors have glossed, and from which we have taken these words together with the interpretation of the aforesaid persons who have taught lately: The Elegy on Colum Chille, the Dialogue of the two Sages, the

Festiology of the Saints, the Festiology of O'Gorman, the Book of Hymns, *Sanasán*, Life of Patrick, old Manuscripts on vellum and an old paper book in which many difficult words with their interpretations were found, *Foras Focal* and the *Deirbhshuir don Eagna an 'Eigsi*, and a great part of the book according to the gloss received from the aforesaid Baothghalach.

Thirdly the reader must know that in setting about this little work we wished only to give a little light to the young and ignorant, and to incite and stir up older and educated persons, to make another such work, better and fuller. And we have not followed at length many of the various meanings which scholars give to many of the words, and we have also omitted to give the etymology of many of the words, because it is particularly to scholars that it belongs, and that people in general have not the same necessity as they to understand and read books.

Fourthly, the young and ignorant who wish to read the old books (a thing which is not difficult for the educated of our country) must know that they rarely guard against writing slender with broad, or broad with slender, and that they very rarely put the aspirate upon the consonants, as *bh, ch, dh, fh*, *etc*, and also that they seldom put the long accent on vowels. Some of the consonants are often written one for another, as *c* for *g*, and *t* for *d*. Here are examples of words by which this will be understood: *clog* the same as *cloc*; *agad, acat*; *beag, beac*; *codladh, cotladh*; *ard, art, etc*. Also *ae* is often put for *ao*, and *ái* for *áoi* and also *oí* for *aoi*. For example *aed*, is often written for *aodh*, and *cael* is the same as *caol*. And *bói* and also *bái* is the same as *báoi*. E is often written instead of *A* in the old books, as *die*, which is the same as *dia*, *cie* which is the same as *cia*, *etc*. I is often written instead of *A*, as *dochuaidh*. *a*, *o*, *u* are commonly written one for the other at the end of a word, as *tompla, tomplo, tomplu, ceardcha, ceardcho, cheardchu, etc*.

3.13 *Nach ait an nós [How Queer this Mode]*, Dháibhidh Ó Bruadair (David Ó Bruadair), ?1643

I

Nach ait an nós so ag mórchuid d'fhearaibh Éireann,
d'at go nó le mórtus maingléiseach,
giodh tais a dtreoir ar chódaibh gallachléire,
ní chanaid glór acht gósta garbhbhéarla.

II

Mairg atá gan béarla binn
ar dteacht an iarla go hÉirinn;
ar feadh mo shaoghail ar chlár Chuinn
dán ar bhéarla dobhéaruinn.

73

I

How queer this mode assumed by many men of Erin,
With haughty, upstart ostentation lately swollen,
Though codes of foreign clerks they fondly strive to master,
They utter nothing but a ghost of strident English.

II

Woe to him who cannot simper English,
Since the Earl hath come across to Erin;
So long my life upon Conn's plain continues,
I'd barter all my poetry for English.

3.14 *Anc. rec. Dublin*, 1657

Whereas certain of the commons preferred petition unto this assembly, showing that whereas by it all persons of this land ought to speak and use the English tongue and habit: contrary whereunto, and in open contempt whereof, there is Irish commonly and usually spoken, and the Irish habit worn not only in the streets, and by such as live in the country and come into this city on market days, but also by and in several families in this city, to the great discontentment of the right honourable his highness council for the affairs of Ireland, [and] the scandalising of the inhabitants and magistrates of the city.

3.15 *Cambrensis Eversus*, Gratianus Lucius (John Lynch), 1662

Showing that Giraldus was absurd in prefixing the title of *Ireland conquered* to his second lucubration.

For as travellers, (bidding adieu for the time to their native homes, and the delightful intercourse of their relations and friends,) explore the wonders of different nations, refine their rougher manners by the polish of foreign intercourse, and soften their domestic rusticity by the purification of external culture; they also imbibe a knowledge of the various languages of the various countries through which they have passed. But if, in their travels, they shall have contracted any vices, they must not ascribe them to those languages, but to the depravity of their own inclinations. Just as the bee extracts honey from thyme, while the wasp extracts poison from the same sweet shrub, so every one, according to his own disposition, acquires good or bad habits from a knowledge of different languages. For there is nothing that can benefit, but may also prove detrimental. Shall he who has tinged his tongue with a foreign idiom, also stain his mind with treason against his country? Did the Welsh, on account of their knowledge of their native language, refuse obedience to the Kings of England? – We do not see the Armoric Gauls, nor the Biscayans of Spain, revolt from their Kings on account of their using a different language. Shall the Irish, however, for having their native idiom in common and general use, be said to conspire the destruction of their sovereign? For I see no other reason why the abolition of the Irish language should be so vehemently insisted upon.

The Irish language is certainly not more adapted for the contrivance of conspiracy than any other, nor less distinguished for its ornamental elegance: for it is so copious, that if it does not equal, it comes very near the Spanish in gravity, the Italian in courtesy, the French in conciliating love, or the German in impressing terror. By the thunder of its eloquence the sacred orator often deters the wicked from their vices, and attracts them, by its blandishments, to virtue. It is numbered as one of the original languages of Europe: For Scaliger says, that in Europe there are eleven primitive tongues; namely, the Latin, the Greek, the Teutonic, the Sclavonian, the Epirotic, the Trataric, the Hungarian, the Finnonian, the Irish, the Basque and the British. Who will deny that the Irish language possesses great energy and elegance, when even Stanihurst himself acknowledges that it is pointedly expressive, abounding in sentimental Phraseology, and perfectly adapted to sharp and witty apothegms, and pleasant allusions. . . . It comprehends indeed facetiousness, mockery and wit in the compass of a few words; and is so appropriate in its flexibility to poetry, that the book entitled *Uirekeacht*, (or the *Precept of the Bards*,) lays down rules for more than one hundred different kinds of verse that can be written in it: So that the Irish poets, in the judgment of such that have been instructed in the knowledge of many languages, yield not to those of any other nation of Europe, in variety of metre, in the art of arrangement, or in poignancy of expression. . . .

Stanihurst however endeavours to obscure, as much as in his power, the brilliancy of the Irish language, when he says that it is so beset with difficulties, that no passage is left open for strangers to arrive at the knowledge of it; notwithstanding that Sir Mathew Doryinge, a German born at Cologne, so penetrated into its recesses, that he has, within our own memory, compiled an Irish grammar. After this he relates of a person possessed of an evil spirit at Rome, that having spoken in other languages, he either could not, or would not, speak Irish, because, forsooth, (as he sneeringly states it) so sacred a language ought not to be profaned by such unhallowed lips; or rather, as he insinuates, because it is so horridly rough and rugged that the Devil himself laboured in utter ignorance of it. His ignorance of the Irish language, indeed, led Stanihurst to form so wild a conjecture concerning it. . . .

But the refined elegance, rather than the uncultivated roughness of the Irish language is established by Stanihurst, when he complains that his brethren of the *English pale* were more desirous to learn it, than the original natives were anxious to become acquainted with the English. – And when he also declares that the Irish would not deign to *distort* their lips by English expression, and complains that his countrymen were not equally averse from the Irish language – nay that they exercised their tongue in prating Irish. . . .

But to renew our discourse concerning the Irish language. It is, at this day, so universally diffused throughout all the country parts of Ireland, that it is almost everywhere the common dialect. It is no wonder, then, that in Giraldus's time, (at the first coming of the English hither, when they had not as yet acquired their more extensive dominion,) it should have flourished, while it was critically embellished with all its ornaments. And therefore the frequent use of the English language among the Irish, could, neither then nor now, be adduced as the criterion of this nation's being totally reduced under the English power.

3.16 *Iomdha Scéimh ar chur na Cluana [Many Pretty Settings]*, Dháibhidh Ó Bruadair (David Ó Bruadair), 1660–63

XXXV

Now Cromadh itself is a miserly, scattered, little town, which is situated on the banks of the Ma[acc]igh, and the beer of that village has no strength in it, except, indeed, that I hear that the good minister of the place has a fine old brew which is delightful to drink. However, I do not fancy that beer, such is the difficulty which I experience in endeavouring to fetter my tongue for fluent speech in the language of the foreigner, so that I always leave the manse on my left hand every time I go near it.

3.17 *Stat.Ire.*, An Act for the Explaining of some Doubts Arising upon an Act Entitled, an Act for the Better Execution of his Majesty's Gracious Settlement of his Majesty's Kingdom of Ireland, 1665

His Majesty taking notice of the barbarous and uncouth names, by which most of the towns and places in this kingdom of Ireland are called, which hath occasioned much damage to diverse of his good subjects, and are very troublesome in the use thereof, and much retards the reformation of that kingdom, for remedy thereof is pleased that it be enacted, and be it enacted by the authority aforesaid, that the lord lieutenant and council shall and may advise of, settle, and direct in the passing of all letters patents in that kingdom for the future, how new and proper names more suitable to the English tongue may be inserted with an *alias* for all towns, lands, and places in that kingdom, that shall be granted by letters patents; which new names shall thenceforth be only names to be used, any law, statute, custom, or usage to the contrary notwithstanding.

3.18 *Caithréim an Dara Séamuis [The Triumph of James II]*, Dháibhidh Ó Bruadair (David Ó Bruadair, 1687)

XVIII

Atá mo shúil re grásaibh iomdha
    an dáilimh d'iompuigh dóthanna
is re teacht na gaoise d'at im ríghsi
    mar ascal taoide i dtócharaibh
d'fhiadh bhar sinnsear niadhta nimhneach
    d'fhiad na thimchioll tóirneacha
do thuathaibh iasachta uaibh nach giallfa
    bruach do bhiadhfadh bóchuingir.

XIX

Atáid bhar bhfírchliar sámh gan dímhiadh
    d'áis an chaoimhniadh chomhachtaigh
is cléirche Chailbhín béas nach anaoibh
    gan pléidh a bpeataoi ar phópaireacht
atáid ar bínnse Dálaigh Rísigh
    sdá n-áileadh saoi do Nóglachaibh
re héisteacht agartha an té nach labhrann
    béarla breaganta beoiltirim.

XVIII

My eye still looks forward to numerous graces
    From the dispenser, who hath changed our despondent oaths,
And the coming of that wisdom that swells in my king
    Like the surge of the tide when by causeways blocked;
Round the land of your ancestors, knightly and vehement,
    He hath called forth the thunders vociferous
Of men who from you will not cede unto foreign tribes
    As much of a bank as would feed a yoke.

XIX

Your true clergy now live in peace, undishonoured,
    By the grace of this powerful, kindly knight,
And the clerics of Calvin – a change not unpleasant –
    Harangue not their pets upon popery;
On the bench now are seated the Dalys and Rices,
    And a sage of Nagles is urging them
To listen to the plea of the man who can't speak
    The lip-dry and simpering English tongue.

3.19 *Diarmuid Mac Muiredhaigh Cecinti [Diarmaid Mac Muireadhaigh Sang This]*, anon., late seventeenth century

1. Gluaisigh ribh a ghlac rannsa
   (ná fuirghe a bfad agamsa)
   go hó Néill na ngruadh ngarrtha
   dó féin sdual gach deaghtarrtha

2. Abruidh uaim ré a fholt tais
   gur cná sibh don chrann iomhais
   do bhean mé (sa taoibh ré tuinn)
   don chraoibh go ngé núir náluinn

3. Innsigh dhósan do shúr suilt
   doighre Cuind et Cormuic
   go bfuil im sdórsa lámh libh
   lán cóffra dona cnóaibh

4. Mac Sir Féidhlim flaith Eamhna
   gion go labhair Gaoidhealga
   do dhéin gáire gléghlan ruibh
   ní náire dhó féin bhar bféuchuin

5. Muidhfigh air a ghean gáire
   tré neart luinde is luathgháire
   an séig súlghlas Ó Theamhair
   a dhúthchas téid tair oileamhuin

6. Mur chídhfe sibh an naoibh sin air
   an flaith do thriall Ó Theamhair
   innsigh dhó brígh bhar dtoisge
   don ghríbh nimhnigh níchoisge

7. Innsigh dhósan gur léur liom
   go bfuilid uaisle Éiriond
   mon-uar ag tréigin a gceirt
   san nGaeidhlig na nuam noirrdheirc

8. Níor thréighte dhóibh í ile
   air bhéurla chríoch gcoigríchthe
   teangaidh aerdha bhlasda bhinn
   béurla do bheannaidh na tailginn

9. Dá dtuigmís (sní tuigthior linn)
   milteanga mhuighe Féidhlim
   níl ceól ná comhrádh bá binde
   lomlán deól is dfhírinne

10. Sgoith gach béurla táinig ón tur
    a ghoirios gach deaghughdar
    (is faghluim sgagtha mar sin)
    do thaghluim gharta Ghaoidhil

11. Tá an dán san diadhacht innte
    san ríghréim go róichinnte
    bí an tsuirghe shaor sna treathain
    sgach ní sduilghe dealathain

12. Féuchtar sní bfhuighthior libh
    air lorg Solaimh na Sigir
    caingne comh-oirrdheirc friu sin
    airrle Coirbmheic do Chairbridh

13. Tochmhairc Ailbhe is Fhinn fheassaigh
    Éimhre is an nilchleassaigh
    mac Prím sa ghrádha ón Ghréig
    ní bhídh óna lámha a leithéid

14. Agallmha na suagh aile
    Néidhe agas Athairnne
    ní bhaoi air sliocht suagh a samhuil
    ní chual o dhraoi a ndeaghshamhuil

15. An tiomna nuagh san tiomna shean
    táid go glan aig an Ghaoidheal
    sgach air labhair an fáidh tré fhios
    na meabhair atáid gan tuathlios

16. Sguiriom dhe so (gá dtám dhe)
    nior sgríobh fallsamh ná file
    mír dhá mhillse don neagna
    nach bídh innte go hinfheadhma

17. Ní hí an teanga do chuaidh Ó chion
    acht an dream dár dhual a dídion
    (mon-uar) dár bhéigin a ndán
    sa nduar do thréigin go tiomlán

18. Dlighidh siadsan dhá dhruim sin
    fíriasma ghléire Gaoidhil
    dán a dtíre bá trom teist
    do ládh go lonn a láincheist

19. Ní bfuil dair liomsa duine
    duaislibh innse Laoghuire

dár chóra a hórdúgh a cceist
ná Górdún is cródha coimhtheist

20. Atámaoid go léir dhá liamhain
ré hoighre Néill Naoighiallaigh
gur dó sdleacht sas dísle go hég
ceart a chríche do choimhéd

21. Tionóladh an chara gan cheilg
a bfuighe feassach san nGaoidheilg
sdo dhéna fínbhriathra dhi
béurla cíndhiamhra a chríche

22. Ó Néill dlighthioch deimhin liom
dá leig a lámh na tiomchioll
do dhén gach éurla duaislibh an fuinn
an réud céudhnna gan choguill

23. Ní beag so dhá chur a gcuimhne
don choin muighe Modhuirnne
gur dó is cinnte mad luinn lais
innte cnó an chruinn iomhais

1. Go, ye handful of verses (stay not long with
me) to O'Neill of the fine cheeks, to him
everything good is due.

2. Say to his soft hair, from me, that ye are a nut
from the tree which I plucked (its side was
towards the ground) from the branch with
fresh beautiful appearance.

3. Tell him, to excite mirth, Conn's and Cormac's
heir, that in my store with ye there is a
cofferful.

4. Sir Féidhlim's son, Emhain's prince, though
he speaks not Irish, shall bestow on ye a clear-
bright laugh, no shame for him it is to look
upon ye.

5. His smile shall on him come through merriment
and delight, the blue-eyed hawk from Teamhair, his nature excels his training.

6. When ye shall see that joy upon the prince
who came from Teamhair, tell the matter of
your business to the griffin, vehement, uncheckable.

7. Tell him that I know well that Ireland's nobles,
   alas! give up their right to the melodious
   Irish.

8. It should never be laid aside for the speech
   of foreign lands, the merry, tasteful, sweet
   tongue, the language the shavelings blessed.

9. If we understood the honeyed tongue of
   Féidhlim's plain (and we do not) no music
   or discourse were sweeter, full of truth and
   knowledge.

10. The flower of every speech that from the
    Tower came (it is thus perfected lore itself)
    which every writer adopts to garner the Gael's
    generosity.

11. In it there is poetry, and piety, accurate
    successions of kings, courtships, the Triads, and
    every difficult composition.

12. Look and you shall not discover, from
    Solomon's or Cicero's hand, a piece so fine
    as Cormac's Advice to Cairbre.

13. The Wooing of Ailbhe by Fionn the Wise,
    of Éimhear by him of the Many Feats, of his
    Grecian Love by Priam's son, they never made
    the like.

14. The Dialogue of the Sages, too, Néidhe and
    Athairne, author never penned its equal,
    wizard I have never heard similar.

15. The Old Testament and the New the Gael
    has in purity, and all the inspired Prophet
    spoke he remembers without a mistake.

16. Let us cease – why continue? No philosopher
    or poet wrote a piece of wisdom, however
    sweet, that it hath not ready for use.

17. It is not the language which has come into
    disesteem but those who should defend it, they
    who have been, alas! obliged to abandon their
    poems and verses all.

18. The true remnant of the best of the Gaedhil
    should, then, strongly support their country's
    poetry, in value great.

19. There is not, I think, one of the nobles of
    Laoghaire's isle to whom it is more proper
    to set it in repute than Górdún, by report
    a warrior.

20. We are all affirming to Niall Naoighiallach's
    heir that for him it is appropriate, and a duty
    till death, to uphold his country's right.

21. Let our guileless friend assemble all skilled
    in Irish, and wine-words he shall make of it,
    the volume-secret language of his country.

22. I am sure, if he, the right Ó Néill, sets his hand
    to it, every prince of the nobles of the land
    will, without hesitation, do the same.

23. This is enough to remind the warrior of
    Modhairne's plain that, if he pleases, there is in
    store for him a nut from the tree in Irish.

4

1690–1800

INTRODUCTION

This period begins and ends with rebellion and punishment. Victory over the Jacobites in the Williamite wars gave the Protestant landed class complete power, which they exercised by the institution of the Penal laws (called the Popery laws at the time). The defeat of the United Irishmen in the 1798 rising led directly to the Acts of Union, passed in the Irish and British parliaments, which incorporated Ireland into the United Kingdom. It is interesting to see again how such periods of unrest are reflected in texts which take historiography and the Irish language as their focus. Cox's *Hibernia Anglicana* (1689–90) disputes the reassertion of the origins of the Irish made by Céitinn, and dismisses Irish as a 'compound' language (linguistic 'purity' was an important criterion of 'authenticity' – Thomas levels precisely the same charge against English in 1787). MacCruitín's reply to Cox, the *Brief Discourse in Vindication of the Antiquity of Ireland* (1717), is claimed to have landed him in jail for a year; though his *Elements of the Irish Language* (1728) was written in English, he took the sensible precaution of publishing it at Louvain. Ledwich's *Antiquities of Ireland* (1790) was a counter to the antiquarian defence of Gaelic culture (highly political in its context) mounted by Catholic campaigners such as Charles O'Conor. Claims regarding the chronological development of the Irish and the origin of their language are subject to particular ridicule.

The Penal laws constituted what was later (in the 1780s) to be called the Protestant Ascendancy. Enacted after 1690, they formed a series of statutes which had the intention of denying civil rights to Catholics and Presbyterians (the 'Protestant' in 'Protestant Ascendancy' referred to the established church). The most important of these Acts was the 'Act to Prevent the Further Growth of Popery' (1704), but one of the first was the 'Act to Restrain Foreign Education' (1695), which prohibited the education of Catholics abroad and forbade Catholics from teaching or organising schools in Ireland. A restatement of Henry VIII's order for the erection of English-speaking schools was made in 1733. The Catholic response, also that of Presbyterians in Ulster, was the

83

system of hedge-schools, a clandestine form of education which lasted into the nineteenth century.

There were Protestants who argued, in a rerun of earlier debates and a fore-taste of what was to come, that the teaching of literacy in Irish was a measure necessary for the taming of the Irish and the banishment of Catholicism. Though it is easy to caricature this position (Richardson notes, for example, that the cost of such a project would amount to no more than the expense of a year's war in Ireland), it is also clearly the case that this type of work was under-taken with due earnestness of purpose. The Presbyterian Synod of Ulster occu-pied itself with this question repeatedly in the first quarter of the eighteenth century, and this was evidently not simply a matter of equipping colporteurs. Resistance from within the established church, however, was often fierce, and grounded, by several ministers, in the significant belief that the extent of spoken English was already sufficient to make the teaching of it unnecessary. It is also important to recall that the Catholic Church in this period hardly promoted the use of Gaelic at all: apart from Gallagher's *Sermons* (1736) and Donlevy's *Teagasg Críosduidhe* (1742) little else was published. The use of English at Maynooth from its opening in 1795 was indicative of the Church's attitude.

As the dangers posed by Jacobitism passed, the Protestant Ascendancy developed in important ways, not least in the increasing political activism of the Protestant middle class, one sign of which was the appearance of Patriot senti-ment. The political consequence of this was the legislative independence of the Irish Parliament between 1782 and the Acts of Union (1800). Culturally, the changes were reflected in the consolidation of the growth of Irish antiquarianism, which had begun earlier in the century. Beginning with the work of Lhuyd (though he was glad to acknowledge his debt to the work of pioneers such as Céitinn and Ware), Irish culture was defended against the attacks made both in the Chronicles and by later opponents such as Cox. The early eighteenth-century work in fact reveals splits in the cultural attitudes of the Catholic community: MacCruitín attacked Cox and 'most of our Nobility and gentry' for their attitude towards the language; Donlevy wrote simply of the 'Dishonour and shame of the *Natives*' in their neglect of it.

As the century progressed, the emergence of a Catholic political movement, based mainly around Dublin business interests and taking the form of the Catholic Committee (O'Conor and Keogh were amongst its leaders), gained important relaxation of the Penal laws. At the same time Protestant Patriots became increasingly engaged with the exploration of Irish antiquity. That some of the research issued in bizarre and speculative claims about the origin and his-tory of Gaelic language and culture (such as Vallancey's assertion that Buddhism was the established religion of the pagan Irish) did not greatly matter. Amongst the other effects of this interest was the founding of the Royal Irish Academy in 1785 (the Royal charter was granted in 1786), later to be the principal centre for Irish scholarship. It was Patriot pride too which inspired Charlotte Brooke's influential *Reliques of Irish Poetry* (1789) and, though it was successfully challenged by his family, Henry Flood's bequest for the establishment of a Chair of 'native Irish' at Trinity College.

Though scholarly attention was being paid to Irish, it is worth pointing out that the English language was also in question. Ó Rathaille, the great Irish poet after Ó Bruadair, followed his predecessor in cursing and mocking English. Swift, though he called publicly for the abolition of Irish (his attitude was in fact more ambivalent), satirised the language of the Planters in his 'Dialogue in Hibernian Style'. Keogh, echoing Swift's piece 'On Barbarous Denominations' and anticipating Maria Edgeworth in her 'Essay on Irish Bulls', denounced the stigma attached to the Irish 'Brogue'. Sheridan, also aware of the 'defects' of Irish pronunciation, sought to correct them as part of his more ambitious project to set himself up in the colonial metropolis as an elocution master teaching the *English* inhabitants how to pronounce their language 'properly'.

4.1 *Hibernia Anglicana*, Sir Richard Cox, 1689–90

Since *Ireland* is reckoned among the Principal Islands in the World, and deserves to be esteemed so, (whether you consider the Situation of the Country, the Number and Goodness of its Harbours, the Fruitfulness of the Soil, or the Temperature of the Climate); it is strange that this Noble Kingdom, and the Affairs of it, should find no room in History, but remain so very obscure, that not only the Inhabitants know little or nothing of what has passed in their own Country; but even *England*, a Learned and Inquisitive Nation, skilful beyond comparison in the Histories of all other Countries, is nevertheless but imperfectly informed in the Story of *Ireland*, though it be a Kingdom subordinate to *England*, and of the highest importance to it.

This could never be so if there were extant any complete or coherent History of that Kingdom; which indeed there is not, those relating to the Time before the Conquest, being Fabulous, and those since, but Scraps and Fragments.

As for those Histories that treat of the Times before the English-Conquest, Doctor *Keating's* is the best, and is exceedingly applauded by some that did, and others that did not know better: *Peter Walsh* thinks 'tis the only complete History that we have of all the Invasions, Conquests, Changes, Monarchs, Wars, and other considerable Matters of that truly ancient Kingdom: But after all, it is no more than *an ill-digested Heap of very silly Fictions*. And *Paul Walsh's* Prospect, which is in effect the Epitome of *Keating* in English, with all the Art he could use to polish it, will never pass for more than a *Utopian* Achievement. And *Mr Flaherty's Ogygia* must expect the same Fate, though he has shown a great deal of Learning and Industry in methodizing the Story, and fitting a Table of Synchronism to it; which with small variation, might serve as well for the History of the Seaven.

But those Tracts that have been written of later times, have most of them another Fault; they generally write true, but not observing Chronology; they jumble Times, Persons and Things together, and so confound the Story. Sir James *Ware* was the first that mended this Error, and is undoubtedly the best Author that has undertaken the Irish History; but he has only the four reigns of *Henry VII*, *Henry VIII*, *Edward VI*, and *Queen Mary*. *Campion* and the rest have but a scrap here and there, and that itself very imperfectly. And *Camden's* Annals, Friar *Clun's*, and others, that were mostly collected by the Monks, are very faulty, and have no coherence; *Spenser's* View of *Ireland* is very well, and Sir *John Davies* his Discourse is better; but both are Commentaries rather than Histories. . . .

But how ungrateful soever the Reader may be to me, I will nevertheless give him the best Help I can to understand the Irish History, which he can never well do, without penetrating into the true Causes of those innumerable Feuds, Wars and Rebellions that have been in that Kingdom; most of which I think were founded on those great Antipathies which were created by Difference in *Nation, Interest* or *Religion*.

The Difference of *Nation* concerned the Irish on one side, and the British on the other; for the Scots, though some of them were extracted from the Irish, yet only such as sympathised with them in Language, Manners, Customs, Religion and Interest, were accounted Irish, as *MacDonald*, *MacConnell*, &c. and the rest who communicated with the English in those five Particulars, are reckoned as such, and justly comprehended under the Appellation of *British*. As for the English, they are undoubtedly a mixed Nation compounded of Britons, Danes, Saxons and Normans: And some think the Irish are also a mingled People of Britons, Gauls, Spaniards and Easterlings, and therefore called *Scots, ie* an Heap: And 'tis certain that they are at this Day a mixed People, if it were for no other Reason, but that there is hardly a Gentleman among them, but has English Blood in his Veins; However, the Irish Antiquaries do Assert, that the Irish are a pure and ancient Nation, and they derive their Pedigree through the famous *Milesius*, and by their Father *Galethus* are descended from *Feinsa Farsa*, and other great Emperors of *Scythia*; and by their Mother *Scota* they were extracted from the mighty Kings of Egypt: But the Jest of it is, That since only two Sons of *Milesius* came into *Ireland* (viz.) *Hiber* and *Herimon*, with about three thousand Soldiers, if all the Irish are of the race of *Milesius*, it must follow that those two Sparks were *Patres Patriae*, in a literal sense, and begot Children for the whole Army; but however that be, it is certain that there were great Antipathies between the Conquerors and the Conquered; but by degrees the English grew so much in love with the Despotick Power of the Lords, and the Licentiousness of the Commons, that they insensibly degenerated not only into Irish Customs, Habits and Manners, but also assumed Irish Names, as *Burk MacWilliam*, *Fitz-Stephen MacSliny*, *Courcy MacPatrick*, *Hodnet MacShery*, *Barry MacAdam*, *Birmingham MacPheoris*, and many others; so that this Difference of Nation was on the Old English Side designed to be buried in Oblivion. But the Irish would not be so served, for they considered the first Conquerors but as unjust Intruders into, and Usurpers of other Men's Estates, and therefore they expected some favourable Opportunity, one time or another, to get rid of them; though for the present they were necessitated to join with them; and therefore they carefully kept up the distinction of Nations, and by no Law or Allurements could be brought to part with their Language or Habit, or even the most of their barbarous Customs. . . .

Who were the *Aborigines* or first Inhabitants of *Ireland*, it was in vain to guess, for the Irish Historians are of no Credit in this Matter, the very Truths they write do not oblige our Belief, because they are so intermixed with Impossible Stories and Impertinent Tales, that it is exceeding difficult to distinguish which is the History and which the Fable. . . . But if we may be permitted to guess at things so obscure, I should think that the World was inhabited by degrees, and from the adjacent Countries, *Asia* peopled *Greece*, *Greece Italy*, *Italy France*, and *France England*; and therefore it is rational to believe, That *England* peopled *Ireland*, being the nearest Country to it, especially in those days when the Art of Navigation was so little understood, that Fleets neither did nor could transport a Colony sufficient to plant that Island from any Country more remote, their Custom being only to sail to the Shore, and so coast it along; which made *Hiram* three Years in his Voyage: Some Welsh Words in the Irish Language, and some Customs used among the Britons, particularly the Bards and the Druids, and many other Circumstances do enforce this Argument: And besides these Britons, the *Belga* and *Danonii* (Inhabitants of the West of *England*, being conquered by *Vespasian*) fled into *Ireland*, and settled there; which gave occasion to the fruitful Fancies of the Irish Historians to forge all those ridiculous Stories which they have published of the *Firbolgs* and *Tuah-de-danans*. Perhaps some Spaniards and more Gauls, ay, and some other Nations, Danes, Norwegians, Eastmen &c. might, in small numbers, by Accident or Design settle themselves in *Ireland*; and therefore the Irish being a mixed People might be called *Scots ie acerva* (a Heap) implying, that as a Heap consisted of many Grains, so the Inhabitants of Ireland were compounded of many Nations. But however that be, 'tis certain, that most of the Original Inhabitants of Ireland came out of Britain. . . . It is certain the Religion and Manners of the Irish and Britons did not differ very much. And their Language did very much agree. The Irish use the Saxon Character to this day, and their use of Bows and Arrows, [b] Bolyes, [c] Mantles and [d] Glibbs are all derived from the Britons, and so are the Bards and Druids aforesaid; their Custom of Gavelkind was British in the Original, and the *Brigantes* of *Ireland* are undoubtedly the Progeny of the *Brigantes* of *England*.

As for the Irish Language, how much soever some of the Bards do brag, That it is a Pure and Original one; yet it is so far from that, that it is the most compound Language in the World, (the English only excepted). It borrows from the Spanish *com estato, ie* how do you do &c. from the Saxon the Words *Rath* and *Doon ie* Hill and many more: From the Danish many Words; from the Welsh almost half their Language: Doctor *Hanmer* gives us a Catalogue of Words Common to both Nations; to which may be added, *Inis, Glas, Caashe, Glin, Yerla, Droum, &c.* From Latin they derive all their Numeral Words, *unus hene, duo dwo, tres three, quator cahir, quinque quooge, sex she, septem shoct, octo hoct, novem ne, decem degh*; and they reckon as the Latins do, *one teen, two teen, undecem henedeag, duodecem dwodeag*; and not as the English do, *eleven and twelve*: The Words *sal, arigut, cabul, aun, aunum, corp, mel, lowre, scribnore, ore, &c.* are also mere Latin; *dy Downig dies Dominicus, dy Lune dies Lunae*; so *dy Mart dies Martis*, and *dy Saturn dies Saturni*. All things that were not in use with them formerly are mere English Words, as *cotah, dublete, hatta, papere, botishy, breesty*, and abundance more. *Holinshed* makes too satirical an Observation, That there is no Irish Word for *Knave*; but I will conclude this Paragraph with this Remark, That *Ulster* has the right Phrase, but not the Pronunciation, *Munster* has the Pronunciation but not the Phrase, Leinster has neither but *Connaught* has both.

4.2 *The Political Anatomy of Ireland*, Sir Wiliam Petty, 1691

If the *Irish* must have Priests, let the number of them, which is now between 2 and 3 thousand Secular and Regulars, be reduced to the competent number of 1000, which is 800 souls to the pastorage of each Priest; which let be known persons, and *Englishmen*, if it may be. So as that when the Priests, who govern the Conscience, and the Women, who influence other powerful Appetites, shall be *English*, both of whom being in the Bosom of the Men, it must be, that no massacring of *English*, as heretofore, can happen again. Moreover, when the Language of the Children shall be *English*, and the whole Economy of the Family *English, viz.* Diet, Apparel, *&c.* the Transmutation will be very easy and quick.

Add hereunto, That if both Kingdoms, now two, were put into one, and under one Legislative Power and Parliament, the members whereof should be in the same proportion that the Power and Wealth of each Nation are, there would be no danger such a Parliament should do anything to the prejudice of the *English* interest in *Ireland*; nor could the *Irish* ever complain of Partiality, when they shall be freely and proportionably represented in all Legislatures. . . .

As for the Interest of these poorer *Irish*, it is manifestly to be transmuted into *English*, so to reform and qualify their housing, as that *English* Women may be content to be their Wives, to decline their Language, which continues a sensible distinction, being not now necessary; which makes those who do not understand it, suspect, that what is spoken in it, is to their prejudice. It is their Interest to deal with the *English*, for Leases, for Time, and upon clear Conditions, which being perform'd they are absolute Freemen, rather than to stand always liable to the humour and caprice of their Landlords, and to have every thing taken from them, which he pleases to fancy. It is their Interest, that he is well-pleased with their obedience to them, when they see and know upon whose Care and Conduct their well-being depends, who have Power over their Lands and Estates. Then, to believe a Man at *Rome* has Power in all these last mentioned Particulars in this World, and can make them eternally happy or miserable hereafter, 'tis their Interest to join with them, and follow their Example, who have brought Arts, Civility, and Freedom into their Country. . . .

The Language of *Ireland* is like that of the *North* of *Scotland*, in many things like the *Welsh* and *Manx*; but in *Ireland* the *Fingallians* speak neither *English*, *Irish*, nor *Welsh*; and the People about *Wexford*, though they agree in a Language differing from *English*, *Welsh*, and *Irish*, yet 'tis not the same with that of the *Fingalians* near *Dublin*. Both these two sorts of People are honest and laborious Members of the *Kingdom*.

The *Irish* Language, and the *Welsh*, as also all Languages that have not been the Languages of flourishing Empires, wherein were many Things, many Notions and Fancies, both Poetical and Philosophical, hath but few words; and all the names of Artificial things brought into use, since the Empire of these Linguists ceased, are expressed in the language of their Conquerors, by altering the Termination and Accents only.

4.3 *Stat.Ire.*, An Act to Restrain Foreign Education, 1695

Whereas many of the subjects of this Kingdom have accustomed themselves to send their children, and other persons under their care, into France, Spain, and other foreign parts, not under His Majesty's obedience, to be educated, instructed, and brought up; by means and occasion whereof, the said children and other persons have in process of time engaged themselves in foreign interests, and been prevailed upon to forget the natural duty and alliegance due from them to the Kings and Queens of this realm, and the affection which they owe to the established religion and laws of this their native country, and returning so evilly disposed into this kingdom, have been in all times past the movers and promoters of many dangerous seditions, and oftentimes of open rebellion: for remedy whereof be it therefore enacted and declared. . . . That in case any of his Majesty's subjects of this realm of Ireland at any time after the end of this session of Parliament shall pass, or go, or shall convey or send, or cause to be conveyed or sent, any child or other person into any parts beyond the seas out of his Majesty's obedience to the intent and purpose to enter into, or be resident or trained up in any priory, abbey, nunnery, popish university, or school, or house of jesuits or priests; or in case any of his Majesty's subjects of this kingdom shall after the time aforesaid pass or go, or be conveyed, or sent out of this kingdom, into any parts beyond the seas out of the king's obedience to the intent and purpose to be resident, or trained up, in any private popish family, and shall be in such parts beyond the seas by any jesuit, seminary priest, friar, monk, or other popish person, instructed, persuaded, or strengthened in the popish religion, in any sort to profess the same, or shall convey or send, or cause to be conveyed or sent, by the hands or means of any person whatsoever any sum or sums of money, or other thing, for or towards the maintenance of any child or other person already gone or sent, or that shall hereafter go or be sent, and be trained and instructed as aforesaid, or under the name or colour of any charity, benevolence, or alms towards the relief of any priory, abbey, nunnery, college, school, or any religious house whatsoever: every person so going, sending, conveying, or causing to be sent, or conveyed or sent, as well any such child or other person, as any sum, or sums of money, or other thing, and every person passing or being sent beyond the seas, contrary to the intent and meaning of this act, and being thereof lawfully convicted in manner and form hereafter mentioned, or upon any information, presentment, or indictment, for any of the offences as aforesaid, to be found by any jury of twelve men of the county, or city, or town corporate, where such person or persons so going or sending shall have any estate of inheritance, when he or they did send or go; such person or persons so going or sending wilfully, from and after such going or sending, shall be for ever disabled, from and after such finding, to sue, bring, or prosecute any action, bill, plaint, or information in course of law, or to prosecute any suit in any court of equity, or to be guardian, or executor, or administrator, to any person, or capable of any legacy, or deed of gift, or to bear any office within the realm, and shall lose and forfeit all his, her, and their goods and chattels, which he, she, or they hath, or any other person or persons have, or hath in trust for him, her, and them, and shall forfeit all his, her, and their lands, tenements and hereditaments, rents, annuities, offices, and estate of free-hold, and all trusts, powers, and interests therein, for and during his, her, and their natural life and lives. . . .

IX. And whereas it is found by experience that tolerating and conniving at papists keeping schools or instructing youth in literature, is one great reason of many of the natives of this kingdom continuing ignorant of the principles of true religion, and strangers to the scriptures, and of their neglecting to conform themselves to the laws and statutes of this realm, and of their not using the English habit and language, to the great prejudice of the public weal thereof: be it further enacted by the authority aforesaid, That no person whatsoever of the popish religion shall publicly teach school, or instruct youth in learning, or in private houses teach or instruct youth in learning within this realm from henceforth, except only the children or others under the guardianship of the master or mistress of such private house or family, upon pain of twenty pounds, and also being committed to prison, without bail or mainprize, for the space of three months for every such offence.

X. And to the intent that no pretence may be made or used, that there are not sufficient numbers of schools in this realm to instruct and inform the youth thereof in the English language, and other literature; be it further enacted by the authority aforesaid, That one act of Parliament, made in the twenty eighth year of the reign of the late King Henry the eighth, called, *An Act for the English order, habit and language*, whereby it is among other things enacted and provided, that every incumbent of each parish within this kingdom shall keep, or cause to be kept, within the place, territory, or parish where he shall have pre-eminence, rule, benefice, or promotion, a school to learn English; and also, one other act made in the twelfth year of the reign of the late Queen Elizabeth, intituled, *An Act for the erection of free-schools*, whereby it is enacted and provided, that a public latin free-school shall be constantly maintained and kept within each diocess of this kingdom, which have generally been maintained and kept but have not had the desired effect, by reason of such Irish popish schools being too much connived at, and all other acts and statutes now in force in this realm concerning schools shall from henceforth be strictly observed and put in execution, according to the good intent and design of the same.

4.4 *Archaeologia Britannica*, Edward Lhuyd, 1707

TIT.X. *Focloir Gaoidheilge-Shagsonach no Bearladoir Scot-Sagsamhuil. An Irish-English Dictionary.*

To the GENTLEMEN and other Learned PERSONS of the *Irish* Nation, whether *Irish*, *Scots*, or other Foreigners, Long Health and Happiness.

It is but reasonable (Generous Gentlemen) that I here make an apology for Undertaking to Write and Publish a Dictionary in a different Language from my Native Tongue; and which I did not learn by Ear from any Person whose Native Language it was.

For though, 'tis true, I travelled through *Ireland* and the North-West of the Highlands of *Scotland*, partly to make Remarks on the Natural Curiosities, and partly to view the Old Monuments of those Nations; yet frequently meeting and conversing with those who spoke *English*, I learned but very little *Irish* in that Progress: And therefore it is from Books, for the most part, that I have acquired the little Knowledge I have in that

Language. Now the Motive that first engaged me in the Study of *Irish* was this:

SOME *Welsh* and *English* Gentlemen laid their Commands on me to write something beyond what has hitherto been Published concerning the Original Antiquity of the *British* Nation; and in this regard the Old and Ancient Languages are the Keys that open the Way to the Knowledge of Antiquity; I found it the more necessary to make myself as much Master as was possible of all the old obsolete Words of my own Native Language. For it was generally owned and taken for granted, (whether true or false) that the *British* was the first and most ancient Language in *Great-Britain*.

As soon as I had made, by the help of a certain Parchment-manuscript, a tolerable progress in the old *British* Language, I found my Knowledge therein not only imperfect and defective, as to the Meaning and Signification of the old Names of Persons and Places, but also that there were many more words in the old Statutes, Histories and Poems, whose Significations still remained to me very dubious and obscure: Notwithstanding the great Benefit and Advantage we have from the *Welsh* and *Latin* Dictionary, compiled by the very learned and ingenious Dr. J. *Davies*, and printed at *London* in the year 1632.

This Difficulty naturally led me to conjecture that a little Skill in the old *Irish* words, would be very useful to me in explaining those ancient *British* words; and therefore I applied myself to read the *Irish* Bible and the Chronological History of *Ireland*, written by the learned Antiquary, Dr.J.Keting, with a few other modern Books that occasionally fell into my hands; and being persuaded, that making a Collection of the words which would very much assist my Memory, I therefore at first made a Dictionary for my own particular Use, which afterwards swelled to the Bulk you now see it in the following Impression. . . .

I think it necessary to address myself to those who ridicule and make a jest of the *Welsh* and *Irish* Languages, and therefore do condemn (as vain and useless) the Labour of those who would endeavour to preserve them: But no wise or knowing Man ought to take notice of such ridiculing Wits; for their Scoffs and Jests proceed either from Ignorance or want of better Education; but I know, from my own Experience (and without doubt many of you are not ignorant of the same) that though there are too many that give themselves great liberty in talking after such a manner; yet the most learned, and Men of the greatest Experience amongst the *English*, discover not only an Inclination to preserve our Languages and Manuscripts, but are also the most bountiful Patrons of Learning, and perhaps of the most extensive Capacities and Understandings in all kinds of Literature and Sciences (take them one with another) of any People in *Europe*. I have no reason to speak partially in this Affair; because I don't profess to be an *Englishman*, but an old *Briton* . . . I have already declared that it was through Ignorance that many Persons would have your Language and ours buried in Oblivion;

and I have no reason upon any account to recall my words, but rather to make this additional Remark, that it argues for a great want of Judgement, that any Man, who would pretend to Learning, ought to be ashamed of it. I. It is undoubtedly true, that they were the first languages of the *British* Isles, under which Denomination, as *Ireland* was formerly included, so it was likewise called *Eire*; and it is as certain that they were the most ancient and best preserved of any Languages in the West of *Europe*, and consequently to suffer these languages to decline and, perish, would be as great an inconvenience to the Society of Knowledge and Literature, as the loss of the old *Celtic*, *Italian*, and *Spanish*, is now found to be, and future ages will have reason to be astonished at the supine Ignorance, in this point, of the two last Centuries, wherein so much Learning has in other respects flourished. II. These being therefore the first and original Languages of the *British* Isles, it follows that it is necessary to acquire them in some degree to be able to explain and account for the Names of Persons and Places; and it is for that reason that these eminent Antiquaries, *Camden*, *Bochart*, and Boxhorn, and other learned persons of that kind were of Opinion, that it was necessary to converse frequently with *Welsh* or *Irishmen*, or both, to be able to make any judgement of their Languages; and withal that they themselves did not write so fully and copiously as they would have done, if they had been Masters of those Languages. III. The famous and learned Nations of *France*, *Italy*, and *Spain*, will not be capable of giving an account of those Languages which *(a)* Menage, *(b)* Aldrete, and many other learned persons endeavoured to do, and indeed made laudable ESSAYS that way; if they do not arrive to some Perfection in the Knowledge of your Language and ours; which without dispute is allowed to have been the best part of the Languages they treated of, before the Arms and Conquests of the *Romans*, *Goths* and *Africans*, laid waste their Countries, and corrupted their Languages. And as concerning even the *Greek* and *Latin* Languages, from which alone the *French* and *Italian* are derived, there are many of their words derived from other Languages; for their *Radices* are not to be found in their own, but sometimes (though I know contrary to the general Rules of Etymologies) in the *Italian*, *Spanish*, and *French*, and sometimes in the *German* Languages, but they were very generally better preserved in your Language and ours, with this distinction only, that you come much nearer to the *Latin*, and we to the *Greek*. . . . Nay, your Language is better situated for being preserved than any other Language to this day spoken throughout *Europe* (I mean so far as to what is contained in your Books, but not to your common Method of Speaking). IV. There are no Languages now extant that are more useful and necessary for explaining the true Names of Rivers, Loughs, Mountains, Rocks, Plains, Countries, Cities, and the Towns throughout *Italy*, *France*, and a great part of *Spain*, than these two Languages. . . .

V. The fifth Motive or Inducement for publishing Dictionaries of our Languages is, that with their help (after being corrected) Men of Learning and other Gentlemen might be the better able to read, for their Pleasure and Diversion, our Poetry, Histories and our Laws, which are still in Being; and which ought never to be lost, but preserved carefully to give some Light to learned Persons, and Knowledge to Antiquaries. . . .

VI. There is a sixth Reason, and I think a very just one, for publishing Dictionaries and Grammars in these Languages; and it is this, That they may be very useful and helpful to those that have taken upon them the Care of Souls, and to those likewise who have any Office or Place of Trust over the common People: As concerning those who propose that it were better to teach all manner of Persons in the three Kingdoms to speak *English*; I will readily agree with them in that, as being of universal advantage in order to promote Trade and Commerce; but those Gentlemen do not inform us how that is to be accomplished. We have been now, for several hundred Years, subject to and conversant with the *English* and *Scots* in the Lowlands of *Scotland*; and yet how many thousands are there in each Kingdom that do not yet speak *English*? And therefore it was my whole design, and what I have still at heart, that this book may prove somewhat useful in this respect, as also in those I have already mentioned.

4.5 *The Church Catechism. Caitecism na Heaglaise,* John Lewis (trans. Revd John Richardson), 1712

The Design of Publishing this Explication of our Church Catechism in Irish is, That such as speak that Language, may thereby be Accomodated with proper Means of attaining to the necessary Knowledge of the Principles of Religion.

It is manifest, that such Books are much wanting; and it can hardly be denied, but that the fittest Method of Instructing that, as well as any other Nation, and Converting them from their Errors, is to propose the Saving Truths of Religion to them, in their Native Language; That being the Language only understood by some, and most acceptable to all of them. I was apprehensive nevertheless, when this Work was begun, That it would meet with some Discouragement and Oposition: But, I resolved to proceed in it, hoping that God would raise up Friends to so well meant an Undertaking. And it is no small Comfort to me, that I have not failed of my Expectation; for ever since I applied to you, and you were fully apprised of the Design, you have Supported me in my greatest Difficulties, and have also Engaged many Worthy persons to Espouse it, by whose Favour and Assistance, in conjunction with yours, it is hop'd, that it may be brought to a prosperous Issue.

All the Return that I can make, is gratefully to acknowledge your Kindness; and to beseech Almighty God (who hath given you Grace, to be so bright an Example of Primitive Piety and Charity, and so Zealous an Instrument of Propagating the Gospel in Foreign Parts, and of Promoting Christian Knowledge in these Kingdoms) to bless you with a Long and Happy Life here, and Eternal Felicity hereafter.

4.6 *A Proposal for the Conversion of the Popish Natives of Ireland*, John Richardson, 1712

It is *humbly proposed*,

I. That a competent Number of Ministers, duly qualified to instruct the Natives, and to perform the Offices of Religion to them in their own *Language*, be provided and encouraged, by a suitable Maintenance, to be sent among them. . . .

III. That the *Bible*, the *Common Prayer Book*, and an *Exposition of the Church Catechism*, be printed in *Irish*, for the Administration of the Ordinances of *Religion* to them in their own Tongue.

IV. That a sufficient Number of *Charity Schools* be erected, for the *Instruction of the Irish Children, gratis*, in the *English Tongue*, and the *Established Religion*; and that some *proper Encouragement* be given to *Irish Children Educated in those Schools*, the Benefit of which Schools may be extended to the Children of *Poor Protestants*.

V. That the *Honourable House of Commons* would be pleased to grant a fund for the carrying on of so *pious* and *charitable* a Design. . . .

It is Objected, That to Print Books in Irish, *and to send Missionaries among the Natives, to instruct them in their own Language, is very destructive of the* English *interest in* Ireland. But I humbly desire that it may be considered.

1. That nothing tends more effectually to preserve the Peace and Tranquility of *Ireland*, and to augment the Improvement thereof, and consequently to promote and secure the Interest which the *English* have therein, than the Conversion of the *Irish* to the Established Religion. . . .

2. Printing Books in *Irish*, and sending Missionaries among the Natives, to instruct them, and administer the Ordinances of Religion to them in a Language which they understand, are the necessary Means of converting them; and therefore cannot be destructive of the *English* Interest; for if the End be good, the necessary Means must be so too.

3. Preaching in the *Irish* Language is not an Encouragement of the *Irish* Interest, any more, than preaching in *French* in *England*, is an Encouragement of the *French* Interest. . . .

4. To administer the Ordinances of Religion to the *Irish* in their own Language, is indeed the most effectual Way to destroy the *Irish* Interest in *Ireland*. . . .

It is objected, *That keeping up a Difference in Language, will keep up a Difference in Religion; so that by Preaching in* Irish, *we shall rather confirm the Natives in* Popery, *than convert them to the* Protestant *Religion.*

I answer, that the different manner of Communicating our Thoughts of any Thing to others, doth neither alter the Nature of the Thing, nor our Thoughts and Notions of it: Otherwise, different Languages would be the Causes of Men having different Conceptions of other Things, as well as of Religion: whereas although there be great Variety in the Languages of the World, yet we have Reason to believe, that all Men agree in their Apprehensions and Conceptions of many Things; and on the other side we find, that Men speaking the same Language, have different Thoughts of the same Thing. Wherefore since a Language hath no Operation upon the Nature of a Thing, or of our Notions and Apprehensions of it, it plainly follows, that Diversity of Religion in the World doth not proceed from the different Way of Speaking which Men use, (for then God would have brought a great Multitude of Religions into the World, by the Multiplication of Languages at *Babel*) but from their different Educations, Tempers, and Constitutions, or from various Abilities and Capacities of their Minds, or sometimes from their different Views and Interests.

2. If Difference in Language keeps up Difference in Religion, our blessed Saviour (who hath enjoined Unity of Religion as earnestly, and as frequently as any other Duty) would not have commanded, and by his Holy Spirit empowered, the Apostles to *preach the Gospel* in different Languages: He would have abolished all Languages but one, otherwise, if this *Objection* holds good, his Command of Unity in Religion had been impracticable.

3. This *Objection* is sufficiently confuted by the Experience of All ages. But to go no higher than the Christian *Aera*. We find, that although the Primitive Christians spoke different Languages, yet they were very unanimous in their Religion. . . . I might quote many instances among the *Mahometan, Popish* and *Protestant* Countries on the Continent, to prove that different Languages do not produce different Religions: But I shall content myself, and I believe every impartial Reader will also be contented with Three or Four in *Great Britain* and *Ireland*. The *English, Welsh,* and *Cornish* Tongues in *England* do not produce Diversity of Religion, among the People who speak them. So in *Scotland*, the *Highlanders* and *Saxons* are for the most part of the same Religion, notwithstanding that their Speech is not the same. On the other hand, Agreement in Language, doth not prevent Diversity of Religion: How many Sectaries are there in these Kingdoms who speak no other Language but the *English*? Have we not *English Papists*, and *Irish Protestants, Irish Papists*, and *English Protestants*?. . .

It is said, That *to print books in* Irish, *and to send Missonaries to teach in that Tongue, is to give too much Encouragement to the Language.*

But this being the only Way to convert such of the Natives, as do not understand *English*, we are indispensably bound to make this Use of the

Language, out of Charity to their Souls, and in Obedience to our Saviour's express Command. And although I should not be for encouraging the Language any farther, than is necessary to promote the Conversion of the *Irish*, and the Salvation of their Souls; yet, it being evident, that Difference of Language doth not keep up Difference of Religion; and that it is not the *Irish* Language, but the *Popish* Religion, that is repugnant to the *English* Interest, I cannot perceive any Harm, even in Point of Policy, in using it. For Diversity of Languages is not hurtful in other Countries; nay, the *Irish* Language itself, is a harmless Thing in *Scotland*, and hath not any Marks of the Beast upon it.

And after all, I do not question, but to make this Use of the Language at present, is the most effectual Way to diminish the Use of it hereafter: For, if we prevail with them to conform to our Church, their Prejudices being thereby in a great Measure removed, they will more readily fall in with our Customs and Language; and being qualified equally with our selves for any Office or Employment, their Interest will soon induce them to speak *English*. . . .

It is objected, That *the best Way to convert the* Irish, *is, to abolish their Language; according to the wise Design of our Ancestors, nigh Two Hundred Years ago.*

How Wise and practicable a Design this is, we may learn from Experience; for, after the Trial of near Two Hundred Years, we find little or no Progress made in it. They still retain their Language, and Religion too. Nay, the *Irish* Tongue is so far from being demolished, that it hath spread as much among the *British*, in proportion to their Number, as the *English* Language among the *Irish*. . . .

As to the great Difficulties of abolishing a Language: When, to defeat the vain and foolish Enterprise at *Babel*, God was pleased, not only so to confound the one Language spoken by the Builders, that they could not understand one another's Speech; but also to scatter them abroad from thence, upon the Face of all the Earth: We have Grounds from Scripture to believe, that (as Bishop *Patrick* observes) 'the same common Dialect (or Way of Speaking) was given to those Families, whom God would have to make one Colony in the Dispersion. For they were divided in their Lands; every one after his Tongue, after their Families, in their Nations', *Gen. 5:20,31.* From which it follows, that where different Languages were spoken, the People speaking them were different Nations, separated from one another, by the Dissolution of that common Bond of Society, which consisted in Unity of Language, and forced into a Plurality of Societies, by the Multiplicity of Languages. Which being premised, the Difficulty of abolishing a Language will more plainly appear: For Difference of Language being generally a Sign of Difference of nation, and Attempt against a Language, will look like a Design against the Nation that speaks it: And all the Nations, or distinct Societies of People, having a natural inclination to favour their

97

own Community, and being apt to glory in their Antiquity, and to boast of the great Merit and Renown of their Ancestors, they will be very loth to part with their Native Language, and apt to give any Design against it all the Opposition they can. . . .

After the best Enquiry that I could make into the Practice of other Nations, with relation to this Point, I do not find in History any Account of the Abolition of a Language. . . . We have several Instances of the same kind among our selves; the *Welsh* and *Cornish* Tongues remain still in *England*, the *Irish* in *Scotland*, and the *Manks* in the Isle of Man: Although all the Laws and Pleadings be confined to the *English* Tongue; and speaking of *English* is a necessary Qualification for any Office of considerable Trust or Profit. In a Word, there cannot any Instance be given, that a Language hath been abolished, even in a conquered Country, except where the Inhabitants were either destroyed, or driven out of it.

Men do not only like, but they are generally fond of, their Native Language. And they will not easily part with any Thing, for which they have a great Love and Affection. An Attempt to take it from them, will very much provoke and exasperate them, and consequently prejudice them against our Instructions, and render them more averse to our Communion. If we shall endeavour to rob them of their Tongue, we shall be sure to lose their Hearts; without which, I doubt, we shall never be able to convert them.

If it therefore be so hard and inconvenient an Undertaking to abolish a Language, how difficult would it be to extinguish a Religion and a Language together? If the strong forces of these two Potentates be united, it will be no easy matter to overcome them. . . .

Upon the whole, it plainly appears, that the Objections against the *Irish* Language have not any Foundation either in Reason or Religion: And it is obvious to observe, that they are grounded altogether upon that National Prejudice and Aversion, which still remains among too many of the *English* and *Irish* Nations to one another. I know some of the Natives of that Kingdom, who can speak *English*, and yet will not, for no other reason, but that it is *English*. The same Motive, on the other side, induceth some to be very earnest for abolishing the *Irish* Language: They have a Dislike to the Nation, and this draweth them insensibly into a Dislike of the Language, for which no other Reason can be given, but that it is *Irish*; if this were not so, there would be the same Necessity for abolishing the *Irish* Language in *Scotland*. Besides, it is not the Language of the Court, but of a poor, ignorant and depressed People, from whom we can have no Expectations; and this, together with the Trouble of Learning an obsolete Language, increaseth Men's Prejudices against it. But whatever may be the Causes of that great Aversion which some have entertained against the Language; an open and avowed Attempt to abolish it, is not the way to unite the two Nations in their Hearts and Affections: Difference of Religion is, that which sets them at the greatest distance from one another; and if that were taken away, all other Differences would dwindle into nothing; or if they continued, they would do no harm. And from what hath been said, it appears that Preaching, and Printing the Bible and Common-Prayer-Book in *Irish*, are the necessary Means for attaining this good End. . . .

That a sufficient Number of Charity-Schools *be erected, for the Instruction of the* Irish *Children* gratis, *in the* English *Tongue, and the Established Church, &c.*

This Article is founded upon the great Usefulness of Religious Education in general, and upon the many Advantages in particular, which the Public will receive, by having these Children instructed in the Church Catechism.

It is proposed, That they be taught to read, not only that they may be more fit for Business; but especially, that they may be more capable of Catechetical Instruction, and improving in Christian Knowledge, which very few illiterate Persons attain to, in any tolerable Measure or Degree.

Now, by the Help of these Schools, great Numbers of Children will be bred up in the Knowledge of Virtue and Religion, who would otherwise be not only abandoned to utter Darkness and Ignorance, but would also be trained up, as it is too much to be feared, in a vicious and dissolute Course of Life. . . .

Ireland is a Nursery to supply some neighbouring Popish Kingdoms with Men, when they have Occasion for them; by which Means the Crown of *Great Britain* and *Ireland*, loses a greater Number of Native Subjects (who might be very useful in War and Peace, at Home and Abroad) than have been got by all the Popish Persecutions. So that in order to complete and establish the Reduction of *Ireland*, and to render it a more useful Branch of our Monarchy, it is absolutely necessary that the Protestant Religion be propagated among the Natives. And as the Expense of effecting this might be easily born,[*] for the Benefits and Accruing thereby to Her Majesty, and to the whole Community, would be great and many.

[*] *The Yearly Charge of four Regiments, or the Expense of one Year's War in Ireland, would do it*

4.7 A Short History of the Attempts that Have Been Made to Convert the Popish Natives of Ireland, to the Established Religion: With a Proposal for their Conversion, John Richardson, 1712

If we expect that Men should hearken to our Instructions, and receive our good Advice, we must treat them very tenderly, and have a great Care not to vex or irritate them; because Nature abhors to follow the Counsels of an Enemy. But to Convert the *Irish*, by attempting to abolish their Language, or by any severe and disagreeable Methods, seems to be the Reverse of this; it is to think of persuading and convincing them, by enraging and exasperating them; and of gaining their Hearts and Affections, (without which they can never be truly converted) by taking from them that which is very dear and valuable to them; which is not the way to expel the morbific Matter, but to poison the Physic of their Souls: And it is not to bind up and heal, but to rankle and envenom their spiritual Wounds. And therefore it is observed, that Men generally lose their End and Design by such Means, which tempt others to dissemble, and to do Violence to their Consciences, but seldom make true Proselytes. And the Truth of this is confirmed to us by what hath been just now related. For the Means that were used to induce, or rather compel, the *Irish* Natives to hear *English* Prayers and Sermons, and to hinder them from receiving any Instruction in their own Tongue, made few or no sincere Converts, and only provoked them (as I have already observed) to rebel on the first Opportunity, and to apostasize, if I may so term it, to that Superstition and Idolatry from which they had not been inwardly converted. . . .

If anyone will look back with an impartial Eye, and consider the Endeavours that have been used to convert the *Irish*, it will be obvious and natural to make this observation on the whole, That the principal Cause, in all probability, why the reformed Religion hath all this Time made no greater Progress among the Natives of *Ireland*, is, that the most fit and effectual, or (to speak in other Terms) the evangelical Means, have not been universally and steadily used to that End: There hath not due Care been taken, to perform the Offices of Religion to them constantly in their own Language. It must be acknowledged indeed, that other Causes have concurred, to keep up Popery in that Kingdom; but the first and greatest is, That the Light of God's Word (*which converteth the soul*, Psal. 19.7.) hath not been sufficiently communicated to them. Politic methods have been depended upon, for accomplishing this Work, and the Means of the Gospel have been neglected: As if we knew better than Christ and his Apostles, how Religion is to be propagated in the World: Or the methods used by them were not seasonable or convenient now.

And that this Omission is the Chief reason, why the Popish Religion continues to have still so many Votaries in *Ireland*, may be presumed, from the greater Progress which the Reformed Religion hath made in *Great Britain*, upon Application made to the People in their own Language. The Inhabitants of *Wales* are generally Protestants; and the Reason is, because they are instructed, and have Religious Offices performed in the *Welsh*, pursuant to an excellent Law now in force in this Kingdom. . . .

By the same Means, the Christian Religion hath begun of late to spread apace in the *East* and *West-Indies*. The Word of God (which is quick and powerful, and which, under the Spirit of God, is the chief Instrument of Conversion) hath been printed in the *Indian* Tongues, and distributed among the Natives; whereby many of them have been turned *from Darkness to Light, and from the Power of Satan unto God.*

100

4.8 Letter to the Secretary, Society for Promoting Christian Knowledge, Revd E. Nicolson, 1715

I have one thing which I cannot forbear mentioning here, that is, the well meaning project of the Reverend Mr. Richardson about preaching to the Irish natives in their mother tongue. I have considered that matter and am absolutely of opinion that it will be utterly insignificant (if it does not do us more harm than good) for tho' such a method be the only way among infidels, yet among our Irish Papists it can have no effect; for in the 1st place their priests have effectual bars by their excommunications and influence over their blind zealots to hinder the hearing us at all. 2dly. the promoting that barbarous language (so intimately fraught with cursing and swearing and all vile profaneness) will but keep up the distinction of their people from ours to make us one people and of one religion, which would have but one language. 'Tis not alike in Wales, where the Protestants have possession of their own language for the major part, and popery is not there rampant in the Welsh tongue as it is here universally among the natives in the Irish language. 3ly. There is hardly a boy of 16 years old in Ireland but can understand and speak English. Their parents encourage them to it for their own trading and dealing with their English landlords. Most of the old people will not learn it, or do scorn to speak it, and those are so stiff in popery and riveted by the superstition of their language and customs that they would never be converted by speaking Irish never so much to them.

I myself could speak Irish from my youth and read it too; yet never could convert any Papist by that means, tho' I have by other means been instrumental, with God's blessing in bringing above 100 to Church of the papists that could understand English, besides the poor boys, whom I don't reckon in that number. But English is now so universally spoken by all the young Irish here that we may hope in the next generation Irish will be quite forgotten. 4thly. This project for promoting Irish books and preaching will deprive us of abundance of money which might go to maintain the poor children at school, among whom all our hope of converting the Irish natives must solely dwell. The old ones will soon die, and if the young ones be rightly educated, popery and Irish barbarism will soon be ended.

4.9 Tarngaireacht dhuinn fhírinne [The Prophecy of Donn Firinne], Aodhagáin Uí Rathaille (Egan O'Rahilly), ?1715

An truagh libh-se faolchoin an éithigh 's an fhill duibh
Ag ruagairt na cléire as dá léirchur fá dhaoirse?
Monuar-sa go tréithlag mac Shéarluis ba rí aguinn,
I n-uaigh curtha in' aonar, 's a shaordhalta ar díbirt!

Is truaillighthe, claonmhar, 's is tréason don druing uilc,
Cruadhmhionna bréige fá shéala 's fá scríbhinn,
'Ga mbualadh le béalaibh ar gcléire is ar saoithe,
'S nár dhual do chloinn tSéamuis coróin tsaor na dtrí ríoghachta.

Stadfaidh an tóirneach le fóirneart na gréine,
Is scaipfidh an ceo so de phórshleachtaibh Éibhir;
An tImpre beidh deorach is Flóndras fá dhaorsmacht,
'S an 'bricléir' go modhmharach i seomra ríogh Séamus.

Beidh Éire go súgach 's a dúnta go haerach
Is Gaedhilg 'gá scrúdadh n-a múraibh ag éigsibh;
Béarla na mbúr ndubh go cúthail fá néaltaibh,
Is Séamus n-a chúirt ghil ag tabhairt chonganta do Ghaedhealaibh.

Beidh an Bíobla sin Liútair 's a dhubhtheagasc éithigh,
'S an bhuidhean so tá cionntach ná humhluigheann don gcléir chirt,
'Gá ndíbirt tar triúchaibh go Neuuland Ó Éirinn;
An Laoiseach 's an Prionnsa beidh cúirt aca is aonach!

Are ye moved with pity because the lying wolves of black treachery
Are scattering the clergy and bringing them to complete servitude?
O woe is me! the son of Charles who was our king is lifeless,
Buried in a grave alone, while his noble son is banished;

It is foul and evil, it is treason in that wicked race,
To brandish audacious perjuries, sealed, and in writing,
Before the faces of our clergy and our nobles,
That the children of James have no hereditary title to the noble crown
    of the three Kingdoms.

The thunder will be silenced by the strength of the sunlight,
And this sorrow will depart from the true descendants of Eibhear:
The Emperor will shed tears, and Flanders will be in dire bondage.
While the 'Bricklayer' will be in pride in the halls of King James.

Erin will be joyful, and her strongholds will be merry;
And the learned will cultivate Gaelic in their schools;
The language of the black boors will be humbled and put beneath
    a cloud,
And James in his bright court will lend his aid to the Gaels.

Luther's Bible and his false dark teaching,
And this guilty tribe that yields not to the true clergy,

Shall be transported across countries to New Land from Erin,
And Louis and the Prince shall hold court and assembly.

4.10 *A Brief Discourse in Vindication of the Antiquity of Ireland*, Aodh MacCruitín (Hugh MacCurtin), 1717

[No indifferent reader, interested in history, would be anything but] surprised at the many fabulous Relations written of the Kingdom of *Ireland* these five hundred and odd years past, all by Foreign Writers, and Styling them Histories of *Ireland*, without any Regard to the Antient State and Affairs of that Nation before the Year of Salvation 1171, when the English first got footing therein. And tho' every one of those Historians pretends to write of the Origin, Monarchy, Custom, Language, &c of the *Gadelians* . . . [the reader] will discover in some of them much Malice and Hatred towards the Antient Inhabitants and their Posterity; insomuch, that setting by the Nobility almost in general, they write only of the Customs and Manners of the Common People; and in the same, collecting several pages full of stuff never found in History, but either invented by themselves, or had from others ignorant in the true Antiquity of the Nation, and setting the same to the Press, under the Title of the History of *IRELAND*. . . .

I doubt not but it will be counted Presumption in me, to attempt the *Vindication of the Antiquity of Ireland*, against a Number of Honourable, Learned, Foreign Writers who have erroneously written thereof: whereas *Sir Richard Cox* has given the following opinions of those that wrote of the same before his Time. As to Doctor *Keating*, he says thus of his Manuscript History of *Ireland*, that *It is an ill-digested Heap of Very Silly Fictions*. . . . He says also, that *Campion* and the Rest, *have but a scrap here and there, and that it fell very imperfectly* . . . He liketh *Spenser's View of Ireland*, and Sir *John Davis's* Discourse; but says at last, *that they are rather Commentaries* than Histories. When Sir *Richard* is pleased to judge thus of those Authors, Men of Learning, Distinction and Quality, what shall I expect, who am inferior to 'em? tho not to any Foreign Writer in the true Knowledge of the *Irish* Antiquity before King *Henry* the Second of *England's* Time. . . .

Sir *Richard*, in his *Introductory Discourse*, says, that, the Irish Language is a Mixture of other Languages, and that, *Com estato* is an Irish word borrowed from the Spanish, and is as much with us, as, *how do you do*; I refer myself to any indifferent man whatsoever that can write the Irish in its true orthography, or understandeth the common Irish language, in what I object herein; for, I say that *com estato* is no way us'd in the Irish Language, and has no affinity to it in orthography, or otherwise that I can find; and the same I say of all the other Words which he mentions in his Apparatus, or Introductory Discourse, to prove the Irish Language to be a mixture of other Languages; and whosoever will be pleas'd to read the most Authentic Irish histories, he shall find sufficient reasons to believe that the Scythian language (and consequently the Irish which is no other but the same) is one of the Antientest in the World, as I shall shew in this following Discourse. . . .

About 49 Yrs after the Confusion of the Tower of Babel, which was building by proud Nimrod and his Complices, Feniusa Farsa was King of Scythia, and studied all Means to come to the knowledge of the languages first known at the said Tower; for there was but one language in the World before that Confusion of Babel; in the Irish language it's call'd Goirtighearn, and after the Confusion there was none of the People that cou'd speak or understand the same; for of the 72 Families there employ'd, each had a peculiar language, which none of the other families cou'd speak or understand, which caus'd them to desist from that foolish Attempt of making a Sanctuary for themselves against the Will of an Omnipotent God.

Heber, the son of Sale, refus'd to assist Nimrod in building the Tower, was found free of this vain Presumption; wherefore he had (in token of God's Favour) the *lingua humana*, ie the *human language*, left to him and his people. And from him it was called the Hebrew language.

The king of Scythia, named Feniusa Farsa, sent 72 of the noblest young men in all Scythia, to learn all those languages, into all parts of the known world, and commanded them to meet him in Achaia, where Heber the son of Sale then liv'd; that, there they may learn the human language from Heber and his People; so he might have all the language taught in that Place.

It was full 60 yrs after the confusion of the Tongue, Feniusa Farsa met in Achaia those he sent abroad out of Scythia. A great many of the young men of Achaia, and of the neighbouring countries, came to learn the languages from Gaoidheal, Son of Eathor, and from Cai, son of Nama, who were constituted chief Masters of the School on the Plain of Senaar in Acaia, which was the first school known in the world. Characters for the primitive languages, as Hebrew, Greek, Latin, Tebidhe, the Scythian language, now call'd Irish with us, with other languages; and engraved those Characters on the Barks of Trees. . . .

This school began 242 years after the Flood, and continued but 20 yrs; when Feniusa Farsa return'd into Scythia, and brought Gaoidheal the son of Eathor along with him, and caus'd him to gather the young Nobles of Scythia, and teach them the languages; and also to learn the characters of the other primitive languages. Those characters Gaoidheal, with much care and diligence, brought to such Protection that he caus'd them to be cut in tables of wood, and on broad flags of stone. The King likewise order'd that the Scythian language should be call'd Gaoidheilge, after this Gaoidheal's name, as a token of his love towards him.

Some say that the Scythian language had its name from Gaoidheal, or Gadelus, the son of Niul; but Cionsaola, Amergin, and many other Irish authors say, that the Scythian language, and Gaoidheal the son of Niul, both had their names from Gaoidheal son of Eathor, by the commands of Feniusa Farsa, for the greater love he bore to this man, who was coadjutor in Achaia, and sole master of the School in Scythia. . . .

All our chieftest Irish authors unanimously agree in this account of Language, and School at Maigh Senaar; and the Scythian language, and consequently the Irish language to be one of the Antientest, without the least contradiction, as to sense or matters of fact. Wherefore I think it strange that any modern Writer, ignorant in the true Antiquities and Histories of Ireland, before the coming of the English, shou'd say that the Irish Language is a mixture of all Languages, contrary to the Authority of all the Antiquity Books, and other True Histories, whereof many are yet extant, and none in any wise contradicting this warrantable account; but all, in a Harmony, asserting the same. And if any will question the Verity of what I say on this purpose, I shall shew such undoubted Monuments of Antiquity, in several authentic parchment books, as shall convince any reasonable Person to believe, that the Scythian language, and consequently the Gadelian or Irish language, are both antient and firm in themselves, without any dependence upon the Spanish, French, German, or British Language.

4.11 *An Milleadh d'imthigh ar Mhór-Shleachtaibh na hÉireann [The Ruin that Befell the Great Families of Erin]*, Aodhagáin Uí Rathaille (Egan O'Rahilly), 1720

Monuar-sa an Chárrth'-fhuil tráighte, tréith-lag!
Gan rígh ar an gcóip ná treorach tréan-mhear!
Gan fear cosnaimh ná eochair chum réitigh!
Is gan sciath dín ar thír na saor-fhlaith!

Tír gan triath de ghrian-fhuil Éibhir!
Tír fá ansmacht Gall do traochadh!
Tír do doirteadh fá chosaibh na méirleach!
Tír na ngaibhne – is treighid go héag liom!

Tír bhocht bhuaidheartha, is uaigneach céasta!
Tír gan fear, gan mac, gan chéile!
Tír gan lúth, gan fonn, gan éisteacht!
Tír gan chomhthrom do bhochtaibh le déanamh!

Tír gan eaglais chneasta ná cléirigh!
Tír le mioscais, noch d'itheadar faolchoin!
Tír do cuireadh go tubaisteach, traochta
Fá smacht namhad is amhas is méirleach!

105

Tír gan tartha gan tairbhe i nÉirinn!
Tír gan turadh gan buinne gan réiltean!
Tír do nochtadh gan fothain gan géaga!
Tír do briseadh le fuirinn an Bhéarla!

Woe is me! weak and exhausted is the race of Carthach,
Without a prince over the hosts, or a strong, nimble leader!
Without a man to defend, without a key to liberate!
Without a shield of protection for the land of noble chieftains!

A land without a prince of the sun-bright race of Eibhear!
A land made helpless beneath the oppression of the stranger!
A land poured out beneath the feet of miscreants!
A land of fetters – it is sickness to me unto death!

A land poor, afflicted, lonely, and tortured!
A land without a husband, without a son, without a spouse!
A land without vigour, or spirit, or hearing!
A land in which is no justice to be done to the poor!

A land without a meek church or clergy!
A land which wolves have spitefully devoured!
A land placed in misfortune and subjection
Beneath the tyranny of enemies and mercenaries and robbers!

A land without produce or thing of worth of any kind!
A land without dry weather, without a stream, without a star!
A land stripped naked, without shelter or boughs!
A land broken by the English-prating band!

4.12 Seanchuimhne ar Aodhagán Ua Rathaille [A Reminiscence of Egan O'Rahilly], Aodhagáin Uí Rathaille (Egan O'Rahilly), 1720s

A BEAUTIFUL precious, green-boughed tree had been growing for ages beside a church which the wicked Cromwell had despoiled, above a well overflowing with cold, bright water, on a green-swarded plain, which a rapacious minister had wrested from a nobleman of the Gaels, who was sent over the wild, raging sea through treachery, and not at the edge of the sword. This foul lubber of a minister was desirous to cut down a green limber limb of this tree to make house furniture of it. But none of the carpenters or other workmen would meddle with the beautiful bough, since it lent them a lovely shade to hide them whilst they mourned in heart-broken sorrow their fair champions who lay beneath the sod. 'I will cut it down,' exclaimed a gawky, bandy-legged, thin-thighed son of this sleek minister's, 'and get ye a hatchet for me at once.'

The thick-witted churl climbed up the tree, like a frightened cat, fleeing from a cry of hounds, and reached a point where two small branches crossed one another. He tried to separate them by the strength of his arms; but in the twinkling of an eye they slipped from his grasp, and closing on his neck held him suspended high between heaven and hell. Then was the confounded Sassenach dangling his feet with the swaying of the bough, while he stood on 'nothing,' and his black-bladed tongue protruded a yard's length, as if in mockery of his father.

The minister screamed and bawled like a pig in a bag or as a goose gripped beneath a gate (and no wonder) while the workmen were getting a ladder to take him down. Egan O'Rahilly from Sliabh Luachra of the heroes was present, attending on the villain of the hemp, and he chanted this song:-

'Good is thy fruit, O tree,
May every branch bear such good fruit.
Alas! that the trees of Innisfail
Are not full of thy fruit each day.'

'What is the poor Irish devil saying?' said the minister.

'He is lamenting your darling son,' replied a wag who stood beside him.

'Here is two pence for you to buy tobacco,' said the sleek badger of a minister.

'Thank'ee, Minister of the Son of Malediction' (*i.e.*, the devil), replied Egan; and he spoke this lay:-

'Huroo! O minister, who didst give me thy two pence
    For chanting a lament for thy child;
May the fate of this child attend the rest of them
    All, even unto the last.'

4.13 *The Church Catechism in Irish*, Francis Hutchinson, 1722

As this *Catechism*, in which both Irish and English are placed in the same English-Letter, in two columns placed over against one another, and Spelt by the same *Alphabet*, is, for aught I know, the first of its Kind, Editors of it must expect to meet with such free Examinations and Objections, as all Projectors of new schemes must allow of: But as this introduction of a new Character, is not a wanton needless changing of a thing well settled, but only Improving a very bad One, with Reasonable Hopes of doing considerable service if it succeeds: Candid Men will be so far from being Severe in

107

censuring Small Defects, that they will rather lend their Assistance towards curing in a second Essay, what we cannot reasonably expect to see perfect in the first.

However, that such kind of Readers may not Condemn without knowing first what it is that is done, we will Premise some few things concerning the old Irish Character which is left. The Reason why the Bible and Common-Prayer-Book were not put into it at the Time of the REFORMA-TION, and the Reason why something ought to be done now, and an Account of this that is here offered, and of the benefits that are hoped for from it.

And first for the old Characters of the Irish-Letters, I need say no more, but that they are not the same, but different from ours. I may say also, that they are awkward, and of an ill Figure, as they must needs be; for they are really the same that ours were about a 11 hundred Years ago, before length of time and PRINTING had given them a smoother and a plainer Turn; but passing over that, I will only say, that Time and want of Use, hath made them unknown; that to us now, they are almost as hard to be learned, as *Greek* or *Hebrew* or any other new *Alphabet* would be.

Then secondly, as they are awkward, and strange, and hard to be learnt; so they are too few for the Expressing any Language whatever. For in their *Alphabet*, they have neither *h* in its proper sound, nor *k*, nor *i* Consonant, nor *v*, nor *w*, nor *x*, *y*, *z*, and yet they have the sounds of them all: But for want of these Eight letters, they are forced to mingle and blend the others, and confound all *Readers*. . . .

Thirdly, Another great fault in the old Character and Spelling, is, that the Compositions are not made by such proper Changes as join the words together with such Convenience, but by adding word to word, and keeping the old Letters, as *Possessive's* or *Heretors* in it. To convince me of the inconvenient Length, and great number of Quiescents that this occasions, two Clergymen have it for their native Tongue, and are chief in making this Traduction of Character that is here presented, chose out the 6th Word found in the Title of the *Church Catechism* as it stands already in the common Character; the word is *ionfhoghomtha* to *be learned*, which is spoken only *inomola*; fourteen letters, and seven of them Quiescents. . . .

But the worse and less intelligible the Language of those Times was, the better it answer'd the Ends of those who were Masters of it. For the Pope's design was to keep Ireland a SACRED, as he call'd it, that is a separate People to himself, And the Popish Priests kept the Laity in Subjection to 'em, by means of their Ignorance; and by the Obscurity of their Language, they did it effectually. For let them make what Representations they would, either of Religion, History, or the Acts and Designs of the Government, neither the King, nor People of England could contradict them, and show the People how much they were impos'd upon.

Now the natural way of Converting these poor People, and delivering them from their Bondage, in my humble Opinion, should have been, by Opening their Eyes, showing them how they had been abused, and making them sensible of the Benefits, that were laid before them by the Protestant Religion.

That was the Method that was taken in England, at the Time of the REFORMATION. The Reformers translated the Bible into English, set up the Holy Scriptures upon the very Walls of the Churches, and read them in the known Tongue. They publish'd and us'd the *Common-Prayer* in the language that every Body understood. They set up schools for the Instruction of Youth, and here in Ireland they did the same within the English Pale, and throu' GOD's Blessing, those good Means, had the same good effect here, that they had in England, and other Places: But the poor Natives lying out of their Power, and having such a language, as I have represented, which cou'd only be spoken, but neither written, nor read, without those difficulties that I have mention'd, the *Parliament* tried to abolish it in the time of Henry the 8th, when they set themselves to root out Popery. And happy would it be for the World, if corrupt Religions, and bad languages could be removed so easily, and Truth, and Wisdom could be planted as easily in their stead . . .The trying to change the Language and Religion of these Natives without these proper Methods, was but forcing Nature; and the Effect was such, as is well known. The poor ignorant People follow'd their old Teachers, and went on in their old Way: For the *Pope* and his *Emissaries* were watchful, and told them they would be damned, if they did not: And the Protestants, who could not speak to them, could not convince them by the contrary, nor by the scriptures of GOD and his Truth before them. . . .

The [catechism] will help them to learn the English Tongue with most Ease. For tho' a little *Irish* is mingled; it is English that is intended to be taught them: And if it shall have the good Effect of bringing them to that, it will do more good than all Laws that have been made for abolishing Distinctions and Incorporating them into one People with us. For the kind Intention, and true Policy of the Government hath been to take away all Difference of Habit, Language, Law and Religion, and make all grow up into one People, as they are in England; where British, Roman, Saxon, Danish or Norman – Blood make no uneasiness or Division: And as the poor Natives, if their Priests, for their own Interest did not deceive them; should of all People be the fondest of this real Union; this learning of them *English* would insensibly bring that Advantage and many other Benefits, which every one must know without our further troubling ourselves with their Innumeration.

4.14 *The Elements of the Irish Language, Grammatically Explained in English*, Aodh MacCruitín (Hugh MacCurtin), 1728

It is certain, most of our Nobility and gentry have abandon'd [Irish], and disdain'd to learn or speak the same these 200 years past. And I could heartily wish, such persons would look back and reflect on this matter; that they might see through the Glass of their own reason, how strange it seems to the world, that any people should scorn the Language, wherein the whole treasure of their own Antiquity and profound Sciences lie in obscurity, so highly esteem'd by all lovers of Knowledge in former Ages . . . I know that there are some ridiculing wits, that condemn as vain and useless, the labours of those who would Endeavour to preserve this Language; but no wise or knowing person ought to take notice of such Critics. And there are many that take great liberty in taking after such a manner, yet some of the Nobility, Bishops, and Doctors of our European Colleges', most Extensive Capacities in all kind of literature, are the most zealous in promoting the language and preserving its monuments.

4.15 *The English Irish Dictionary. An Focloir Bearla Gaoidheilge,* Conor Begly and Hugh MacCurtin (Conchobar Ó Beaglaoich agus Aodh MacCruitín), 1732

[The Irish have complained] in regard of the injury done to their language, which, without being understood, has hitherto been cried down and ridiculed by the English in general, and even by some Gentlemen in particular, whose fine sense and good manners in other respects have deserved Praise and Imitation. . . . Of all the dead or living languages none is more copious and elegant in the expression, nor is any more harmonious and musical in the Pronunciation than the IRISH, though it has been declining these five hundred years past, along with the declining Condition of our country; whereas most of the modern Tongues of Europe have been polishing and refining all that long series of Time. This is a circumstance in favour of the IRISH which no other national Tongue can pretend to; and shows that a language which was so polite, when the ENGLISH arms first put a stop to the Progress of, would have been much more so than at present, had it the like Opportunities that the others have met with. Nevertheless, as it is, it will be found inferior to none. Our Authors affirm it to be the old Scythian Language, and upon that account well deserves to be rescued from oblivion. . . .

That a People so naturally ambitious of Honour and so universally covetous of Glory, as several generous British Historians have described the IRISH to be, can so strangely neglect cultivating and improving a language of some Thousands of Years standing may seem surprising to all learned Foreigners, and I believe will do so to the Irish themselves, when they recover out of their Error, and take a little time to consider how much they deviate, in this particular, from the Practice and Policy of their Ancestors, and how inexcusable they are for neglecting so sacred a Depository of the Heroic Achievements of their Country. . . . The Irish Gentry have therefore opportunities enough, still left, for recovering and preserving their Mother Language, and, consequently, are without the least Colour of Excuse if they shamefully continue to neglect it.

4.16 His Majesty's Royal Charter for Erecting English Protestant Schools in the Kingdom of Ireland, 1733

George the Second by the Grace of God of Great Britain, France and Ireland, King, Defender of the Faith, &c. To all persons to whom these Presents shall come. Forasmuch as we have received information. . . . That in many Parts of our said Kingdom there are great Tracts of Mountainy and Coarse Land, of Ten, Twenty and Thirty Miles in Length, and of considerable Breadth, almost entirely inhabited by Papists, and that in most Parts of the same, and more especially in the Provinces of Leinster, Munster and Connaught, the Papists do exceed the Protestants of all Denominations in Number. That the Generality of the Popish Natives appear to have very little sense or knowledge of Religion, but what they implicitly take from their clergy, to whose Guidance in such matters they seem wholly to give themselves up. . . . So that if some Effectual method be not made use of to instruct these great Numbers of People in the Principles of True Religion and Loyalty, there is little prospect but that Superstition and Idolatry . . . will from generation to generation be propagated among them. That among the ways proper to be taken for converting and civilising of the said deluded Persons . . . one of the most necessary, and without which, all others are likely to prove ineffectual, has always been thought to be the Erecting and Establishing of a sufficient Number of *English* Protestant Schools, wherein the children of the *Irish* Natives may be instructed in the *English* Tongue, and the Fundamental Principles of True Religion. . . .

We do hereby give to the said Society full Power and Authority to nominate and appoint fit and able persons to be approved and Licensed by the Archbishops and Bishops of this Kingdom, in their respective Dioceses, to be the Schoolmasters and Schoolmistresses therein . . . to teach the Children of the Popish and other poor Natives of our said Kingdom, the English Tongue, and to teach them to read, especially the Holy Scriptures, and other good and pious Books, and to instruct them in the Principles of the Protestant Religion . . . and to teach them to Write, and to instruct them in Arithmetick, and such other parts of Learning, as to the said Society shall seem meet, and to bring them up in Virtue and Industry; and to cause them to be instructed in Husbandry and Housewifery, or in Trades or Manufactures, or in such manual Occupations as the said Society shall think proper.

4.17 'A Dialogue in Hibernian Style', Jonathan Swift, c.1735

A. *Them* apples is very good.
B. I am *again* you in that.
A. Lord, I was so bodderd t'other day with that prating fool Tom!
B. Pray, how does he *get* his health?
A. He's often very *unwell*.
B. [I] hear he was a great pet of yours. Where does he live?
A. Opposite the 'Red Lyon'.
B. I think he behaved very ill the last sessions.
A. That's true, but I cannot forbear loving his father's child. Will you tast a glass of my ale?
B. No, I thank you; I took a drink of small bear. You have a country house, are you [a] planter?
A. Yes, I have planted a great many oak trees and ash trees, and some elms round a loough.
A. And a good warrant you have, it is a kind father for you. And what breakfast do you take in the country?
B. Why, sometimes, sowins, and sometimes stirabout, and in summer we have the best frawhawns in all the county.
A. What kind of man is your neighbor Squire Dolt?
B. Why a meer buddogh. He sometimes coshers with me, and once a month I take a pipe with him, and we shoh it about for an hour together.
A. Well, I'd give a cow in Connaugh to see you together! I hear he keeps good horses.
B. None but garrawns, and I have seen him often riding on a sougawn. In short, he is no better than a spawlpeen, a perfect Monaghan. When I was there last, we had nothing but a maddor to drink out of, and the devil a night-gown but a caddow. Will you go see him when you come into our parts?
A. Not *without* you go with me.
B. Will you lend me your snuff-box *till* I take a pinch of snuff?
A. Do you make good chese and butter?
B. Yes, when we can get milk; but our cows will never keep a drop of milk without a puckawn.

4.18 *Sixteen Sermons in An Easy and Familiar Style On Useful and Necessary Subjects*, Bishop James Gallagher, 1736

I do not know whether to blame myself for the novelty of this attempt, or the rest of my countrymen for not publishing sermons in their own language, that I could hear of; contrary to the established practice of all other Christian countries, who in their mother tongue compose and print sermons for the benefit of beginners, who either copy or model their discourse by such precedents. It may be objected that the generality of our clergy have sermon books in Latin or French, or other languages, I allow they have; but generally in a style not so well adapted to our country. But surely they are not the worse to have some in their mother tongue, which may furnish them with thoughts or proper expressions, very often wanting to such as gather discourses from foreign languages. . . .

I have made them in an easy and familiar style, and on purpose omitted cramped expressions, which might be obscure to both the preacher and the hearer. Nay, instead of such, I have sometimes made use of words borrowed from the English, which practice, and daily conversation have intermixed with our language; choosing, with St. Augustine, rather to be censured by the critics, than not to be understood by the poor and illiterate, for whose use I have designed them. . . . If my brethren will admire, why Irish sermons should come clothed in English dress, which seems not to suit so well the Irish language, one reason is, that our printers have no Irish types: and another, that our mother tongue, sharing so far the fate of her professors, is so far abandoned, and is so great a stranger in her native soil, that scarce one in ten is acquainted with her characters. Lest any, then, should be discouraged from making use of this little work, by being strangers to its very elements, I have made choice of letters, which are obvious to all; and in spelling, kept nearer to the present manner of speaking, than to the true and ancient orthography. This seeming difficulty being removed, I hope that as many as can speak, or tolerably pronounce the Irish, if furnished with any stock or zeal to discharge their duty, will with little pains soon read and understand the following discourses.

4.19 'On Barbarous Denominations in Ireland', Jonathan Swift, *c*.1740

I have been lately looking over the advertisements in some of your Dublin newspapers, which are sent me to the country, and was much entertained with a large list of denominations of lands, to be sold or let. I am confident they must be genuine; for it is impossible that either chance, or modern invention, could sort the alphabet in such a manner, as to make those abominable sounds, whether first invented to invoke, or fright away the Devil, I must leave among the curious.

If I could wonder at any thing barbarous, ridiculous, or absurd among us, this should be one of the first. I have often lamented that Agricola, the Father-in-law of Tacitus, was not prevailed upon by that petty King from Ireland, who followed his camp, to come over and civilise us with a conquest, as his countrymen did Britain, where several Roman appellations remain to this day; and so would the rest have done, if that inundation of Angles, Saxons, and other nothern people, had not changed them so much for the worse, although in no comparison with ours. In one of the advertisements just mentioned, I encountered near a hundred words together, which I defy any creature in human shape, except an Irishman of the savage kind, to pronounce; neither would I undertake such a task, to be the owner of the lands, unless I had liberty to humanise the syllables twenty miles round. The Legislature may think what they please, and that they are above copying the Romans in all their conquests of barbarous nations; but I am deceived, if any thing hath more contributed to prevent the Irish from being tamed, than this encouragement of their language, which might easily be abolished, and become a dead one in half an age, with little expence, and less trouble.

How is it possible that a gentleman, who lives in those parts, where the Town-lands (as they call them) of his estate produce such odious sounds from the mouth, the throat, and the nose, can be able to repeat the words, without dislocating every muscle that is used in speaking, and without applying the same tone to all other words, in every language he understands? As it is plainly to be observed, not only in those people, of the better sort, who live in Galway and the Western parts, but in most counties of Ireland.

It is true, that in the city-part of London, the trading people have an affected manner of pronouncing; and so, in my time, had many ladies and coxcombs at Court. It is likewise true, that there is an odd provincial cant in most counties of England, sometimes not very pleasing to the ear: and the Scotch cadence, as well as expression, are offensive enough. But none of these defects derive contempt to the speaker; whereas, what we call the Irish Brogue is no sooner discovered, than it makes the deliverer, in the last degree, ridiculous and despised; and, from such a mouth, an Englishman expects nothing but bulls, blunders, and follies. Neither does it avail whether the censure be reasonable or not, since the fact is always so. And, what is yet worse, it is too well known that the bad consequence of this opinion affects those among us who are not the least liable to such reproaches, further than the misfortune of being born in Ireland, although of English parents, and whose education hath been chiefly in that kingdom. . . .

But I have wandered a little from my subject, which was only to propose a wish, that these execrable denominations were a little better suited to an English mouth, if it were only for the sake of the English lawyers; who, in trials upon appeals to the House of Lords, find so much difficulty in repeating the names, that if the plaintiff or defendant were by, they would never be able to discover which were their own lands. But besides this, I would desire, not only that the appellations of what they call the Town-lands were changed, but likewise of larger districts, and several towns, and some counties; and, particularly, the seats of country-gentlemen, leaving an *alias* to solve all difficulties in points of law.

4.20 *An Teagasg Críosduidhe do réir agus ceasda agus freagartha. The Catechism, or Christian Doctrine by way of Question and Answer*, Andrew Donlevy, 1742

It is no Wonder then, seeing the *English Tongue*, although in the Opinion of all it be otherwise much improved, is thus maimed and confronted, *even in prose*, that a *Language* of neither Court, nor City, nor Bar, nor Business, ever since the Beginning of *King James* the *First's* reign, should have suffered vast Alterations and Corruptions; and be now on the Brink of utter Decay, as it really is, to the great Dishonour and Shame of the *Natives*, who shall pass everywhere for *Irish-Men*: Although *Irish-Men* without *Irish* is an incongruity, and a great Bull. Besides, the *Irish Language* is undeniably a very Ancient *Mother Language*, and one of the smoothest in Europe, no way abounding with Monosyllables, nor clogged with rugged Consonants, which make a harsh Sound, that grates upon the Ear. And there is still extant a great Number of old valuable Irish Manuscripts both in the public and private hands, which would, if translated and published, give great light into the Antiquities of the Country, and furnish some able Pen with Materials enough, to write a complete History of the *Kingdom*: what a Discredit then must it be to the whole *Nation*, to let such a Language go to wrack, and to give no Encouragement, not even the Necessaries of life, to some of the Few, who still remain, and are capable to rescue those *venerable Monuments of Antiquity* from the profound obscurity, they are buried in?

4.21 *A Vindication of the Antiquities of Ireland,* John Keogh, 1748

The Irish Nation, from the very Beginning, took so much care of their Antiquities and Histories, in order they should be fairly transmitted down to Posterity without Corruption, that anciently there have been in Ireland two hundred chief Annalists or Historians by Place and Office, who had Estates in Land assigned to them and their Issue after them in Perpetuity, as

Dr. Keating in his Preface mentions. I do not think they could be paralleled by any Nation in this Affair.

And as they took care of their Antiquaries, so they did also, as Camden mentions, of their Poets, Physicians, and Harpers, by assigning them Estates in Land.

Now notwithstanding what I have hitherto mentioned concerning the Learning and Piety of the Irish, (which I have sufficiently proved by undeniable Authorities), I extremely admire that the English call them a rude, ignorant, and illiterate People; whereas it plainly appears to the contrary, and that they and most of the Western Nations were beholden to them for divine as well as human Learning. Sure it must be some national Prejudice, which occasions them to cast such Calumnies and Aspersions on the Irish, without any manner of Foundation; but Prejudice I know cannot speak well of any one. As for the vulgar sort of English, I cannot much blame them, because they know no better; but as for the better sort, specially the People of Quality, whom are Men of Letters, and have the Advantage of Books to inform themselves, I cannot well believe they, without wronging their Judgments, can entertain such mean Notions of the Natives of this Kingdom, since their own Authors, which I have hitherto produced to confirm what I have said, can fully direct them.

I cannot say but that there are some of the common People of this Kingdom rude and illiterate; but it is therefore a bad way of reasoning to conclude from thence that the whole Nation is so, that is, from particular Premises, to draw a general Conclusion. In answer to this, are not the Peasants, or English Boors, as rude, ignorant, and unmannerly, as any People in Europe; they will scarcely give you a civil Answer of the Road, or direct you where you intend to go; but here it is not so, for a poor Man will not only direct you, but go a Mile or two along with you, without asking any Reward, and if you want a Lodging, he will entertain you after the best manner he can.

There are some places in this Kingdom, where the very Herdsmen speak the latin Tongue fluently: from hence I conclude, that a great Number of the common People here have Humanity, Manners and Learning, which one in a thousand of the plebeain English has not. Now it would be a wrong way of arguing, to say, that the English Nation is rude and illiterate, because the common People are so; I know by Experience the contrary, that there are in England as fine Gentlemen, as any in Europe, endowed with good Nature, Liberality, and Humanity; and the very Enemies of Ireland will allow, that there are as polite Gentlemen in Ireland, as in any Part of the World, and are distinguished in most Courts of Europe for their undaunted Courage, Learning, Generosity, and martial Discipline. The Irish are reflected on by the English, because they have a kind of Tone, or Accent, in their Discourse, (which they are pleased to call a Brogue). I think this ought to be no Disgrace to them, but rather an Honour, because they distinguish themselves by retaining the Tone of their Country Language; which shows, that they have a Knowledge of it.

Would it not be an odd Thing for a Man to declare himself an Irishman, an Englishman, or a Frenchman, in a foreign Country, and not be able to speak the Lingua of the Nation from whence he came, or even retain the Tone of it? The Irish have a greater Right to cast this Reflection on the English; for there is hardly a Shire in England, but has a different Tone in pronouncing the English Tongue; so that oftentimes one Shire cannot understand another; sure this is more culpable, to have so many different Tones in the same Kingdom, than one among the Irish: nay in London they refine and mince the English Tongue to that degree, that it is scarcely intelligible, but by those who are acquainted with it. You may as well reflect upon the French, Dutch, Germans, Danes, Spaniards, Swedes, &c. because they retain the Tone of their respective Languages by which you may readily distinguish them. Now most other Nations may escape the Censure of the English, but the unfortunate Irish, who must have Calumnies heaped on them.

The Vulgar sort of people in England, called the natives of this Kingdom Wild Irish, and formerly thought they were caught in Nets and Toils, like wild Beasts; but I am sure the Better sort have had no such Notion. It is certain, that they must have had a very mean, despicable, base and barbarous Opinion of them. I shall make no other Answer to this Aspersion, but to tell them, that I pity their Ignorance and Stupidity.

4.22 *Dissertations on the Ancient History of Ireland,*
Charles O'Conor, 1753

The nation was never thoroughly undone nor vanquished by *itself*, until after the expulsion of the *Normans*: And to this is owing the Preservation of a Language near as old as the Deluge. . . .

Celtic was originally the language of the *Gomerians* and *Scythians*; what in after Times, branched forth into the various Dialects of the *Gauls*, *Teutons*, *Persians* and *Spaniards*; this was certainly a language as old and extensive as any in the world, and yielded not to the most celebrated, either in Force or Harmony. . . .

Our *Scotic* we think, hath the Preference, in point of Purity, if not Antiquity, to all other *Celtic* Dialects; and as it is evident we had the Use of Letters since our first Settlement in *Ireland*, there can be no dispute that it comes nearest the original Language of the Posterity of *Japeth*, and must be, consequently, (what Sir *William Temple* judiciously owns it) the *most original* and UNMIXT Language yet remaining in any part of *Europe*.

[Irish orthography is not Greek or Roman but] our Style and Manner of writing wonderfully corresponds with that of the Orientals from whom we borrowed, as before observed, the elements of Literature. Had our ancient

117

History been silent on these Heads, such Signatures of our ancient early commerce with the *Phoenecians*, would, we think, be self-evident. . . .

The Original and Preservation of our language thus being accounted for, we may pronounce of it, in the general, that it not only answered all the Commodious ends of Speech, but bestowed all those Decorations of Harmony and Expression which a great Genius for Poetry or Oratory can require, to become Master, both of his Subject and Auditors; for it was copious, without luxuriance; and laconic, without Obscurity; nervous, pathetic and figurative. . . .

Our Language is the most original Dialect of the Language of Japhet, and that from which the *Grecians* and *Latins* borrowed more than from any other in the world; it ought, one should think, to engage the attention, or rather care, of this learned Age.

4.23 *Focalóir Gaoidhilge-Sax-Bhéarla, Or An Irish-English Dictionary*, Archbishop John O'Brien, 1768

The tedious and difficult task both of compiling and correctly printing the *Irish Dictionary* now offered to the public, hath been undertaken by its editor with a view not only to preserve for the natives of *Ireland*, but also to recommend to the notice of those of other countries, a language which is asserted by very learned foreigners to be the most ancient and best preserved Dialect of the old Celtic tongue of the Gauls and the Celtiberians; and at the same time, the most useful in investigating and clearing up the antiquities of the Celtic Nations in general . . . a [further] consideration regarding this language, and which is grounded on a fact that is solidly proved by Mr. Edward Lhuyd, a learned and judicious antiquary, viz. that the Guidhelians or old *Irish*, had been the primitive inhabitants of Great *Britain* before the ancestors of the *Welsh* arrived in that island, and that the Celtic Dialect of those GUIDHELIANS, was then the universal language of the whole British isle . . . [another consideration] is the very close and striking affinity it bears, in an abundant variety of words, not only with the old *British*, in its different dialects the Welsh, and Armoric, besides the old Spanish or Cantabrian language preserved in *Navarre, Biscaye*, and *Basque*; but also with *Greek* and *Latin*; and more especially with the latter, as appears throughout the course of this work, wherein every near affinity is marked as it occurs, whatever language it regards. . . .

The plain fact of this abundant affinity of the Iberno-Celtic dialect with the Latin in such words of the same signification as no language could want, should I presume be esteemed a strong proof that the *lingua-prisca* of the *Aborigines* of Italy, which the Latin of the twelve tables and afterwards the Roman language, were derived, could be nothing else but a Dialect of the primitive Celtic, the first universal language of all Europe; but a Dialect indeed, which in the process of time received some mixture of the Greek, especially the Aeolic, from the colonies or rather Adventurers which anciently came to Italy from Peloponesus. . . . But it shall appear from this Dictionary, and partly what shall be laid down in the Preface, that the Greek itself had a strong mixture of the primitive *Celtic*, which was a more universal language, and more simple in the radical formation of its words. . . .

The Latin has borrowed much less of its words from the Greek than is generally imagined, and that a vast number of those Latin words which are supposed to be of Greek extraction, have been really and immediately derived from the Celtic and not from the Greek, whose words of this nature are likewise derivatives of the Celtic; or which is the same thing, either of the Phrygian or Thracian; this latter people being unquestionably Celts, as well as the parents of the former, according to the best authorities: and this confirms the truth of Plato's opinion in his *Cratylus*, that the Greeks have borrowed a great deal of their language from the *Barbarians*. . . .

For a conclusion of this Preface, I have a remark to add, which tends to show the perfection and politeness, as well as the antiquity of the Irish language. It consists in this one remarkable circumstance, that before the Irish came to the knowledge of the *Gospel*, or *Christian* morals, their language had words for all moral duties and virtues, and their opposite vices or sins; nay, and for those acts which are called Theological virtues, *faith*, *hope*, and *charity*, and whose Irish names are *Creidiomh*, *Dóchas*, *Gradh*, all three were original Irish words. . . . All this plainly shows that the Druids, who were the Doctors of morality and religious discipline among the *Celts*, and particularly in Ireland, were a *learned* body of people, and fully instructed of all moral duties and virtues.

4.24 *An Essay on the Antiquity of the Irish Language*, Charles Vallancey, 1772

The positive assertions of all the Irish Historians, that their Ancestors received the Use of *Letters* directly from the *Phoenecians*, and the Concurrence of them all in affirming that several Colonies from *Africa* settled in *Ireland*, induced the Author of the following Essay, who had made the ancient and modern Language of *Ireland* his peculiar study for some years past; to compare the *Phoenecian Dialect* or *bearla Feni* of the Irish with the *Punic* or Language of the *Carthaginians*.

The Affinity of the Language, Worship and Manners of the *Carthaginians* with those of the *ancient Irish* appeared so very strong, he communicated his Discoveries from time to time to some Gentlemen well skilled in the antiquities of *Ireland* and of the Eastern Nations; their Approbation of this rude Sketch induced the author to offer it to the Consideration of those who have greater Abilities and more leisure to prosecute such a work.

Well knowing the ridiculous light most Etymologists are held in, the Author has trod with all possible Caution in this very remote path of

Antiquity. The arbitrary Liberties taken by some Etymologists have justly drawn on them the Censure of the learned. Their general Rule of the commutation of Letters has often led many astray, and caused them to lose sight of the radical word and its primitive Sense: thus for Example, the word *adder* may by an Etymologist unacquainted with the English Language be turned to *otter*, for the *a* and *o* being both broad vowels are commutable, and the word may be written *odder*; the *d* being also commutable with *t* the word may be formed to *otter*, an Animal of a very different Species from the primitive word *adder*. . . .

If there be an Affinity of the *Irish* Language, this discovery will throw great lights on the darker periods of the *Heathen Irish* History. It will show, that although the details be fabulous, the foundation is laid in Truth. It will demonstrate the early use of *Letters* in this Island, because nothing but *that use* could preserve the least Affinity from the flourishing era of *Carthage* to the present, a space of more than 2300 Years. It will account for the Irish assuming to themselves the names of *Feni* or *Fenicians*, which they have retained through all Ages. It will with the same certainty account for their giving the name of *Bearla Feni* (the Phoenecian Tongue) to one of their native Dialects. In fine, it will show, that when they adopted the *Phoenecian Syntax*, they confined their *Language* to Oriental Orthography, while *it* harmonized itself out of *its* primitive consonantal *Celtic* harshness, by the suppression of many radical Letters in the Pronunciation of Words.

An Essay on the Antiquity of the Irish *Language*

It has been generally thought, that the Irish Language, is a compound of the Celtic, and old Spanish, or Basque; whoever will take the pains to compare either of these Languages with the ancient Manuscripts of the Irish, will soon be convinced, that the Irish partakes not the least of the Biscayan.

On a collation of the Irish with the Celtic, Punic, Phoenecian and Hebrew Languages the strongest Affinity, (nay a perfect Identity in very many Words) will appear; it may therefore be deemed a Punic-Celtic Compound; and the following Essay will prove this to be somewhat more than a bare Conjecture.

The Irish is consequently the most copious Language extant, as from the Hebrew proceeded the Phoenecian, from the Phoenecian, Carthaginian or Punic, was derived the Aeolian, Doric and Etruscan, and from these, was formed the Latin; the Irish is therefore a Language of the utmost Importance, and most desirable to be acquired by all Antiquaries and Etymologists. . . .

All Etymologists agree that where the Letter and the Sense correspond in any two Languages, they must be *identically* the same; before we proceed to the Collation it may not be improper to advertise the young Etymologist, that in most Languages the Letter *d* is commutable with *t*; *b* with *p*; *c* with g; *bh*, *mh*, with *v* consonant; that the broad vowels *a*, *o*, *u*, are indifferently written one for the other, as also the small Vowels *e*, and *i*, are often substituted one for the other; that in the Irish Language an adventitious *d* with an hiatus, or *dh*, is often introduced in Syllables, where two or more Vowels are connected. . . .

Punica Maltese	Irish
Alla, God	*All*, mighty, omnipotent.
	Ailt-dhe paenates.
Samem, the Heavens	*Samh*, the Sun, *Samhra*, Summer.
Sema, an Assembly.	*Samhadh*, a Congregation.
Baal, Sidoniorum seu	*Bel*, *Bal*, *Beal*, the chief Deity of *Iall*
Phoenicum, & *Belus*	(pro ealta Lhuyd)
Kartaginiensium numinis	
nomen est: ut *Bel*	
Chaldeorum *Saturnus*.	*beira dhuit* may you repent.
	God forgive you.
Allai hier eq. God bless you	
Iva h'alla, a Curse.	*Jobhadh* (*pronounced iva) bi o*
	may Death come from the Almighty.
Alla, *tummin*, truly	*tam ann*. that's true, truly.
Ara! interjectio.	*Arah*! an Interjection.
Ardu, the End or Summit.	*Arda*, high, haughty.
	Ard, a hill. . . .

4.25 *A Grammar of the Iberno-Celtic or Irish Language*, Charles Vallancey, 1773

The author of the following sheets is an Englishman, who employed his leisure hours in the study of the laws and manners of the ancients. The mists spread over the dark regions of antiquity have not discouraged him; he sought lights which laziness can never purchase; and found them in the laborious study of ancient languages.

Where the language of any ancient nation is attainable, a criterion is discovered for distinguishing accurately, the more remarkable features in the national character. Should the language be found destitute of the general rules of grammatical construction, and concordance; barren of scientific terms; and grating in its cadence; we may without hesitation pronounce, that the speakers were a rude and barbarous nation. The case will be altered much, where we find a language masculine and nervous; harmonious in its articulation; copious in its phraseology; and replete with those abstract and technical terms, which no civilised people can want. We not only grant that the speakers were once a thinking and cultivated people; but we must confess that the language itself, is a species of historical inscription, more ancient, and more authentic also, as far as it goes, than any precarious hearsay of old foreign writers, strangers in general, to the natural, as well as civil history of the remote countries they describe.

In this view of tracing the original and antiquities of ancient nations, the author has been at the pains of making himself master, as far as his leisure would permit, of the old language of Ireland, still fortunately preserved in ancient books, not in any jargon yet spoken by the unlettered vulgar; and he now offers the fruit of a part of his labours, in the following sketch of an Irish Grammar, that other curious enquirers may learn with less difficulty, what he has acquired with toil and labour, and he offers it in confidence, that some abler pen may complete a task, now cleared from the many disadvantages it heretofore laboured under. . . .

The earnest labours of many learned men, not only of Great Britain and Ireland, but of many other states of Europe, to restore the primitive Iberno-Celtic, or Irish language, which by being preserved in all its purity in this sequestered island, is the only key to the ancient history of those great European nations, which like great rivers are never thoroughly known, unless you trace them to their springs, have produced this work sooner than intended.

The Irish language is free from the anomalies, sterility, and heteroclite redundances, which mark the dialects of barbarous nations: it is rich and melodious; it is precise and copious, and affords those elegant conversions which no other than a thinking and lettered people can use or require. . . .

In any other but the learned age we now live in, the Iberno-Celtic, or Irish language, although the living language of at least one third of His British Majesty's subjects, would have continued to be despised. Interest, that powerful incentive of the human mind, has induced Europeans to study the *Asiatic* languages, and without that charm, the laborious works of the learned *Jones*, had been perused by the few only, who delight in antiquated languages.

The language we are now going to explain, had such an affinity with the *Punic*, that it may be said to have been in great degree the language of Hannibal, Hamilcar, and of Asdrubal; it must consequently be as acceptable to the classic scholar, as useful to the historian. It is the root from whence sprung the *lingua prisca* of the Aborigines of Italy, from which the Latin of the 12 tables, and afterwards the *Roman* language, was in great measure derived; it was in its original simplicity, the universal language of all Europe. . . .

If we were to judge of the Celtic language from its affinity with almost every language of the known world, we might conclude with *Boullet*, that it was the primeval language. There is not only a great affinity between the Iberno-Celtic and the Hebrew, Persian, and other oriental dialects; but what is more remarkable, there is a surprising affinity also, between the old Iberno-Celtic, and the dialects spoken on the vast continent of North America.

Baron la Hontan in his voyage to North America, published in 1703, assures us that the *Algonkin* language is the master language of that country, and is understood by all the Indian nations, except two. The Algonkins say they are the most ancient, and the most noble tribe on that continent: their name in Irish indicates as much, *cine algan*, or *algan cine*, i.e. the noble tribe: *all gain cine* i.e. the most renowned nation. . . . The Baron has favoured us with a small vocabulary of this Algonkin language, from which we have extracted a few words for example.

Algonkin		Irish
bi laoua	it is charming	*bi luaig'* (*g* not pron.)
kak ina	every thing	*cac' eini*
kak eli	all	*cac' uile*
na biush malatat	it is not worth bartering	*na bi fiu she malarta*
ta koucim	come hither	*tar c'uigim*
ma unia	assist me	*me uait'nig'e* (pro. *uani*). . . .

The following pages will demonstrate, that the Irish did not borrow from the Latins any words, except such are as indicative of the rites of the Christian religion, and that there is a great correspondence of syntax, idiom, and structure between the Iberno-Celtic, or Irish, and the Hebrew, Chaldaic, and Phoenecian languages.

Many learned men have observed that the modern Spanish retains a great number of words, names, and idioms of Hebrew extract, but have been at a loss how to account for it. Had *Aldrete* known any thing of the affinity there is between the Hebrew and the Celtic, he would easily have concluded that all these words and idioms in the modern Spanish, must have come from the latter, and not from the former; which would have removed all the difficulty, without having recourse to the Arabic. He was led into this notion by the great conformity between this last language and the Celtic. Hence that surprising number of words and idioms, common to the *High Dutch* and *Arabic*, which has puzzled so many critics, and cannot otherwise be accounted for, than by supposing them to be of old *Celtic* original, which like the old *Arabic* was a dialect, or as some choose to suppose it, both the Hebrew and they were dialects of the *original tongue*. . . .

As for the language of the Irish, says Sir William Temple, it must be confessed, there is not left the least trace by which we may seek out the original of this nation; for it is neither known, nor recorded to have been used *any where else* in the world besides Ireland, the Highlands of Scotland, and the Isle of Man, and must be allowed to be an *original* language, without any affinity to the old British, or any other upon the continent; and perhaps with *less mixture* than any other of those original languages yet remaining in any part of Europe. . . .

This strange sentiment of Sir William, proves he was not skilled in antiquated languages, yet he has here laid a fair foundation, for an ancient history of Ireland to be built on; for a nation and a language are both of an age; and if the language be ancient, the people must be as old. In a former work we have proved this language to be as nearly allied to the *Punic*, as it is possible for any two dialects to be, proceeding from the same mother tongue; in a future work we propose to go further, to show the Hebrew root from whence sprung each Iberno-Celtic word. . . .

4.26 *A Tour in Ireland*, Arthur Young, 1778

Lord Shannon's bounties to labourers amount to 50l a year. He gives it them by way of encouragement; but only to such as can speak English, and do something more than fill a cart.

4.27 *A General Dictionary of the English Language*, Thomas Sheridan, 1780

Scheme of the Vowels

	First	Second	Third
a	h$\overset{1}{a}$t	h$\overset{2}{a}$te	h$\overset{3}{a}$ll
e	b$\overset{1}{e}$t	b$\overset{2}{e}$ar	b$\overset{3}{e}$er
i	f$\overset{1}{i}$t	f$\overset{2}{i}$ght	f$\overset{3}{i}$eld
o	n$\overset{1}{o}$t	n$\overset{2}{o}$te	n$\overset{3}{o}$ose
u	b$\overset{1}{u}$t	b$\overset{2}{u}$sh	bl$\overset{3}{u}$e
y	love-l$\overset{1}{y}$	l$\overset{2}{y}$e	

Rules to be observed by the Natives of Ireland in order to attain a just Pronunciation of English

The chief mistakes made by the Irish in pronouncing English, lie for the most part in the sounds of the first two vowels, *a* and *e*; the former being generally sounded å by the Irish, as in the word bår, in most words where it is pronounced $\overset{2}{a}$, as in d$\overset{2}{a}$y by the English. Thus the Irish say, påtron, måtron, the vowel, å, having the same sound as in the word fåther; whilst the English pronounce them as if written paytron, maytron. The following rule, strictly attended to, will rectify this mistake through the whole language.

When the vowel, *a*, finishes a syllable, and has the accent on it, it is invariably pronounced å [day] by the English. To this rule there are but three exceptions in the whole language, to be found in the words fåther, papå, mamå. The Irish may think also the word *rather* an exception, as well as *father*; and so it would appear to be in their manner of pronouncing it, rå-ther, laying the accent on the vowel *a*; but in the English pronunciation, the consonant, th, is taken into the first syllable, as thus, rath'-er, which makes the difference.

Whenever a consonant follows the vowel *a* in the same syllable, and the accent is on the consonant, the vowel *a* has always its first sound, as håt', mån'; as also the same sound lengthened when it precedes the letter *r*, as få'r, bå'r, though the accent be on the vowel; as likewise when it preceded *lm*, as bå'lm, pså'lm. The Irish, ignorant of this latter exception, pronounce all words of that structure as if they were written, bawm, psawm, quawm, cawm, &c. In the third sound of *a*, marked by different combinations of vowels, or consonants, such as *au*, in Paul; *aw*, in law; *all*, in call; *ald*, in bald; *alk*, in talk, &c. the Irish make no mistake, except in that of *lm*, as before mentioned.

The second vowel, *e*, is for the most part sounded *ee* by the English, when the accent is upon it; whilst the Irish in most words give it the sound of second å, as in hate. This sound of ě [ee] is marked by different combinations of vowels, such as, *ea*, *ei*, *e* final mute, *ee*, and *ie*. In the last two combinations of *ee* and *ie*, The Irish never mistake; such as in meet, seem, field, believe, &c; but in all others, they almost universally change the sound of ě, into å. Thus in the combination *ea*, they pronounce the words tea, sea, please, as if they were spelt tay, say, plays; instead of tee, see, pleese. The English constantly give this sound to *ea*, whenever the accent is on the vowel *e*, except in the following words, a pěar, a běar, to běar, to forběar, to swěar, to těar, to wěar. In all which the *e* has its second sound. For want of knowing these exceptions, the gentlemen of Ireland, after some time of residence in London, are apt to fall into the general rule, and pronounce the words as if spelt, beer, sweer, &c.

Ei, is also sounded *ee* by the English, and as å by the Irish; thus the words de*ceit*, re*ceive*, are pronounced by them as if written de*sate*, re*save*. *Ei* is always sounded *ee*, except when a *g* follows it, as in the words, *reign*, *feign*, *deign*, &c. as also in the words *rein* (of a bridle), *rein*-deer, *vein*, *drein*, *veil*, *heir*, which are pronounced like *rain*, *vain*, *vail*, *air*.

The final mute *e* makes the preceding *e* in the same syllable, when accented, have the sound of *ee*, as in the words, suprěme, sincěre, replěte. This rule is almost universally broken through by the Irish, who pronounce all such words as if written, supråme, sinsåre, replåte, &c. There are but two exceptions to this rule in the English pronunciation, which are the words, *there, where.*

In the way of marking this sound, by double *e*, as thus, *ee*, as the Irish never make any mistakes, the best method for all who want to acquire the right pronunciation of these several combinations, is, to suppose that *ea, ei,* and *e* attended by a final mute *e*, are all spelt with a double *e*, or *ee*.

Ey is always sounded like $\overset{2}{a}$ by the English, when the accent is upon it; as in the words, pr$\overset{2}{e}$y, conv$\overset{2}{e}$y, pronounced pray, convay. To this there are but two exceptions, in the words k$\overset{3}{e}$y and l$\overset{3}{e}$y, sounded *kee* and *lee*. The Irish, in attempting to pronounce like the English, often give the same sound to *ey*, as usually belongs to *ei*; thus for pr$\overset{2}{e}$y, conv$\overset{2}{e}$y, they say *pree, convee*.

A strict observation of these few rules, with a due attention to the very few exceptions enumerated, will enable the well-educated natives of Ireland to pronounce their words exactly in the same way as the more polished part of the inhabitants of England do, so far as the vowels are concerned. The dipthongs they commit no fault in, except in the sound of $\overset{2}{i}$; which has been already taken notice of in the Grammar. Where likewise the only difference in pronouncing any of the consonants has been pointed out; which is the thickening the sounds of *d* and *t*, in certain situations; and an easy method proposed of correcting this habit.

4.28 *Observations on the Pamphlets Published by the Bishop of Cloyne, Mr.Trant, and Theophilus, On One Side, and Those by Mr.O'Leary, Mr.Barber, and Dr.Campbell On the Other*, Daniel Thomas, 1787

His Lordship considers as great impediments to the further advancement of the established religion, first, the immoderate extent of the parishes, secondly, the want of churches, fourthly [*sic*] the ignorance of the Irish language under which the clergyman generally labours. . . . His fourth observation must excite indignation in the breast of every Irishman. What, shall a language confessedly derived from one of the first tongues which subsisted among polished nations, be abolished, merely to make room for another compounded of all the barbarous dialects which imperfectly communicated the thoughts of savages to each other? No, my Lord, the natives of Ireland must ever be instructed in their vernacular tongue. . . .

No change could be lasting, which took place in contradiction to the passions of the people, who in all nations have been more affected by changes in local manners and customs, but particularly in language, than by political innovations; for any attack upon their former habits wounds them in a part (where they possess the most exquisite sensitivity, where they are capable of perceiving the full extent of insult, or of injury) . . . to alter speech is to inhibit speech to the lower ranks, and to reduce men to the lower ranks. . . .

Be so good to consider, what is the distinctive mark of the natives of different countries? What but language. Any design therefore to destroy the vernacular tongue, is an attempt to annihilate the nation, and let your Lordship well weigh, whether the mouths which you now wish to close, may not soon open with harsh thunders in your ears.

4.29 *Reliques of Irish Poetry*, Charlotte Brooke, 1789

In a preface to a translation of ancient Irish poetry, the reader will expect to see the subject elucidated and enlarged upon, with the pen of learning and antiquity. I lament that the limited circle of my knowledge does not include the power of answering to just an expectation; but my regret at this circumstance is considerably lessened, when I reflect, that had I been possessed of all the learning requisite for such an undertaking, it would only have qualified me for an unnecessary foil to the names of O'CONOR, O'HALLORAN and VALLANCEY. . . .

It is impossible for imagination to conceive too highly of the pitch of excellence to which a science must have soared which was cherished with such enthusiastic regard and cultivation as that of poetry, in this country. It was absolutely, for ages, the vital soul of the nation; and shall we then have no curiosity respecting the productions of genius once so celebrated, and so prized? . . .

I am aware that in the following poems there will sometimes be found a sameness, and repetition of thought, appearing but too plainly in the English version, though scarcely perceivable in the original Irish, so great is the variety as well as the beauty peculiar to that language. The number of synonima in which it abounds, to repeat the same thought, without tiring the fancy or the ear.

It is really astonishing of what various and comprehensive powers this neglected language is possessed. In the pathetic, it breathes the most beautiful and affecting simplicity; and in the bolder species of composition, it is distinguished by a force of expression, a sublime dignity, and rapid energy, which it is scarcely possible for any translation fully to convey; as it sometimes fills the mind with ideas altogether new, and which, perhaps, no modern language is entirely prepared to express. One compound epithet must often be translated by two lines of English verse, and, on such occasions, much of the beauty is necessarily lost; the force and effect of the thought being weakened by too slow an introduction on the mind; just as that light which dazzles, when flashing swiftly on the eye, will be gazed at with indifference, if let in by degrees.

But, though I am conscious of having, in many instances, failed in my attempts to do all the justice I wished to my originals, yet still, some of their beauties are, I hope, preserved; and I trust I am doing an acceptable service to my country, while I endeavour to rescue from oblivion a few of the invaluable reliques of her ancient genius; and while I put it in the power of the public to form some idea of them, by clothing the thoughts of our Irish muse in a language with which they are familiar, at the same time that I give the originals, as vouchers for the fidelity of my translation, as far as two idioms so widely different would allow. . . .

The productions of our Irish Bards exhibit a glow of cultivated genius, – a spirit of elevated heroism, – sentiments of pure honour, – instances of dis-interested patriotism, – and manners of a degree of refinement, totally astonishing, at a period when the rest of Europe was nearly sunk in barbar-ism: And is not all this very honourable to our countrymen? Will they not be benefited, – will they not be gratified, at the lustre reflected on them by ancestors so very different from what modern prejudice has been studious to represent them? But this is not all.

As yet, we are too little known to our noble neighbour of Britain; were we better acquainted, we should be better friends. The British muse is not yet informed that she has an elder sister in this isle; let us then introduce them to each other! Together let them walk abroad from their bowers, sweet ambassadresses of cordial union between two countries that seem formed by nature to be joined by every bond of interest, and of amity. Let them entreat of Britain to cultivate a nearer acquaintance with her neighbouring isle. Let them conciliate for us her esteem, that the portion of her blood which flows in our veins is rather ennobled than disgraced by the mingling tides that descended from our heroic ancestors.

4.30 *Antiquities of Ireland*, Edward Ledwich, 1790

Of the Ogham Characters, and Alphabetic Elements of the Ancient Irish.

The origin of letters among the Celts is thus delivered by the fabulous Berosus. The great giant Samethes, the brother of Gomer and Tubal, promulged a Code of Laws for the Celtic nations, taught them the courses of the planets and the nature of sublunary things, gave them the Sagae or Phoenecian letters, and led colonies into the Celtic regions 143 years after the deluge, and into Britain 252 years after the same event.

Now for the Irish elements. The celebrated Fenius Farsa, according to Keating, was the son of Magog, and King of Scythia. Desirous of becoming Master of the seventy-two languages created at the confusion of Babel, he sent seventy-two persons to learn them. He established an University at Magh-Seanair near Athens, over which he, Gadel, and Caoith presided. Therefore the Greek, Latin and Hebrew letters. Gadel was ordered to digest the Irish into five dialects: the Finian, to be spoken by the Militia and Soldiery; the poetic and historic, by the Senachies and Bards; the medical, by Physicians, and the common idiom by the Vulgar.

Mr.O'Conor's account of the Bethluisnion of the Ogham is in the same wild romantic strain. 'This', observes he, 'has not the least resemblance with either the Greek or Roman alphabets. Had our Bards been silent on the original of our letters from a celebrated Phenius or Phoenecian, yet the signatures of an early commerce between our predecessors and an oriental lettered people, would appear evident. These letters are arranged in a different order from the alphabet of the Greeks, or abecedarium of the Romans: their ancient virgular figures were peculiar to this western nation alone: and their names partly Phoenecian and partly Vernacular, not only show their Asiatic original, but their great Antiquity in this island.' Mr. Pinkerton very justly calls such writers, 'visionaries, who detail superficial dreams to the public, upon no antient authority, and upon the most silly and irrational ratiocination'. 'Hence', adds he, 'what no foreign Antiquary, what no man of sound learning would even imagine, has been seriously advanced, that the Phoenecians settled colonies in the South of Britain, and in Ireland, and that traces of the Phoenecian language may be found in the Irish!. . .'

Truth, though clouded, will at length burn the thick envelope of fable. 'What, says O'Flaherty, if I should affirm that our Phenisius was the Phoenecian Cadmus, who depicted the ancient Greek letters, and which resembled the Latin.' Here he states an indisputable fact, that the Irish elements are from the Latin, (the greater part at least,) and the Latin from the Greek: but how painful to a liberal mind is the diffidence with which he expresses himself? He had written too large a work, and staked his reputation with his countrymen too deeply, to make the proper allocation of his learning and abilities to the subject of Irish Antiquities. Like many others, to be confident he was obliged to be absurd, and to be patriotic he sacrificed his fame on the altar of national prejudice.

O'Conor, whose dissertations on the ancient History of Ireland, are nothing but scraps translated form Lynch's Cambrensis Eversus and O'Flaherty, grants the letters used by the old Irish, since the reception of Christianity, are evidently borrowed from the first christian Missioners, as more commodious than the old, uncouth and virgular forms imported into Ireland by the Celto-Scythian colony from Spain. What a direct contradiction is this of his former assertion, and how changed in tone from the tumid and bombastic verbosity of his former citation? Sir George Mackensie and Bishop Stillingfleet had examined the Irish claim to remote history and literature, and found it to be an heap of impertinence and imposture. Father Innes, the two MacPhersons and Mr. Whitaker have since totally subverted it. Ashamed of persevering in gross errors, and unable to stand the conviction flashed on him from every quarter, the Irish Antiquary gives up his fables, and reluctantly owns the triumph of learning and criticism.

For the reprobation of these puerile figments no great extent of reading, or strength of judgement is requisite: nor should they have farther engaged the reader's attention, did I not imagine the subject has hitherto been totally misunderstood, and of course imperfectly treated. The Irish ground their pretensions to an original alphabet on the traditions of the Bards, (who bring their ancestors from the East) and the agreement of these traditions with allowed history. Thus O'Conor compares the accounts in the Leavar Gabhala and Leavar Lecan, two MSS. which have never seen the light, with the facts given in Newton's chronology. In his way of concluding this matter, he might have parallels equally accurate, in Amadis de Gaul or any other romance, as in these leavars. . . .

But to obviate every doubt respecting the oriental colonisation of Ireland, the Irish language is adduced as proof, 'that the Speakers were a civilised and lettered people, which could only be derived from an eastern connection: that the language is masculine and nervous: harmonious in its articulation, copious in its phraseology, and replete with abstract and technical terms; free from anomalies, sterilities and heteroclite redundancies.' – We are told, says Mr.Pinkerton of many abstract terms in the old Irish language, as a proof that the people were civilised; yet no such terms are produced, and if they were, how old are they? The use of Latin abstract terms is quite modern. There is not one Irish MSS. extant older than the 11th century, long after metaphysics and such trifling sort of learning had been success-fully studied there. To which I add, that its copiousness arises from its corruption, and so does its harmony; for in the 4th and 5th centuries, and much earlier, it is branded by the ancients with the harshest expressions for its barbarism; and a native writer, about the year 700, calls it a vile tongue. As no genuine specimen of Celtic has been produced, or possibly can, to warrant the praises bestowed on it, it clearly follows, that to speak of it in such panegyrical terms must be to deceive the unlearned reader, while at the same time it reveals the writer's profound ignorance. . . .

The aid of etymology is called in to demonstrate the eastern complexion of the Irish tongue, by [Vallancey]. . . . If he designed to prove the Celtic to be originally the same, as the Hebrew or any other Oriental language, he ought, as a scholar, to have shown their agreement in matter and form, for it is these, and not from resemblances in sound, the affinity of languages is to be inferred. The Celtic, in its structure, varies from every other tongue. In it, words are declined by changing not the terminations but the initial letters in the oblique cases. Its pronouns alter the beginning of nouns, and its grammar cancels every rule of language. Not to insist on the uncertainty of etymology from the vicious orthography of words by Lexicographers, and the vicious orthoepy of sounds by the natives themselves, the Irish leavar for liber, litur for litera, and scriptuir for scriptura, abundantly demonstrate that we had neither letters, writing or books, until received through a Roman discourse. This Innes has long since observed. The corrupt state of ancient tongues has, at all times, been a fine field for literary trifling, and a rich soil for sciolists and alphabetarians to flourish in. On the whole, the pretension of the Irish to an eastern origin is a vain, groundless notion, generated in ignorance and mistaken patriotism, digraceful to the good sense of the nation, and not to be supported by reason, history, or learning.

4.31 Henry Flood's Will, 1795

[Leaves his lands, houses, inheritances and estates to Trinity College in order that:] they do institute and maintain, as a perpetual establishment, *a professorship of and for the native Irish or Erse language*, and that they do appoint, if he shall then be living, Colonel Charles Vallancey to be the first professor thereof, with a salary of not less than three hundred pounds sterling a-year, seeing that by his eminent and successful labours in the study and recovery of that language, he well deserves to be so appointed; [and] to *the purchase of all printed books and manuscripts in the said native Irish or Erse language, wheresoever to be obtained*, and next to the purchase of all printed books and manuscripts of the dialects and languages that *are akin to the said native Irish or Erse language.*

4.32 *Bolg an tSolair: Or, Gaelic Magazine*, Patrick Lynch, 1795

When it is considered that the main design of the following work, is nothing else than to recommend the Irish language to the notice of Irishmen, any arguments laid down on that head, to persuade the natives that their own language is of some importance to them, would appear quite superfluous in the eye of foreigners, but seeing that the Gaelic has been not only banished from the court, the college, and the bar, but that many tongues and men have been employed to cry it down, and to persuade the ignorant that it was a harsh and barbarous jargon, and that their ancestors, from whom they derived it, were an ignorant and uncultivated people, – it becomes necessary, to say something in reply. . . .

The Irish will be found by the unprejudiced ear, to excel in the harmony of its cadence; nor was any language fitter to express the feelings of the heart. It is also a rich and copious language, abounding with terms of art, and words to express every thought of the mind; and it has this advantage over all the modern dialects, that it compounds all its words within itself – so that the unlearned could never be at a loss for their meaning. . . .What a degree of perfection must a language attain, that was spoken by the same race of people, in the same place, without mixture, for more than two thousand years, and *that* under the inspection of learned men. . . .

Thus we see that an acquaintance with Gaelic, as being the mother of all the languages in the West, is necessary to every antiquary who would study the affinity of languages, or trace the migrations of the ancient races of mankind; of late it has attracted the attention of the learned in different parts of Europe – SHALL IRISHMEN ALONE REMAIN INSENSIBLE?. . .

Notwithstanding that Ireland had been subject to England from the time of Henry II and that English colonies had remained for centuries in this country, no attempt was made to change the national language, nor to force a foreign jargon on the natives. The Irish enjoyed their own laws and language, till the reigns of Elizabeth and James I. When the English laws were universally established, and English schools were erected, with strict injunction that the vernacular tongue should be no longer spoken in the seminaries. . . .

At present, there are but few who can read, and fewer that can write with the Irish characters; and it appears, that in a short time, there will be none found who will understand an Irish manuscript, so as to be able to transcribe or translate it. . . . It is chiefly with a view to prevent in some measure the total neglect, and to diffuse the beauties of this ancient and once-admired language, that the following compilation is offered to the public.

4.33 *Projects for Re-Establishing the Internal Peace and Tranquility of Ireland*, W.Stokes, 1799

For the diffusion of religious knowledge, it is necessary, that it should be conveyed in the language the people understand. . . . One of the fundamental principles of the Reformation was, that every person should address his Maker, and read His word, in his native tongue; yet this was neglected in Ireland, with a view of making the English language universal; but it is easier to alter the religion of a people than their language.

5

1800–1876

INTRODUCTION

The first half of the nineteenth century witnessed the continuation of two modes of interest in Irish culture. The first was antiquarianism, as the Patriotic attention to Irish literature, history and language developed in a number of societies. Chief among them were the Gaelic Society (1808), the Iberno-Celtic Society (1818), and later the Irish Archaeological Society (1840). This activity coincided with the start of the Townland Survey of Ireland, better known as the Ordnance Survey. Originally established as a branch of the British military in the 1790s as part of the defences against the threat of French invasion, the Survey in Ireland was commissioned for the purpose of the assessment of taxation. Undertaken between 1824 and 1841, in its detail the Survey amounts not only to a notable achievement in cartography, but also to a labour of love for Irish scholars of such standing as O'Reilly, Petrie, O'Donovan and O'Curry. The result was a fascinating account, at once synchronic and diachronic, of the place-names, commerce, geology and natural history of the country.

The second strand of continuity was linked to Protestant proselytising in the first quarter of the eighteenth century. As in the earlier period, both the Presbyterians and the established Church were to the fore in this movement, known as the Second Reformation. The establishment of the Irish Society for Promoting the Education of the Native Irish through the Medium of their Own Language (formed in 1818 mainly at the instigation of the Church of Ireland, though at least partly in response to a pamphlet by the Baptist minister Anderson) was an important development. Debates around this issue were hotly contested, though again the contributions of the Catholic Church were limited. Preaching in Irish was viewed by some as the only means by which Protestant truths could be made available to the poorer rural Irish in particular, though many of those involved reiterated the point made by Richardson in the previous century: teaching literacy in Irish would inevitably lead to the spread of the use of English. A number of writers also argued that knowledge of Irish was a practical necessity for such as the clergy, legal professionals and government officers in their everyday dealings with the native population. The force of this contention struck none more forcefully than the native population itself, though it turned the argument on its head and learned English instead.

The campaign for the emancipation of Catholics from the restrictions which still applied after the late eighteenth-century Catholic Relief Acts continued and was dominated by the same mix primarily of the Catholic middle and landed class. O'Connell's tactic of the Catholic Rent, however, a membership subscription of a penny per month to the emancipatory Catholic Association, transformed the campaign into a national mass movement which also had the support of the Catholic clergy. Following electoral successes, not least by O'Connell himself, the threat of a breakdown of order brought emancipation in 1829. Yet if this gave the Catholic population political confidence, it did not spread to their regard for their culture. There was already a split between the political and cultural wings of Irish nationalism, which was to deepen as the century progressed. Grattan saw the Irish language as an unnecessary divisive factor and O'Connell, a native speaker, held that the superiority of English as a language of modernity was sufficient cause to think of the passing of Irish without regret. The 1830s was also a fateful decade for the Irish language in that it saw the introduction of State provision of elementary education. The Board of Commissioners for National Education (1831) was instituted in answer to the demand, primarily from Catholic representatives, for education which was based neither on the unregulated hedge-school system, nor that offered by the Protestant proselytising societies. Teaching in the National Schools was conducted in English, a fact which caused Archbishop MacHale (one of the few members of the Catholic hierarchy to take a public stance in favour of Irish) to describe them as 'the graves of the national language'. Faced by a political and clerical leadership which took little or no interest in Irish, and a system of education which used English as its medium, it seems hardly surprising that the Irish-speaking population should renounce its language. In fact, however, this was a process which had started many years before, and was grounded more than anything else in the need for economic survival. Petty, writing in 1691, had argued that for the poorer Irish, 'it is their interest to deal with the *English*, for Leases, for Time, and upon clear Conditions' and, therefore, 'to be transmuted into *English*' and to 'decline their language'. To confirm the point, Arthur Young noted in 1778 the differential pay given to Irish labourers who could speak English. These lessons were not lost on a population facing stark poverty; Coneys pointed out that for the Irish speaker, his native language is 'the language of his heart' but English is 'the language of his commerce'.

The split between the political and cultural wings of nationalism became particularly clear in the relations between O'Connell and the Young Irelanders in the 1840s. The Repeal of the Act of Union gave them common ground, but O'Connell's tactics of pragmatic political nationalism, supported by the Catholic clergy and grounded in the mass support of the populace, was at odds with the romantic nationalism of the Young Irelanders, a group of mainly middle-class graduates of Trinity with its leaders drawn in the main from Protestant and

Ascendancy backgrounds. Inspired by the centrality of national languages to the political programmes of contemporary European cultural nationalist movements, one of the leaders of Young Ireland, Thomas Davis, argued for the Irish language as the key to national revival. His essay 'Our National Language', published in Young Ireland's organ *The Nation*, was to be influential for a later generation of cultural and political activists. What it signalled in fact was another continuity with a theme articulated earlier: the stress on the political importance of the language and the identification of those responsible for its neglect (MacCruitín and Donlevy expressed it in the previous century). Picking up on this, Hardiman, the anthologiser of *Irish Minstrelsy* (1831), laid the blame squarely with the benighted practices of colonial rule (a claim which infuriated Samuel Ferguson). For others, the social pretensions of those whose particular lot had improved were culpable; *The Nation* featured satires which connect back to *Pairlement Chloinne Tomáis* in the seventeenth century. Interestingly, on this score the Catholic clergy did not escape censure, and its role became a contentious issue later.

The greatest blow to Irish, however, was inflicted by that natural and man-made disaster, the Great Famine. The failure of the potato crop in three out of four harvests between 1845 and 1849 had devastating consequences for the Catholic rural poor, particularly in those areas where, for many, Irish was still the language of everyday life. The death of up to a million, and the emigration of more, led to a decline in Ireland's population of some 20 per cent in the five years between 1845 and 1851. Those who could escape to cities in America or Britain needed English for survival, and this became another damaging factor for the language. Early in the century Dewar observed a truth which had held for a considerable time: that Irish was associated with Catholicism and English with Protestantism. After the Famine the Gaelic language was linked, even by its native speakers, with poverty and backwardness. Though Irish emigrants who were successful in their new countries soon began to organise themselves politically and often to regret the loss of their culture and language, for those left behind the imperative was simply to get English. As the saying went, the Irish may love their language, but they love their children more.

5.1 'Essay on Irish Bulls', Maria Edgeworth, 1802

THE BROGUE

Much of the comic effect of Irish bulls, or of such speeches as are mistaken for bulls, has depended upon the tone, or *brogue*, as it is called, with which they are uttered. The first Irish blunders that we hear are made or repeated in this peculiar tone, and afterward, from the power of association, whenever we hear the tone we expect the blunder. Now there is little danger that the Irish should be cured of their brogue; and consequently there is no great reason to apprehend that we should cease to think or call them blunderers.

Of the powerful effect of any peculiarity of pronunciation to prepossess the mind against the speaker, nay, even to excite dislike amounting to antipathy, we have an instance attested by an eye-witness, or rather an ear-witness.

'In the year 1755,' says the Revd James Adams, 'I attended a public disputation in a foreign university, when at least 400 Frenchmen literally hissed a grave and learned *English* doctor, not by way of insult, but irresistibly provoked by the quaintness of the repetition of sh. The thesis was, the concurrence of God *in actionibus viciosis*: the whole hall resounded with the hissing cry of *sh*, and its continual occurrence in *actione, viciosa,* &c.'

It is curious that Shibboleth should so long continue a criterion among nations!

What must have been the degree of irritation that could so far get the better of the politeness of 400 Frenchmen as to make them hiss in the days of *l'ancien régime*! The dread of being the object of that species of antipathy or ridicule, which is excited by unfashionable peculiarity of accent, has induced many of the *misguided* natives of Ireland to affect what they imagine to be the English pronunciation. They are seldom successful in this attempt, for they generally overdo the business. . . . There are Irish ladies, who, ashamed of their country, betray themselves by mincing out their abjuration, by calling tables *teebles*, and chairs *cheers*! To such renegadoes we prefer the honest Quixotism of a modern champion for the Scottish accent, who boldly asserted that 'the broad dialect rises above reproach, scorn, and laughter,' enters the lists, as he says of himself in Tartan dress and armour, and throws down the gauntlet to the most prejudiced antagonist. 'How weak is prejudice!' pursues this patriotic enthusiast. 'The sight of the Highland Kelt, the flowing plaid, the buskined leg, provokes my antagonist to laugh. Is this dress ridiculous in the eyes of reason and common sense? No; nor is the dialect of speech: both are characteristic and national distinctions'. . . .

How angry has this grave patriot reason to be with his ingenious countryman Beattie, the celebrated champion of *Truth*, who acknowledges that he never could, when a boy or a man, look at a certain translation of Ajax's speech into one of the vulgar Scots dialect without laughing!

We shall now with boldness, similar to that of the Scotch champion, try the risible muscles of our English reader; we are not, indeed, inclined to go to quite such lengths as he has gone: he insists that the Scotch dialect ought to be adopted all over England; we are only going candidly to suggest, that we think the Irish, in general, speak *better English* than is commonly spoken by the natives of England. To limit this proposition so as to make it appear less absurd, we should observe, that we allude to the lower classes of the people in both countries. In some counties in Ireland, a few of the poorest labourers and cottagers do not understand English, they speak only Irish, as in Wales there are vast numbers who speak only

Welsh; but amongst those who speak English we find fewer vulgarisms than amongst the same rank of persons in England. The English which they speak is chiefly such has been traditional in their families from the time of the early settlers in the island. During the reign of Queen Elizabeth and the reign of Shakespeare, numbers of English migrated to Ireland; and whoever attends to the phraseology of the lower Irish, may, at this day hear many of the phrases and expressions used by Shakespeare. Their vocabulary has been preserved nearly in its pristine purity since that time, because they have not had intercourse with those counties in England which have made for themselves a jargon unlike to any language under heaven. The Irish *brogue* is a great and shameful defect, but it does not render the English language absolutely unintelligible. There are but few variations of the brogue, such as the long and the short, the Thady brogue and the Paddy brogue, which differ much in tone, and but little in phraseology; but in England, almost all of our fifty-two counties have peculiar vulgarisms, dialects, and brogues, unintelligible to their neighbours. Herodotus tells us that some of the nations of Greece, though they used the same language, spoke it so differently, that they could not understand each other's conversation. This is literally the case between the provincial inhabitants of remote parts of England. Indeed the language peculiar to the metropolis, or the *cockney* dialect, is proverbially ridiculous. The Londoners, who look down with contempt on all that have not been *bred and born* within the sound of Bow, talk with unconscious absurdity of *weal* and *winegar*, and *v*ive and *v*indors, and ask you *ow* yo so? and '*ave ye bin taking* the *h*air in 'yde park? and '*as* your 'orse 'ad any *h*oats &c? aspirating always where they should not, and never aspirating where they should.

5.2 *Transactions of the Gaelic Society of Dublin*, Theophilus O'Flanagan, 1808

The friends of literature, and of Ireland, are invited to join an institution, whose purpose is to preserve and cultivate a Language the most ancient, copious and elegant of Europe; by far the best preserved from the changes and corruptions incident to other languages. . . .

The affinities and connections of the ancient and modern Languages, elucidated from the Mother Tongue, formed by FENIUS from the radical terms of the Languages that sprang from the confusion of Babel; the truth of which tradition is proved by the fact, since the Gaelic will be found to contain most of the radical and primitives of the various Dialects spoken from Aurora and the Ganges, to the Atlantic, the South Sea Islands, and America. The Gaelic, says Shaw, is the language of Japhet, spoken before the Deluge, and probably the Language of Paradise. . . .

The Society intend, as soon as may be, to publish every fragment existing in the Gaelic Language. The History of Ireland, by Dr. Keating, in the original Gaelic, with a new Translation, will shortly be put to press. There are still, in existence, a variety of Tracts in History, Genealogy, Law, Physic, Poetry, and Romance. The Books of Ballymote and Lecan, in the Library of the Royal Irish Academy, contain much valuable Historic matter, a large work on Irish Topography, several curious Poems, and a vast quantity of Genealogy. In the Library of Trinity College, (to which, indeed, Ireland is much indebted for preserving her valuable Records,) are many Fragments of Laws, well worth public attention, and several volumes of Annals. We have still, in several private hands, copies of the Annals of Innisfallen, of the four Masters of Donegal, in five large volumes; Annals of Tigernach, Boyle, Connacht, and Ulster; the Book of Conquests; numbers of fine Poems, many Volumes of History, Biography, Romance, &c.&c. which may soon be laid before the Public. . . .

'Observations on the Gaelic Language, Communicated by P.McElligot'

The Gaelic Society having for one of their foremost objects, the revival of the language and literature of the Gaels; the following observations are offered to the attention of those gentlemen, who are intended to form, very shortly, a Committee for the purpose of compiling a Dictionary and Grammar of our language, without which all attempts to restore that ancient parent tongue, and all hopes of cherishing the present ardour for studying it, must fall to the ground; 'while,' says Ledwich, (a writer who, without the *slightest* knowledge of our *language*, has yet dared to obscure and ridicule our antiquities) 'the Irish preserved their ancient LANGUAGE and dress, there was no hope of civilising them, or bringing them to an acquiescence in English dominion or English laws.'

The short-sighted policy of endeavouring totally to eradicate the native dialect of any conquered country, (so contrary to the practice of the most enlightened nations of antiquity, who, far from the vain attempt of utterly abolishing, wisely adopted the very language, laws, customs, and superstitions of the vanquished, and endeavoured, as far as possible, to incorporate with and assimilate to their own,) has long been considered unnecessary and ineffectual, all arguments then on this head we shall pass over as nugatory. . . .

The daily decrease of piety, the narrow limits of true religion, and the little dissemination of it from the difficulty of intercourse with the lower classes of the people, the uncertainty and danger attending decisions on the lives and properties of millions of our fellow-subjects, and the mutual distrust of the different orders of society; these, I say, are more than sufficient to rouse the energy, and awaken the attention of the legislature, the Clergy, and every man who wishes well to his country. The present state of

Gaelic literature is nearly what that of the Persian was when the great Sir William Jones wrote his grammar of that beautiful language. 'Since the literature of Asia,' says that admirable scholar, 'was so much neglected, and the causes of that neglect so various, we could not have expected that any slight power would rouse the nations of Europe from their inattention to it; and they would, perhaps, have persisted in despising it, if they had not been animated by the most powerful incentive that can influence the mind of man: interest was the magic wand which brought them all within one circle; interest was the charm which gave the languages of the East a real and solid importance. By one of those revolutions, which no human prudence could have foreseen, the Persian language found its way into India; that rich and celebrated empire, which, by the flourishing state of our commerce, has been the source of incredible wealth to the merchants of Europe. A variety of causes, which need not be mentioned here, gave the English nation a most extensive power in that kingdom: our India company began to take under their protection the princes of the country, by whose protection they gained their first settlement; a number of important affairs were to be transacted in peace and war, between nations equally jealous of each other, who had not the common instrument of conveying their sentiments; the servants of the company received letters which they could not read, and were ambitious of gaining titles of which they could not comprehend the meaning; it was found highly dangerous to employ the natives as interpreters, upon whose fidelity they could not depend; and it was at last discovered, that they must apply themselves to the study of the Persian language, in which all the letters from the Indian princes were written.'

The old objections, of want of encouragement, scarcity of books &c. will now soon be removed; our fine poems and other literary productions will no longer rot in the dust of libraries neglected and unknown; and amidst the present general taste for learning, the ardour of studying the Gaelic, now happily excited, will, I trust, not be suffered to abate. The beauties and excellence of our language must soon be seen and admired; a language copious, elegant, and harmonious, ancient above all the languages of the world, yielding to none, not even to the Greek, in the beauty and elegance of its compounds, its flexibility, the sweetness of its cadences, and peculiar aptness for music and poetry; a language, in fine, highly cultivated and admired by the most polite and learned princes of the world, at a time when the Gaels alone, of all the nations in Europe, were free from barbarism and ignorance, and stood unrivalled in the cultivation of letters. If this were not confessedly the character of the Gaelic, the impartial testimonies of the best scholars of Europe, of Leibniz, Usher, Vallancey, Lhuyd, Boulet, Davies, and others, would be more than sufficient to establish it, and excite, at least, a curiosity among the learned, and enquiries into its merits.

5.3 *Uraicecht na Gaedhilge. Grammar of the Gaelic Language*, Edmond O'Connell [William Haliday], 1808

The Language of a people, it has been universally admitted by all literary men, is the true criterion of their limitation or advancement in Civility. If harsh, grating, irregular, barren and incongruous, it is pronounced the dialectic medium of a rude and barbarous people; if harmonious, elegant, flexible, copious and expressive; it is admitted to be the sentimental communication of a people highly cultivated in mental improvement, and consequently far advanced in civilisation. The latter character has been impressed on the Gaelic Language, by the testimonies of the venerable Ussher, Leibniz and Lhuyd, and of many other respectable personages in the walk of Literature. It must seem strange, therefore, that the study of this language should be so little cultivated, at a time when a taste for general and diffusive learning seems universally to prevail; but although it has been generally neglected, to the shame of literature, for nearly three hundred years, yet there have been from time to time, some Luminaries that dared to diffuse their vivid rays through the gloom of prejudice; and have excited a glow of research, by which this valuable mine is now, at length, on the point of being explored; Prejudice has been put to flight, and in its place, appears triumphant the fair Spirit of Liberal Investigation.

5.4 *An Introduction to the Irish Language*, Revd W.M.Neilson, 1808

That the Irish is the best preserved dialect of the ancient and extensive Celtic language, is allowed by the most liberal and enlightened antiquarians. To the general scholar, therefore, a knowledge of it is of great importance; as it will enable him to trace the origin of names and customs, which he would seek in vain in any other language. To the inhabitants of Ireland [it] is doubly interesting. In this language are preserved the venerable annals of our country, with as much fidelity as is usually found in the primitive records of any nation; while the poetic and romantic compositions, with which the Irish Manuscripts abound, afford the finest specimens, of elegant taste and luxuriant imagination.

But it is, particularly, from the *absolute necessity* of understanding this language, in order to converse with the natives of a greater part of Ireland, that the study of it is indispensable. If Irish be no longer that language of the court, or the senate, yet the pulpit and the bar require the use of it; and he that would communicate moral instruction, or investigate the claims of justice, must be versed in the native tongue, if he expects to be generally understood, or to succeed in his research. In travelling, and the common occurrences of agriculture or rural traffic, a knowledge of Irish is absolutely necessary.

It has been said that the use of this language be abolished, and the English prevail universally. But without entering into the merits of this position, while the Irish exists, and *must* exist for many years to come, it is surely reasonable and desirable, that every person should be able to hold converse with his countrymen, as well as to taste and admire the beauties of one of the most expressive, philologically accurate, and polished languages that has ever existed.

5.5 Rt. Hon. Henry Grattan, to the Secretary of the Board of Education, 1812

In obedience to the Wishes of the Board I venture to submit, what I do not presume to call a plan, but instead of one, a few ideas . . . I would pursue the suggestion of the Act that established Parish Schools, with such alterations as must arise from the change of time, circumstances, and condition. . . .

And I would submit, as a proper subject matter of education in those schools, not only the study of the English tongue, reading, writing and arithmetic; but also the study of certain books of horticulture and agriculture, together with treatises on the care and knowledge of trees.

I should recommend that in those Parish Schools the Christian religion be taught; but that no particular description of it should form part of their education – in the place thereof, it might perhaps not be improper to devise some instruction regarding the four great duties of man – duty to God, duty to one another, duty to the country, and duty to the government.

I beg to add, that one great object of national education should be to unite the inhabitants of the island, and that such an event cannot be well accomplished, except they are taught to speak one common language; I think the diversity of language, and not the diversity of religion, constitutes a diversity of people. I should be very sorry that the Irish language should be forgotten; but glad that the English language should be generally understood; to obtain that end in Ireland, it is necessary that the schools formed on a plan of national education, which teach the English language, should not attempt to teach the English religion, because the Catholics who would resort to our schools to learn the one, will keep aloof if we attempt to make them proselytes to the other; and we should by that attempt, reject one great means of uniting our people; and we should continue to add to the imaginary *political* division, supposed to exist in a difference of religion, a real political division formed on the diversity of language.

5.6 *Observations on the Character, Customs and Superstitions of the Irish*, Daniel Dewar, 1812

To some the wild enthusiasm, the ardent love of kindred and country, may seem inapplicable to the Irish character. But I can assure such that I have witnessed a considerable share of this even among the low and uneducated part of [the Irish] people in London. When I spoke to them in their own language, their national enthusiasm was kindled, and for a while they seemed to forget that they were in the land of strangers. And though doomed to ignorance, penury, and toil, at home as well as abroad, yet, so fond are they of their country, and of everything connected with it, that he who will talk to them in the tongue of their fathers, which they regard as sacred, and who seems not displeased with their customs, will be considered as their countryman and friend. . . .

The Irish is very idiomatic, and possesses so little in common with the other languages of modern Europe, except the Celtic, and at the same time so very figurative, that it is difficult for any one who *thinks in it* not to make *bulls*. It is partly on this account that an unlettered Irishman speaks in glowing and metaphorical diction. It is impossible for him to separate the language of his early years from his habits of thinking; he, therefore, very naturally accommodates the acquired tongue to the idiomatic construction and phraseology of his own, and imperceptibly enriches it with all the tropes and figures with which his mind is familiar. . . .

It has already been remarked, that it is altogether idiomatic in its construction, or, to speak more correctly, its idioma are different from those of all the languages of Europe. It is extremely copious, especially on any subject connected with the passions; though it can scarcely be considered a good vehicle for philosophy. No tongue can beter suit the purpose of the orator, whose object is to make an impression on a popular assembly, and who, regardless of precision seeks only to accomplish his end. Hence also, it is admirably adapted to poetry. . . .

The number of people who speak this language is much greater than is generally supposed. It is spoken throughout the province of Connaught by all the lower orders, a great part of whom scarcely understand any English; and some of those who do, understand it only to conduct business: they are incapable of receiving moral or religious instruction through its medium. The Irish is spoken very generally through the other three provinces, except among the descendants of the Scotch in the north. It cannot be supposed that calculations on this subject should be perfectly accurate; but it has been concluded on good grounds that there are about two millions of people in Ireland who are incapable of understanding a continued discourse in English. . . .

Now, to proscribe the language of a whole people because it does not happen to be the same with the speech of the conqueror and the court, to leave those who speak it in ignorance in order to accelerate its extinction, and even actively to discourage every attempt to instruct and enlighten unless it be in the *protected* tongue, are maxims which appear to me to be not only barbarous, but absolutely inefficient as to the end in view. . . .

The reformation, it is well known, has made very little progress in [Ireland]: the mass of the people remain in connection with the church of Rome. Of these, as has been already observed, there are a million and a half, who understand no tongue but the Irish. Now the established church has made no provision whatever for this population; there is not one of its ministers that preaches in this language. . . . It is true most of these people are Roman catholics. Are they not forced, however, to remain in the bosom of the Roman church? Their priests give them that instruction in the venerable tongue of their fathers, which the protestant teachers have always denied them. And yet, these teachers complain of the increase of papists, and of the gross ignorance of the people. . . .

It appears to me to be a dictate of reason, and of common sense, that if ever a people be informed and enlightened, it must be by means of the language, which they understand. Will it not answer a good end to enlighten, and inform, and improve the native Irish? Will it not answer the most noble and beneficent purposes to inculcate those principles, which will make them good men, and good subjects? But this measure will perpetuate the Irish tongue. What then? its existence surely can do no harm; whereas ignorance, and vice, and superstition, will always produce evil.

The truth is, however, that the cultivation of either the Irish or the Gaelic is the most effectual, as well as the most expeditious plan that can be adopted for their extinction. Make any people intelligent and rational, and they will gradually lose their prejudices; many of them will acquire a taste for general knowledge, and they will seek for it in the general tongue of the empire. Besides, all their interest must incline them to this measure: if they wish to improve their condition, or to have their sons advanced in the service of their country, they will find it necessary to have some English *book-learning* themselves, and to be at some pains to impart it to their children. . . .

From the foregoing observations this particular must have been anticipated. It has been stated, that the priests, wherever it is necessary, are all acquainted with this tongue, while the protestant teachers are all ignorant of it, or at least do not take the trouble of making it the vehicle of religious instruction. This circumstance has become the occasion of considerable rancour and animosity. For, on the one hand, the understanding of English is the characteristic of Protestantism; on the other, the Irish tongue is the mark of Catholicism. This man hates his neighbour, because he speaks no Irish; and his neighbour treats him with contempt because he is not acquainted with English. By the principle of association, the Protestant confounds Irish with disloyalty and rebellion, and the Catholic considers English as allied to protestantism and damnable error. . . .

Ought that population [of Ireland] to be instructed or not? If they ought, is it not singularly perverse to disregard the only possible way in which this can be effectually accomplished? This mode of communicating knowledge may perhaps be neglected; in that case the people will remain ignorant and superstitious; they will be the source of poverty and wretchedness to themselves; they will continue turbulent and barbarous, and that empire which might have made them its glory and defence, will have them for a thorn in its side. And is this a time coldly to speculate on the advantages of abolishing for ever the Irish language, – of refusing to instruct a people who want to be instructed, unless they understand a dialect which they cannot and will not understand? When the whole of Europe is prostrate at the 'foot of the tyrant, when it has become the duty and destiny of Britain to contend for the liberties of the world, to contend for its own independence and existence, how great is the infatuation, not to embrace every measure of uniting the people, of removing every cause of suspicion in the government, every cause of even seeming grievance in the subject, of enlightening, improving, and civilising every part of the population!. . .

As to the expediency and necessity of adopting, with regard to Ireland, some such plan as I have here been recommending, it will readily be admitted by all who are capable of judging on the subject, and on which, therefore, I think it idle to enlarge. But surely I may say, that while Christian Missionaries are sent forth to the Islands of the South Sea, to India, and Africa, the moral and religious instruction of a people so closely linked to us, in civil and political interest as the Irish should not be entirely neglected.

5.7 *An English-Irish Dictionary, Intended for the Use of Schools*, Thaddeus Connellan, 1814

It is obvious, that when tribes of men are intermixed who speak different languages, a great part of the advantages which man should afford his neighbour, must be diminished or lost. The magistrate cannot address his subjects, the pastor his flock, but by the imperfect medium of an interpreter. Lawyers, Divines, Physicians, Merchants, Manufacturers, and Farmers, all feel more or less this inconvenience when they have to do with those, with whom they have no common language. . . .

Some, I believe, may fear that my encouragement to the revival of the Irish language may be injurious, by delaying its decline, and the consequent extension of English. To me this decline does not appear so rapid as it may to others; but with respect to the extension of the English language, it appears likely to be promoted at present by the cultivation of the Irish. This is what will open to the native student, an easy path to the first rudiments of knowledge; when these are obtained, and emulation and interest will soon stimulate him to the acquisition of the English language, on which his hopes depend. . . .

Let us then diminish the inconvenience of distinct languages, by multiplying interpreters. All the intercourses of society will be conducted with more facility, and the tribes so long separated, may at length begin to blend into one nation.

5.8 *Sanas Gaoidhilge Sagsbeurla. An English Irish Dictionary*, E.O'Reilly, 1817

The great utility that a knowledge of the Irish language to those who wish to give a satisfactory account of the vernacular dialects and antiquities of most nations in Europe, has been confessed by Lhuyd, Bullet, Leibniz, and other learned foreigners; and its absolute necessity to all who are desirous of becoming acquainted with the emigrations, history, laws, manners, customs, religion and learning of the early inhabitants of Ireland is so obvious, as to preclude the necessity of impressing it on the mind by any species of argument. To strangers it is therefore interesting, but to the natives of Ireland, the preservation of this beautiful and expressive language should be of the utmost importance. In the several hundreds of ancient Irish manuscripts which still survive the erosive tooth of time, or the devastating hands of barbarous invaders, are to be found the venerable memorials of the piety, learning, wisdom, valour, and achievements of our ancestors. In the composition of our *Senachies*, in our annals, and other historical documents, the migrations, contentions, settlements and domestic policy of the primitive inhabitants of the country, are related with at least as much fidelity, and deserving as much credit, as the early records of any other nation. In our laws will be seen strong proofs of the civilisation of our forefathers; in them provision is made for the protection of property, the reward of virtue and merit, the prevention of crime, and the punishment of vice. In our medical books it will be found that our physicians had as much knowledge of the human frame, and as much skill in the treatment of disease, as the physicians of any other country of the same period. And in the works of our bards may be discovered the grandest and most pathetic descriptions, the most sublime flights of fancy, and the most romantic tales of luxuriant imagination, displayed in elegant and appropriate language. . . .

That a great portion of our language should be nearly forgotten at the present day, will not be much wondered at, when it is considered, that for some hundreds of years it had been the policy of Government to use every means in their power to eradicate our language, and to deprive our people of every opportunity to obtain education. For this absurd purpose our books were destroyed, acts of parliament passed, schoolmasters persecuted, and where laws of severity were found ineffectual, recourse was had to ridicule, to shame the people out of the most energetic, and as Sir William Temple has since described it, the most original and unmixed language now remaining in Europe. But even ridicule, that powerful engine over weak minds, has failed in producing the desired effect; and the Irish language still exists as a living memorial of the refinement to which our ancestors had attained, and the encouragement given by them to learning and learned men. This silly policy is at length laid aside; the reign of prejudice has expired, and is in great measure succeeded by candid inquiry and rational investigation. . . .

Independently of the claims which this language has upon the general scholar for consideration, and upon the descendants of the aborigines for protection, it merits the attention of the Divine, the Lawyer, the Physician, and all those who have to converse with the people, whose living and only language it is. It is the only medium through which instruction can be conveyed to at least four fifths of the people of Ireland. The Divine, therefore, who neglects this language, should consider how far he is competently to discharge the duty he owes to those souls committed to his care. The great utility of this language to the Lawyer, is proved frequently in the year. In every county, at every sessions, trials occur in which prisoners or witnesses can be heard only through the medium of an interpreter, probably but ill qualified for such an office, and who, by the mistake of a simple word in the evidence, may cause the acquittal of a murderer, or the murder of an innocent. . . . To the Physician several cases must have occurred where his scientific skill was buffeted by his ignorance of the language in which only his patient could clearly point out the nature of his complaint. And every person who has dealings in the country, has daily proof of the inconvenience arising from the want of the language of the people with whom he has to converse.

5.9 Reasons for Giving Moral Instruction of the Native Irish through the Medium of their Vernacular Language, J.S.Taylor, 1817

Remember that a people with the sensibilities of the Irish cannot be your slaves, without being dangerous, or your free brethren without being affectionate; and they can hardly *be free* till *instruction* has made them appreciate the *value* of the blessing, and taught them its genuine enjoyment and best security. I know that there are many who think, that there is something radically defective in the Irish character; something that sets it at variance with the regular habits of well-ordered society, and renders it averse from the respect even of the wisest legislation; but let them remember that it is but lately that my countrymen have had reason to learn the docility which a judiciously mild, and conciliatory treatment produces from the human mind. It is but lately that they have been told that there is a virtue in obedience, because authority has shown itself virtuous – and that there is wisdom in submission, because demanded by an intelligent control. Yes, I perceive that the British people, advised by the examples of the past, counsel better for the future interests of Ireland; they now perceive it is a *mental* authority which must mould the heart of Ireland in confrontation to British sentiment, and the interests of a united empire; and they have discovered that the great instrument of this must be EDUCATION. . . .

Is it strange that such a people, influenced as they are by the traditions of ancient times, should love a language which bears with it the endearing memory of their independence – breathing the spirit of their bards, celebrates the achievement of their heroes, contains the names which embellish their romantic history – and in their legendary songs, like the voice of departed days, is full of a mournful fascination! That the Irish should be attached to their native language, when it has been attempted to drive them out of it by persecution, is not a curious thing in the history of mankind. All nations so circumstanced, have been fond of the relics of their former freedom, however barbarous, and have clung to whatever reminds them of their recorded glories, however dimly seen through the fables, and mist of antiquity. . . .

[On objectors to teaching in Irish:] They suppose, that by thus countenancing the love for their *native* language, you will roll back upon them in tenfold darkness that cloud of barbarism which they say is beginning to break, and that you will finally shut out every ray of civilisation . . . morality will not be less moral – nor religion less pure, nor its civilising spirit less corrective of impetuous passions, and erratic sensibilities, *because introduced through the medium of the Irish language*; and when such information is conveyed to the mind of man, what matters it in what language he speaks? . . . No, *let the mind be informed and the habits well-directed*, and men's language will accommodate itself to their moral improvement, it will become polished and pleasing, or if it be inflexibly barbarous, they will *take advantage of a language already formed*, for the expression of their new wants. . . .

That dominion which was commenced in dark and barbarous times, has, through a series of ages established over the Irish population a terrible ascendancy. It has reduced them I am sorry to say, almost to a state of *satisfied* servitude, that kind of habitual slavery, in which chains of darkness are so familiar, that we have no remembrance of liberty and light! To this infatuating influence, under which reason must be *silent* or rebellious, nothing can be proved with such probable chance of success as The Gospel, conveyed through the medium of the Irish language. . . .

I repeat it, the most effectual means to introduce to the Irish peasant a salutary influence, which must correct an injurious and hereditary teaching, is to make the language of truth address him – in what, *in his own tongue*. Yes, let him have the advantage which was given to the Capadocians, and the Phrygians of old, and the Indian of the present day; let not *him alone* be the exception to the rule of an intelligent philanthropy . . . he will become sensible of the odious deformity of that gothic superstructure whose gloomy and fantastic battlements have so long thrown their shadow over his country, chilling its moral bloom, and causing its virtues to perish untimely.

147

5.10 *A Brief Sketch of Various Attempts which have been made to Diffuse a Knowledge of the Holy Scriptures through the Medium of the Irish Language,* Revd Christopher Anderson, 1818

Through the medium of what language can moral, religious, or indeed any other instruction whatsoever, be most speedily and most efficiently conveyed to a people; the answer would undoubtedly be, through the medium of that language which they understand best; and to which they are most warmly attached, the language of their thoughts and feelings. . . .

Persons residing in the metropolis, and large cities, and in those parts where English is the prevailing language, are not in general aware how large a population occupies the less frequented parts of the southern, western, and north-western counties, including peninsulas and islands, together with the wild sequestered glens and mountainous districts of even some of the inland counties, who still cherish, with an almost exclusive attachment, the language of their fathers . . . Irish is to them the language of social intercourse, of family communion; every feeling connected with moral duty is closely interwoven with that language. If consciousness of guilt sting the bosom of one of these, the reflections it excites, the anguish of remorse, the terrible paintings of a smitten conscience, the brightening hopes of mercy, all pass in a rapid succession before his mind, clothed in the habilments which his native tongue has given to them. . . . Man, to whom he owes kindness, God, to whom he owes devotion, are presented before him in the mirror of his native tongue. Thus all those principles in which morality is founded, are embodied in his own language, in that language in which he conceives, in which he reasons what he feels. Can the same be said of English? It is to him the language of barter, of worldly occupations; taken up solely at the market, laid aside when he returns home, a very confined vocabulary. . . .

Perhaps it will be said that in keeping up the language you keep up a mark of distinction between the different classes of the community who use the different tongues. It cannot be denied indeed that diversity of languages tends much to prevent that free intercourse which every philanthropist would wish to promote, and that therefore considered in this light, it would be desirable that the language not only of every state, but even of the whole earth, were one. But must not every one acknowledge that a unity of sentiment, a unity of customs, a unity of laws, tend much more to the amalgamation of the people than a mere unity of language? Is there anything in diversity of tongue alone which must of necessity induce diversity in these respects? Does not the history of past ages – does not the history of the present time – furnish abundant evidence of whole tribes of people who using different languages, live peaceably under the same government? Look at Great Britain; there we see the Gael in Scotland, the Briton

in Wales, and the Saxon in England, living together in the utmost h
Are we then to suppose there is something peculiar in the combi
the sounds or characters that constitute the Irish language, rendering it ⌐
involuntary and necessary agent for the production of all the ills of disaffection and disunion? Can we continue of this opinion when we reflect how
harmless and inoffensive the same language has proved in Scotland?. . .

It is said Irish is calculated to revive recollections of past transactions,
which it were better were forgotten, as the tendency of these recollections
is to disunite the people. If it was intended to publish details of the
mutual struggles of adverse sects contending for ascendancy, there might
perhaps be some force in this objection: such is not the intention here: to
enable the native to read the Scriptures in his own tongue is the sole
object. You thus afford him that knowledge which is most calculated to
heal every irritable feeling, and to allay every animosity which such recollections he may unhappily still cherish. If the only language they know has
hitherto carried the poison of disaffection and disunion through every part
of the system which it has visited in its circulation, let it now convey,
through ramifications not less extensive, the antidote to that poison. . . .

Can it be imagined on the one hand, that principles of obedience to the
constituted authorities will be weakened in the minds of an Irishman, by
perusing such passages as these? – 'Render unto Caesar the things which
are Caesar's'. 'Let every soul be subject to the higher powers; for there is no
power but of God: the powers that be are ordained of God. Whosoever,
therefore, resisteth the power, resisteth the ordinance of God'. 'Wherefore
you needs must be subject, not only for wrath, but also for conscience
sake'. 'Render therefore to all their dues: tribute to whom tribute is due;
custom to whom custom; fear to whom fear; honour to whom honour'.
'Submit yourselves therefore to every ordinance of man for the Lord's sake:
whether it be to the King, as supreme, or unto governors, as unto them
that are sent by him for the punishment of evil doers, and for the praise of
them that do well'. 'Honour the King'. . . . Such truths, whether expressed
in English or the Irish language, are equally well calculated to infuse the
most exalted and firmly grounded sentiments of loyalty to the ruling
powers, and of mutual affectionate attachment of man towards man. . . .
Nor is this a matter of mere speculation. Mr. Dewar informs us that an
Irish man, into whose hands a New Testament had been put, exclaimed, on
reading it, 'If I believe this, it is impossible for me to remain a rebel'.

5.11 *Remarks on the Irish Language*, J.Scurry, 1827

It is now ascertained that the Irish language is spoken in the interior of
many of the West Indian islands, in some of which it may be said to be
almost vernacular. This curious fact is satisfactorily explained by documents
in the possession of my respected friend, James Hardiman, Esq., author of

the history of Galway. After the reduction of Ireland by Cromwell and his myrmidons, the thousands who were 'shipped to the Carribes', so these islands were then called, 'and sold as slaves', carried with them their language. *That* they preserved, and *there* it remains to this day.

5.12 *Facts Afforded by the History of the Irish Society*, H.M.Mason, 1829

The Irish language is the most effectual medium for conveying to the people spiritual instruction . . . the two inveterate prejudices in the Irish peasant's mind, are that against the Saxon language, and that against the creed of the Protestant . . . but by employing the Scriptures in the much loved native tongue, you neutralise the second prejudice with the first. . . .

The Irish peasant is assiduously instructed to consider the Protestant Bible to be an heretical book, but nothing can persuade him that heresy can be uttered in his native tongue. . . .

[Nothing] can now be done to prevent the gradual progress of the English tongue, which is the commercial, the legal, the political, the fashionable medium of communication, towards its finally becoming the universal language of the country.

5.13 *Irish Minstrelsy, Or Bardic Remains of Ireland*, James Hardiman, 1831

After ages of neglect and decay, the ancient literature of Ireland seems destined to emerge from obscurity. Those memorials which have hitherto lain so long unexplored, now appear to awaken the attention of the learned and the curiosity of the people; and, thus, the literary remains of a people once so distinguished in the annals of learning, may be rescued from the oblivion to which they have been so undeservedly consigned. That the ancient Irish possessed ample stores in their native language, capable of captivating the fancy, enlarging the understanding, and improving the heart, is well known to those acquainted with the mouldering membranes which have survived to our times. The historical importance of our annals has been acknowledged by the most learned men of Europe for the last three centuries. They are written in the language of the first inhabitants of Europe; and, with a simplicity of detail which truth only can confer, they record the primaeval state of this island, the origin of its early inhabitants, their history, religion, and laws, and the arts known amongst them for several generations. . . .

The language invariably used [in the compositions of ancient and modern times] was that of the country. To it [the Irish] were attached for many reasons, independent of nationality. The most learned men of Europe, since the revival of letters, have been loud in its praise. Usher has ranked it among the first for richness and elegance, and Leibniz and Lluyd have left on record their opinions of its value. The latter observes, that 'The Irish have preserved their letters and orthography beyond all their neighbouring nations.' The ancient language was very different from that spoken at the present day. It was divided into several dialects, of which the *Bearla Feine*, or *Phoenecian*, was in highest estimation, and without a knowledge of that dialect it is impossible to understand the early poets. The introduction of Christianity, and Latin, had not that effect on this primordial language, which might be supposed. For a long period after it suffered no material alteration. At length, in the sixteeenth century, our learned men began to turn their thoughts to the subject; and if they had not been impeded by the jealous interference of the English, it is probable that it would have undergone a change similar to that of most of the other dialects of Europe. How far that circumstance is now to be regretted, by one who contemplates the present, and probable future political amalgamation of the interests of these islands, it may be difficult to determine. From the days of Henry VIII. the English rulers were bent upon the total annihilation of our national language, but time has shewn the folly of the undertaking. The late Bishop Heber, in his life of Bedel, has stigmatized it as 'narrow and illiberal policy, which, though it has in part succeeded, has left a division in the national heart, far worse than that of the tongue.' Most grants of lands from the crown, in the reigns of Henry and his successors to Charles I., contained special provisos, for the disuse of the native, and the encouragement of the English tongue. But all these efforts would have proved abortive, were it not for the fatal disasters of the seventeenth century. Immediately before the civil war of 1641, a momentary gleam of hope lightened over this devoted language. The learned antiquaries of Donegal associated to collect and publish the remains of our ancient literature; but their patriotic intentions were unhappily frustrated by the succeeding troubles, and the language which had withstood the shock of so many ages, at length sunk in the general wreck. Thenceforth it was banished from the castle of the chieftain, to the cottage of his vassal, and, from having been the cherished and cultivated medium of intercourse between the nobles and gentry of the land, it became gradually limited to the use of the uneducated poor. No wonder then that it should have been considered harsh and un-polished when thus spoken, but it was as unjust to estimate our language by such a standard, as it would be to judge of the English by the jargon of Yorkshire. The measure of its vicissitudes was not yet, however, full. In the last century, the inquisitors of the Irish parliament denounced it as the dialect of that phantom of their political frenzy, popery. According to a favourite model of native reasoning it was resolved to reduce the poor Catholics to a state of mental darkness, in order to convert them into enlightened protestants. A thick cloud of ignorance soon overspread the land; and the language of millions ceased to be a medium of written communication. To these circumstances, perhaps, may be attributed its preservation from the written corruptions which pervade the present Gaelic of Scotland. The bards of modern times were the principal scribes in Irish. In it they were educated; to its orthography and grammatical structure they carefully attended; and in this last stage of its eventful history, it appears in their writings in a degree of purity, which, considering the disadvantages under which they laboured, is truly remarkable.

Although colloquially debased, many of the original characteristics of our language remain unimpaired. Its pathetic powers have been particularly celebrated. '*If you plead for your life, plead in Irish,*' is a well known adage. But the revilers of the people have not spared even their speech. Of the species of abuse usually resorted to, a curious specimen may be found in the prejudiced Stanihurst, who assures his readers, that the Irish was unfit even for the prince of darkness himself to utter, and to illustrate this, the bigoted Saxon gravely adduced the case of a possessed person in Rome, who 'spoke in every known tongue except Irish, but in that he neither would nor could speak, because of its intolerable harshness.' This notable story is said to have made such an impression on the witch-ridden mind of James the first of England, that he conceived as great an antipathy to our language, because the devil would not speak it, as he is known to have had to the sight of a drawn sword. It was, however, differently estimated by a celebrated scholar of a later date, even the renowned William Lily, astrologer, celestial intelligencer, and chamber prophet of the royal martyr, Charles the first. That noted authority informed the world, that the Irish language was like that spoken in heaven. 'It is very rare, yea even in our days, for any operator or master, to have the Angels speak articulately; when they do speak it is like the Irish, much in the throat.' How is it possible while reciting these ludicrous specimens of prejudice and imposture, to avoid reflecting, with bitter feelings, how often the best interests of Ireland have been thoughtlessly sacrificed by its rulers, to the extremes of bigotry, rapacity, and ignorance? Even in matters connected with our subject, we are informed, that Queen Elizabeth was prevented from sending to Denmark for certain ancient Irish records, said to be there, by the remark of one of her council, that it would be better all such evidences of our independence were annihilated. So late as the reign of Queen Anne, we are told that the intention of that princess to promote the cultivation of the Irish language, was frustrated by the Duke of Ormond, who repeated in her presence, an unmeaning sentence of broad sounding words as a proof of its barbarity. At a later period, we find an Irish Catholic, in the fervency of his zeal, to make Ireland 'thoroughly British,' wishing that 'the Irish language were entirely obliterated;' and recommending that 'if it were possible to pump St. George's channel dry, and unite the two islands physically, it ought to be done, at whatever expence.'

5.14 Daniel O'Connell on the Irish Language, 1833

Someone asked him whether the use of the Irish language was diminishing among our peasantry. 'Yes,' he answered, 'and I am sufficiently utilitarian not to regret its gradual abandonment. A diversity of tongues is no benefit; it was first imposed on mankind as a curse, at the building of Babel. It would be of vast advantage to mankind if all the inhabitants spoke the same language. Therefore, although the Irish language is connected with many recollections that twine around the hearts of Irishmen, yet the superior utility of the English tongue, as the medium of modern communication, is so great, that I can witness without a sigh the gradual disuse of the Irish.'

5.15 *A Dissertation on Irish Grammar*, Owen Connellan, 1834

My task has been undertaken, from a wish to serve the cause of Irish literature, to point out the real nature of the grammatical construction of the Irish language, and above all, to prevent the student from being misled by a compilation abounding in so many errors and inconsistencies as Mr. Mason's work. . . . It is to be lamented, that whenever an Elementary work on the Irish language has appeared, it has almost invariably been of an inferior and defective character. To this cause may be attributed the general neglect into which the language has fallen. . . .

It is also a current but mistaken opinion on the part of many literary men, that the study of the Irish language retards the progress of the English. But the fact is otherwise. The more the Irish is studied, by the peasantry of Ireland (it being their vernacular language) the better are their minds prepared and their taste formed to learn and understand the English. . . . The Synod of Ulster have latterly come to this conclusion, and have enacted a law by which it is imperative on their students to attend an Irish class for one season at least, and have actually appointed a Professor for that purpose.

5.16 *Ancient Ireland*, P.Barron, 1835

PRAYER-BOOKS

The different Persuasions wish to have versions of their Prayer-Books and Catechisms &c., printed in Irish. Let them send me those versions, approved of respectively, and they shall have them printed, in the greatest abundance, and at the cheapest possible rate. *Tros Tyriusve mihi nullo discrimine agetur.* Trojan or Tyrian shall meet no distinction from me.

THE PROTESTANT CLERGY

I need not remind the Protestant Clergy that some of their most learned and illustrious Prelates have been the most strenuous advocates for the revival of the ancient literature of Ireland. They are all well acquainted with the fame and literary labours of the celebrated Primate Ussher, the Protestant Archbishop of Armagh, who lived over 200 hundred years since (having been born in 1580,) and who has been described as *'The great Luminary of the Irish Church.'* At an early age he formed the resolution of making himself master of all languages. He applied his powerful mind to the antiquities and language of Ireland, and has left us his opinion in the most emphatic words. The opinion of such a scholar cannot be too highly valued or too widely circulated. He ranks the Irish language amongst the very first of languages for 'elegance' and 'richness'. He then goes on to express his deep regret at the manner in which this beautiful language is neglected. . . .

THE PRESBYTERIAN CHURCH

The heads of the *Presbyterian Church* have also, in the most decisive manner, given evidence of their anxiety to promote the cultivation of the Irish language, as I learn by a letter from the Irish professor at the College of Belfast, from which the following is an extract:

'The Synod of Ulster have passed a law, making the study of the Irish *imperative* on their candidates for holy orders. They will not now ordain, without that qualification. Also, Dr. Crowley, the Catholic Bishop of this Diocese (Down and Connor), is about to establish an Irish class, in a seminary which he has lately founded. The Irish Professorship in the Belfast College is, as yet, but an experiment. In the article of *class-books* a great want exists. The chief obstacle to reviving the cultivation of the Irish language is the want of elementary books. . . .

THE CATHOLIC CLERGY

And then, need I remind the Catholic Clergy that to their predecessors Ireland was, in a great degree, indebted for the high literary renown which she so long maintained. They were, in their monasteries, colleges, and abbeys, the chief cultivators and propagators of learning. Many of them, in later times, when in exile, in the different countries of the Continent, still persevered in the fond effort to save from utter oblivion their much-loved language. They made there a last struggle, but their efforts failed, and they could only mourn over the literature of Ireland, as they saw it descending to that grave in which it has ever since lain. The Catholic Clergy of the present day are now standing over its cradle, at this first dawn of its revival, solicitously affording it all the fostering protection in their power. . . .

The knowledge of the Irish language is not so general amongst the Protestant as the Catholic clergy, as I learn by letters from themselves. In fact, it is particularly fortunate for the revival of learning in Ireland, that there happens to be such a body as the Roman Catholic clergy, who possess the two great requisites, viz. -*A practical knowledge of the Irish Language, and a Classical Education*. These two requisites are not combined in any other body of persons in the country. . . .

Irish Teachers will now be in great request. Persons, therefore, competent to teach the language, or even the elements of it, had better announce themselves – perhaps, their most effectual way of doing so will be to advertize in this Magazine which will have such a wide circulation. The charge for such advertisements will be 4s . . . I have reason to think this Magazine will present the singular circumstance of numbering amongst its subscribers *every clergyman in Ireland, of all persuasions, and of all ranks*.

It is earnestly to be hoped, that the Ladies of Ireland will lend their all-powerful aid and example in reviving that language which abounds in such rich and beautiful poetry – which was once the language of courts and castles, when no other was spoken by the fair and noble-born 'daughters of Erin' – that sweet language which was modelled, made and melodized upon the harp, and which resounded every night in the halls of the nobles to the praise of the fairest of Erin's daughters, and the bravest of her warrior chiefs – of those who were –

> The boldest and bravest in war,
> As the fondest and truest in love.

For the constant themes of Erin's Harp were the captivating virtue of her daughters, and the chivalrous gallantry of her sons. . . .

The Ladies should feel that they owe much to a language, which was for ages and ages unceasingly employed in singing their praises and lauding, in the highest and most ardent strains, their charms, attractions, beauty and virtues. It is but fair at the same time, to state, for the Ladies, that to one of their own sex, is the Irish language more indebted than perhaps to any other individual of latter days, for a strenuous and fascinating effort towards its revival, viz. to the talented amiable and accomplished Miss Brooke. . . .

I have had, from several Ladies, assurances that they will form themselves into classes, in their respective neighborhoods, for the study of the Irish language, and that they will also interest themselves about having it taught in the schools within their reach. This resolution, I trust, will be adopted universally, indeed I have little doubt but it will.

Ladies have been the subjects of the greater part of the poetry in the Irish language, and it would, therefore, now appear to be a duty incumbent, *in a particular degree upon them*, to promote its revival by every means in their power.

5.17 *Irish Sermons with Translations*, P.Barron, 1835

Our arrangement was to have kept back these Sermons, till we should have an entire volume of them printed; but so great is the anxiety of the clergy generally, and so earnest their requests to let them have, without delay, even one Sermon, in their native language, that we have been induced to issue the present Number, in order to comply with their wishes: and we can anticipate with what gratification it will be received.

In the selection of a Sermon to commence with, we have not sought for the most eloquent, or the most elevated in style; but, on the contrary, the most simple and easy, feeling that the great object is to afford, in the outset, every facility. It will, therefore, be perceived, that the Sermon which we now publish is remarkable for its plain and easy style, at the same time conveying sound moral instruction.

We would guard the reader, however, against inferring that tameness, or coldness, are characteristic of pulpit eloquence in the Irish language – the contrary being the fact. That the Irish language is particularly powerful, and suited to the highest order of eloquence, has been avowed by all who have ever examined it. Again it is admitted that Irishmen are endowed beyond the ordinary degree, with the gift of eloquence; insomuch, that it is one of the characteristics of the nation, and pervades all classes. . . .

The Irish clergy are singularly circumstanced. Their case has no parallel in the civilised world. The language in which they are obliged to preach, is neither read, written, nor printed. They are thus labouring under a disadvantage which no other clergy in the world have laboured under. The clergy of all other countries have the advantage of reading the finest productions of all those who have gone before them. But in Ireland all is lost as soon as uttered: the Irish clergy have no sermons to read; neither can they write down or record their own ideas. And hence many a volume of the richest sacred eloquence has been lost forever, for want of the mere mechanical means of recording it. . . . This is a wrong to Ireland; and at the same time, it is productive of a grievous injustice to the clergy.

Why, therefore, should not the clergy of Ireland have sermons in their own language, as well as the clergy of England, France, Spain, or Italy? Have they not as important a mission to fulfil? Have they not flocks as numerous, and duties as multifarious to perform? Have they not, as a body, talent and eloquence equal to any other clergy in the world? and have they not a language as rich, as powerful, and as persuasive as that of any other nation? Whence, therefore, comes this strange anomaly? It comes from the shameful and discreditable neglect of the Irish language hitherto – a neglect which has been productive of much disadvantage and substantial injury. . . . Another great consideration is this – that it is to the altar and to the clergy we must look for improving the Irish language, and bringing it back to what it was.

5.18 'The Irish Language', *The Nation*, Revd Coneys, 1842

I entered a cabin near Lord Bantry's, at Glengariff, with a friend. It was Watch Saturday; and I asked him what it meant, and what were Good Friday and Easter Sunday the days before and after? He could not tell. 'You don't recollect,' said my friend, 'you are speaking to him in a foreign tongue'. I asked him the same question in Irish. His countenance brightened up, and he told me of the death and burial of the Lord, of the Angels' watch over His incorruptible body, of His ascension and glory. 'The English' said my friend, 'is the language of his commerce – the Irish the language of his heart'. Thus would Ireland – if dull to the foreign tongue, and intractable to the foreigner's ways – grow bright and eloquent, dutiful and devoted, at the sound of the Irish tongue and the Irishman's bidding.

5.19 *Songs of the Irish*, Conor McSweeny, 1843

The Highlanders have this advantage over us, that they have been taught their language, that it has been made the subject of education amongst them. Their clergy, whether Presbyterian or Catholic, not only learn the language themselves, but are careful to put Gaelic books into the hands of the peasantry. In the chapel of Eskedale in Invernesshire, most of the prayer-books, which I observed before and on either side of me, were Gaelic; and in the Catholic and Gaelic districts of Lochaber, Strathglass, and Arasig, the peasant has the same advantage both for private devotion and public worship. In the towns, grammars, books of instruction of every kind, and original Gaelic works, are to be seen in the booksellers' shops. An Irish prayer-book is a thing which the poor Irish peasant has never seen. Not only has he not been taught the language which he speaks, but his clergy have never encouraged, and have sometimes forbidden him to learn it. This objection arose chiefly, I believe, from the impudent intermeddling of Bible Societies with the religion of the people. By their patronage of the Irish language, they had desecrated it in the eyes of the Irish themselves. I have seen an Irish bishop, with mitre on head and crozier in hand, delivering an elaborate English discourse to an Irish congregation, while a priest stood in the pulpit interpreting it sentence by sentence. This prelate was the son of an Irish peasant, born and reared in one of the most Irish districts in Ireland. Many of his audience might have been, and very probably were his playmates in childhood and boyhood, and must have heard him speak the language of his father and mother; but he had never learned it, and was now too distinguished a dignitary of the church, to remember anything of the language of the vulgar herd he had left below him. With the exception of one or two distinguished names, we have done little for our language, not half as much as the Scotch, nor one-tenth as much as the Welsh, who live in an English atmosphere, have done and continue to do. The Welsh have newspapers in their native tongue. All our patriotism is of the mouth. It vanishes in the evaporations of speech. That patriotism, patient and laborious, which works on silent, obscure and unrequited, with *country* for its subject and its end, has no charms for us. While we boast of love of country, we are servilely following our oppressor in every path he takes, we must learn his language, and his accent, and his fashions; everything original or pertaining of ourselves is *vulgar* amongst us. What is this but to prostrate ourselves like slaves and arrant cowards at his feet.

But the poor Irish peasant has not been idle. In despite of tyranny, in despite of a still more dangerous influence, the neglect and discouragement of his own clergy, the only protectors who remained to him, and in spite of the necessity of learning for civil purposes a foreign jargon, he has preserved his own language triumphant all through. I am proud of being that peasant's countryman.

5.20 'English Schools and Irish Pupils', *The Nation*, anon., 1843

From Mrs O'Rourke, Formerly Miss Biddy Fudge, To Her Sister in England. Ballysassenagh, March 29, 1843.

> . . . Above all, 'tis the *accent* I'm anxious about;
> Good accent's the main point beyond any doubt.
> You remember last year how your own dear Kitty
> Delighted us all here, her talk was so pretty.
> When you asked her to sing about Margery Daw,
> And she said with her sweet little frown, '*Au* mamm*au*,
> Don't *ask* me I pray, since you know that I *caunt*.'
> Had she sung it, she couldn't have more pleased her aunt.
> Yes! England's the place for an accent – it's there
> One imbibes the pure sounds with the pure English air;
> Besides 'tis the place where a young man will learn
> All his more vulgar Irish attachments to spurn.
> While he talks with a tone he will act with one, too,
> That will show he has little with Ireland to do.

5.21 'The Irish Language', *The Nation*, anon., 1843

I

The Irish language is, indeed, phoenix-like, it is unique and has no parallel among the living or dead languages of Europe, nay, of the world. Let no person suppose that it was sought to be extinguished on account of its inutility, or of its rude or barbarous construction. Such was not the case; but the barbarians who sought to do so had political reasons strong enough to warrant the course they were taking. They plainly saw that while so powerful, copious and feelingly expressive a language continued to be in use among the people, their nationality sooner or later would grasp the rights of which it was unjustly deprived. . . .

Such was and still is the Irish language — the language of saints and heroes, and now the language of the most moral, religious, generous and brave people on earth. The Irish language is copious, expressive and important. It is copious and rich in itself because it borrows nothing and lends much: many of the living and dead languages and tongues of Europe and of the world are deeply indebted to it; yet all of its own words, syllables and even letters, all *meaning*, are to be traced only within and from itself. Its importance need not be questioned, even if we begin with the Garden of Eden — and in doing so I do not for a moment think we assume too high a position. We find the meaning of the first word that necessarily had been spoken by the Creator to his creature pure Irish . . . — Adam, ie *Ead, am, As yet Fresh*, which was very appropriately addressed by the Deity to the object He had just created in his own likeness, and hence was our first father called Adam. The names of Cain and Abel, his sons, are also Irish. Cain *-ie Bondage*, because he was born after the fall of his parents, when the human race had been subject to the bondage of sin and death . . . I believe that most, if not all the names in Scripture will be found to be also pure Irish, or, at least, are more satisfactorily radix than any other language we know affords them, will be found in the Irish language. . . . If we take into consideration the near affinity the languages of the near east — the Hebrew, Chaldaic, Sanscrit, Chalmuc, Egyptian . . . bore to the Irish; that the roots of many words in Greek, Latin, etc, not forgetting the English itself, are to be found in it; its maternal relation to the Welsh, Manx, Waldenese etc etc, at home, and even its relative is found, it is said, in the language of the Aborigines of America; and the length of country it must embrace in both the old and new world — the vast importance of the Irish language must at once be considered. Many learned philologers have considered it to be the *master key* to most other languages, living and dead. Upon the whole it can be seen how important must be the knowledge of such a language to the commentator on sacred and profane history, the Christian missioner, the traveller, and the antiquary.

To the people of Ireland themselves it is of the utmost importance; to every grade of individual moving in every grade of society, and discharging every relation in life, from the poor peasant and his wife who go to the market to dispose of the pig, or poultry, to the clergyman who addresses his flock in a language not half understood by them, to the magistrate and the judge who sits on the judicial seat to pass sentence of life or death from the knowledge of facts obtained through the very imperfect medium of the interpreter. Seeing the great antiquity, sweetness, power, expressive copiousness, and utility, nay necessity, of a knowledge of the language of Ireland, a society, to be denominated the Hibernian Gaelic Society, which has principally *in view the wider diffusion of a knowledge of the Irish language*, antiquities, poetry, etc., of Ireland, intends to struggle to remove the barriers that hitherto stood in the way of that knowledge – first, by distributing cheap, amusing, and useful publications among the people; and next, if Irishmen will duly appreciate the project by coming forward to its support, by establishing schools wherein the language will be taught in its purity.

II

Oh England! you who loudly boast of your just and equitable laws – your laws to promote education – it was you who made laws (too disgraceful to bear that sacred name) to suppress education in Ireland and barbarise the Irish people; and thus you plundered and tyrannised over them, under the plausible pretence of civilising them – but what did this civilisation amount to? . . . Blush, England, I say, if a blush yet remains in your brazen face! – you who put the gibbet and the axe between the Irish people and education, that you might totally eradicate the Irish language. . . .

Do Irishmen wish to see their language again revived? Would Irishmen wish to hear their native strains once more accompanied by the soul-stirring, vivifying melody that flows from the trembling strings of the Irish harp, and feel it gladdening their souls, and blessing their leisure hours? Will they be Irishmen again? or will they not? If they will, let them come forward like true Irishmen, and join the Hibernian Gaelic Society, which has for its object the revival, or rather the wider propagation of the language and music of Ireland . . . it should be a great national movement.

And soon shall Ireland hear her own dear language spoken once more, and the hearts of her people gladdened by the sweet, heavenly music of her national instrument, the harp; and then shall Ireland again be Ireland as she was of old – the land of the saint, and the land of the brave.

5.22 'Our National Language', *The Nation*, Thomas Davis, 1843

I

Men are ever valued most for peculiar and original qualities. A man who can only talk common-place, and act according to routine, has little weight. To speak, look, and do what your own soul from its depths orders you, are credentials of greatness which all men understand and acknowledge. Such a man's dictum has more influence than the reasoning of an imitative or common-place man. He fills his circle with confidence. He is self-possessed, firm, accurate, and daring. Such men are the pioneers of civilisation, and the rulers of the human heart.

Why should not nations be judged thus? Is not a full indulgence of its natural tendencies essential to a *people's* greatness? Force the manners, dress, language and constitution of Russia, or Italy, or Norway, or America, and you instantly stunt and distort the whole mind of either people.

The language which grows up with a people, is conformed to their organs, descriptive of their climate, constitution, and manners, mingled inseparably with their history and their soil, fitted beyond any other language to express their prevalent thoughts in the most natural and efficient way.

To impose another language on such a people is to send their history adrift among the accidents of translation – 'tis to tear their identity from all places – 'tis to substitute arbitrary signs for picturesque and suggestive names – 'tis to cut off the entail of feeling, and separate the people from their forefathers by a deep gulf – 'tis to corrupt their very organs, and abridge their power of expression.

The language of a nation's youth is the only easy and full speech for its manhood and its age. And when the language of its cradle goes, itself craves a tomb.

What business has a Russian for the rippling language of Italy or India? How could a Greek distort his organs and his soul to speak Dutch upon the sides of the Hymettus, or the beach of the Salamis, or on the waste where once was Sparta? And is it fitting the fiery, delicate-organed Celt to abandon his beautiful tongue, docile and spirited as an Arab, 'sweet as music, strong as the wave' – is it befitting in him to abandon this wild liquid speech for the mongrel of a hundred breeds called English, which, powerful though it be, creaks and bangs about the Celt who tries to use it?. . .

A people without a language of its own is only half a nation. A nation should guard its language more than its territories – 'tis a surer barrier, and more important frontier, than fortress or river. . . .

There is a fine song of the Fusians, which describes –

'Language linked to liberty.'

To lose your native tongue, and learn that of an alien, is the worst badge of conquest – it is the chain on the soul. To have lost entirely the national language is death; the fetter has worn through. . . .

How unnatural – how corrupting – 'tis for us, three-fourths of whom are of Celtic blood, to speak a medley of Teutonic dialects. If we add the Celtic Scots, who came back here from the thirteenth to the seventeenth centuries, and the Celtic Welsh, who colonised many parts of the Wexford and other Leinster counties, to the Celts who never left Ireland, probably five-sixths, or more, of us are Celts. What business have we with the Norman-Sassenagh?

Nor let any doubt these proportions because of the number of English *names* in Ireland. With a politic cruelty, the English of the Pale passed an Act (3 Edw. IV, chap 3), compelling every Irishman within English juris-diction, 'to go like to one Englishman in apparel, and shaving off his beard above the mouth,' 'and shall take to him an English surname of one town, as Sutton, Chester, Trym, Cork, Kinsale; or a colour, a White, Black, Brown; or art or science, as Smith, or Carpenter; or office, as Cook, Butler; and that he and his issue shall use this name, under pain of forfeiting his goods yearly.'

And just as this parliament before the Reformation, so did another after the Reformation. By the 28th [year of] Henry VIII, *c*.15, the dress and language of the Irish were insolently described as barbarous by the minions of that ruffian king, and were utterly forbidden and abolished under many penalties and incapacities. . . .

But this is not all; for even the Saxon and Norman colonists, notwith-standing these laws, melted down into the Irish, and adopted all their ways and language. For centuries upon centuries, Irish was spoken by men of all bloods in Ireland, and English was unknown, save to a few citizens and nobles of the Pale. 'Tis only within a very late period that the majority of the people learned English. . . .

Nothing can make us believe that it is natural or honourable for the Irish to speak the speech of the alien, the invader, the Sassenagh tyrant, and to abandon the language of our kings and heroes. What! give up the tongue of Ollamh Fodhla and Brian Boru, the tongue of Sarsfield's, Curran's, Mathews', and O'Connell's boyhood, for that of Strafford and Poynings, Sussex, Kirk, and Cromwell!

No! oh no! the 'brighter days shall surely come,' and the green flag shall wave on our towers, and the sweet old language be heard once more in college, mart, and senate.

II

Now, reader, don't be alarmed, we are not going to ask you to call your wife *machree*, or your child *mavourneen* instead of 'my heart' and 'my dear,' as you do or ought to do now. We do not want you to learn names for those imple-ments of agriculture and trade, those articles of furniture and dress, those relations of love, and life, and religion, other than you in infancy lisped.

For *you*, if the mixed speech called English was laid with sweetmeats on your child's tongue, English is the best speech of manhood. And yet, rather, in that case you are unfortunate. The hills, and lakes, and forts and castles, the churches and parishes, the baronies and counties around you, have all Irish names – names which describe the nature of the scenery or ground, the name of founder, or chief, or priest, or the leading fact in the history of the place. To you these names are hard to pronounce, and without meaning. . . .

The usual objection to attempting the revival of Irish is, that it could not succeed.

If an attempt were made to introduce Irish, either through the national schools or the courts of law, into the eastern side of the island, it would certainly fail, and the reaction might extinguish it altogether. But no one contemplates this save as a dream of what may happen a hundred years hence. It is quite another thing to say, as we do, that the Irish language should be cherished, taught, and esteemed, and that it can be preserved and gradually extended.

What we seek is, that the people of the upper classes should have their children taught the language which explains our names of persons or places, our older history, and our music, and which is spoken in the majority of our counties, rather than Italian, German, or French. It would be more useful in life, more serviceable to the taste and genius of young people, and a more flexible accomplishment for an Irish man or woman to speak, sing, and write Irish than French.

At present the middle classes think it a sign of vulgarity to speak Irish – the children are everywhere taught English and English alone in schools – and, what is worse, they are urged by rewards and punishments to speak it at home, for English is the language of their masters. Now, we think the example and the exertions of the upper classes would be sufficient to set the opposite and better fashion of preferring Irish; and, even as a matter of taste, we think them bound to do so. And we ask it of the pride, the patriotism, and the hearts of our farmers and shopkeepers, will they try to drive out of their children's minds, the native language of almost every great man we had, from Brian Boru to O'Connell – will they meanly sacrifice the language which names their hills, and towns, and music, to the tongue of the stranger?

About half the people west of a line drawn from Derry to Waterford speak habitually, and in some of the mountain tracts east of that line it is still common. Simply requiring the teachers of the National Schools in these Irish-speaking districts to know Irish, and supplying them with Irish translations of the schoolbooks, would guard the language where it now exists, and prevent it from being swept away by the English tongue, as the red Americans have been by the English race from New York to New Orleans.

5.23 'Repeal Reading Rooms', *The Nation*, Thomas Davis, 1844

To the districts where the Irish language is spoken, they should send a purely Irish Grammar, and an Anglo-Irish Grammar and Dictionary for each room, to be followed by other works containing general information as well as peculiarly Irish knowledge, in Irish. Indeed we doubt if the Association can carry out the plan which they began by sending out Dr. MacHale's Translations without establishing a newspaper, partly in English and partly in Irish, like the mixed papers of Switzerland, New Orleans and Hungary. . . . Were such a Room in every village you would soon have a knot connected with it of young men who had abjured cards, tobacco, dissipation and more fatal laziness, and were trying to learn some science, or art, or accomplishment – anything that best pleased them, from mathematics to music.

5.24 *The History of the Origin and Progress of the Irish Society*, H.J.M.Mason, 1844

The truth is that the English, from the time of their first settlement in Ireland, were possessed with a jealousy of the Irish tongue. It was manifest, that it operated greatly to prevent a complete subjection of the people, and was an idiom in which treason might be hatched, even in the hearing of the Viceroy himself; and it was ever to be the badge of that degeneracy among their fellow country-men, of which they were always complaining. . . .

It is not a fact that the Irish is a barbarous tongue; it has been, it is true, for a long time the vernacular idiom of a very uncivilised people; but it is an original language, the purest dialect of the Celtic; and it derives from this circumstance and advantage also, of which no vulgar use can deprive it, that it is better suited to convey truths to the mind of the unlearned, than the English or any compound tongue. Having its roots within itself, the meaning of all those terms that express justification, regeneration, repentance, charity, etc. etc. is at once obvious, without the interference of any learned expositor; an advantage which, in a country and religion where a reference to human authority and teaching is an evil of great prevalence, counterbalances any fastidious imagination respecting the barbarism of the tongue . . . this use of the Irish tongue . . . has not only reconciled the people to the use of English, but led to its adoption as a means of advancing in education, civilisation, and spiritual knowledge.

5.25 *An tIliad*, Bishop MacHale, 1844

Without insisting on the pre-eminence of the Gaelic language beyond all others ancient or modern, or defending the learned paradox of Parsons, one of our enthusiastic antiquarians, that it was in Irish the Iliad was originally written, in which case it should be confessed that the Greek was an excellent translation; I may venture, in all seriousness, to assert, that there is no European tongue better adapted than ours to a full and perfect version of Homer. It is true that in radical structure the Irish bears a stronger resemblance to the Hebrew than to the Greek language. But in the happy flexibility of the latter to the most varied and harmonious combinations, there is such an analogy between it and the Irish language, as to render the one the fittest medium for the transfusion of the other. . . .

Even in its present condition, the Irish language is one of the most effective instruments of oratorical persuasion, by which the feelings of a religious and sensitive people could be roused to any pitch. Were there no other monument to attest the early and superior civilisation of our nation, it is indelibly impressed on its truly philosophical language. For if, as is universally confessed, language be one of the most unequivocal standards by which you can ascertain the degree of refinement reached by any people, the sententious and expressive aphorisms that give such a complexion to ours, prove that those, to whom it is familiar even only as a spoken dialect, must necessarily be a highly intellectual people.

5.26 *Annual Report of the Commissioners of Education*, P.J.Keenan, 1856

It is natural to inquire how this strong passion for education could have possessed a people who are themselves utterly illiterate. Neither at Tory, Inisboffin, Gola, Owey, Rutland, nor Innisfree, is there a resident clergyman; Arranmore being the only one of the islands which enjoys such an advantage; nor is there anyone above the rank of a peasant living amongst the inhabitants to give a direction to their tastes, or to counsel them to have their children educated. Their passion may be traced to one predominant desire – the desire to speak English. They see, whenever a stranger visits their islands, that prosperity has its peculiar tongue as well as its fine coat; they see that whilst the traffickers who occasionally approach them to deal in fish, or in kelp, or in food, display the yellow gold, they count it out in English; and if they ever cross over to the mainland for the 'law', as they call any legal process, they see that the solemn words of judgment have to come second to them, through the offices of an interpreter. Again English is spoken by the stray official who visits them, by the sailors of the ships that sometimes lie occasionally in their roadsteads, and by the schoolmaster himself; and whilst they may love the cadences, and mellowness, and homeliness of the language which their fathers gave them, they yet see that obscurity and poverty distinguish their lot from the English-speaking people; and accordingly, no matter what the sacrifice to their feelings, they long for the acquisition of the 'new tongue', with all its prizes and social privileges. The keystone of fortune is the power of speaking English, and to possess this power there is a burning longing in their breasts that never varies, never moderates. It is the utilitarian, not the abstract idea of education which influences them, for they know nothing of the pleasures of literature, or of the beauties and wonders of science. The knowledge which they thirst for in the school is, therefore, confined to a speaking use of the English Language. I met with some remarkable cases, illustrative of their ardent desire to know English. At Tory, a man who expressed himself in English pretty well, told me that he had been in a boat with a party of fellow-islanders at Moville, in Inishowen, and, to use his own expression, when speaking of his own companions, who spoke Irish only, he said he 'was ashamed of them; they stood like dummies; the cattle go on as well as them'. . . . At Owey the teacher is an intelligent young man, who has been well trained in a most superior school on the mainland; a fair attempt had been made at teaching grammar, geography, and arithmetic; the senior pupils knew a tolerable share of English; the juniors were still without a word. The master adopts a novel mode of procedure to propagate the 'new language'. He makes it a cause of punishment to speak Irish in the school, and he has instituted a sort of police among the parents to see that in their intercourse with one another the children speak nothing but English at home. The parents are so eager for the English, they exhibit no reluctance to inform the master of every detected breach of the school law; and, by this coercive process, the poor children in the course of time become pretty fluent in speaking very incorrect English.

5.27 *The College Irish Grammar*, Canon U.J.Bourke, 1856

The children of Ireland are no longer, as of old, flogged for lisping in the broad Celtic of their fathers . . . [though] there are hundreds of persons still living who, 'in boyhood's days', had suspended from the neck 'scores' or tablets, the number of incisions on which showed how often the prohibi-tion to speak Irish had been violated, and for which the schoolmaster inflicted upon the delinquent a proportionate number of stripes. Verily that was beating the language out of the country with the vengeance! yet depart it would not, till the lash of fashion and corruption were employed against it. . . .

[The cause of the decay of the language is] chiefly to that desire which the humbler classes of our people naturally have, of speaking the language spoken by their more enlightened countrymen; and to that total exclusion of everything related to the Irish language from our *National* Schools; to the want also of elementary treatises, written with philological taste, in a style at once simple, pleasing, and attractive, published withal at a moderate price, so that they might become readily accessible to the great majority of the reading public. . . .

Should it not be our pride and our boast to have such a language, while other countries rejoice in their jargon – in their compound of various languages. Why do Welsh and Scots do better? Because they are used as the common language of the country; because they are taught in their elementary schools and encouraged by the nobility and gentry, instead of being ashamed of their mother tongue – as I am sorry to say we should generally be found of ours – or rather, are sought to be made so, by those who are interested in suppressing it as a mark of our nationality. . . .

The Board of our *National Education* could do much for the language of Ireland. In fact without their cooperation, or that of the Christian Brothers, it will, it is to be feared, soon become a dead language; for it never can be *nationally* revived unless nursed again in the *national* cradle of the schools of Ireland. . . . The Archbishop of Tuam calls the National Schools 'the graves of the National Language'.

Within [the language] are interwoven a thousand national recollections which we fondly cherish; with it is wound up the history of our glory, of our triumphs, of our fame. It ought to be fostered even for its own sake. . . . If we do not cherish it for its own sake, why let us do it for our own. We know the language of a nation is the exponent of the nation's antiquity – the index of their refinement – the mouthpiece of their history – the echo of a nation's greatness and fame; shall we, then, let our language die?

'The Celtic Tongue', Revd M.Mullin

I

It is fading! it is fading! like the leaves upon the trees!
It is dying! it is dying! like the Western Ocean breeze!
It is faintly disappearing, as footsteps on the shore
Where the Barrow, and the Erne, and Lough Swilly's waters roar
Where the parting sunbeam kisses the corrib in the West,
And the ocean, like a mother, clasps the Shannon to its breast!
The language of old Erin, of her history and name –
Of her monarchs and her heroes, of her glory and her fame –
The sacred shrine where rested, through her sunshine and her gloom,
The spirit of her martyrs, as their bodies in the tomb!
The time wrought shell where murmured, through centuries of wrong,
The secret voice of freedom, in annal and in song –
Is surely, fastly sinking into silent death at last,
To live but in the memories and relics of the Past!

II

The olden tongue is sinking, like a Patriarch to rest,
Where youthhood saw the Tyrian, on our Irish coasts a guest,
Ere the Saxon or the Roman – ere the Norman or the Dane
Had first set forth in Britain, or the Visigoth in Spain.
Whose manhood saw the druid rite at forest tree and rock –
The savage tribes of Britain round the shrines at Zernebock,

And for generations witnessed all the glories of the Gael,
Since our Celtic sires sang war-songs round the warrior fires of Baal!
The tongues that saw its infancy are ranked among the dead;
And from their graves have risen those now spoken in their stead.
Ah the glories of old Erin, with her liberty, have gone,
Yet their halo lingered round her while her olden Tongue lived on;
For, mid the desert of her woe, a monument more vast
Than all her pillar-towers, it stood – that old Tongue of the past!

III

And now tis sadly shrinking from the land that gave it birth
Like the ebbing tide from shore, or the spring-time from the earth;
O'er the island dimly fading, as a circle o'er the wave –
Still receding, as its people lisp the language of the slave.
And with it, too, seems fading as a sunset into night,
All the scattered rays of Freedom, that lingered in its light!
For, ah, though long with filial love it clung to Motherland,
And Irishmen were Irish still, in *tongue*, and heart, and hand!
Before the Saxon tongue, alas! proscribed it soon became;
And we are Irishmen today, but Irishmen in name!
The Saxon claim our rights and tongue alike doth hold in thrall,
Somewhere among the Connaught wilds, and hills of Donegal,
And the shores of Munster, like the broad Atlantic past,
The olden language lingers yet – an echo of the Past!

IV

Through cold neglect 'tis dying, like a stranger on our shore,
No Teamore's halls shall vibrate to its thrilling tones e'ermore –
No Laurence fire the Celtic clans round leaguered Athacleith –
No Shannon waft from Luimneach's towers their war-songs to the sea.
Ah! the pleasant Tongue, whose accents were music to the ear!
Ah! the magic Tongue, that round us wove its spell so soft and dear!
Ah! the glorious Tongue, whose murmur could each Celtic heart
enthrall!
Ah! the rushing Tongue, that sounded like the swollen torrent's fall!
The tongue that in the senate was the lightning flashing bright,
Whose echo in the battle was the thunder in its might;
The tongue that once in chieftain's hall swelled loud the minstrel's lay,
As chieftain, serf, or minstrel old is silent there today;
Whose password burst upon the foe at Kong or Mulaghmast,
Like those who nobly perished there, is numbered with the Past.

V

The Celtic Tongue is fading and we coldly standing by –
Without a pang within the heart, a tear within the eye –
Without one pulse for freedom stirred, one effort made to save
The language of our fathers, lisp the language of the slave!
Sons of Erin! vain your efforts – vain your prayers for freedom's crown
Whilst you crave it in the language of the foe that clove it down.
Know you not that tyrants ever, with an art from darkness sprung,
Strive to make the conquered nation slaves alike in limb and tongue.
The Russian bear ne'er stood secure o'er Poland's shattered frame,
Until he trampled from her breast the tongue that bore her name.
Oh, be *Irish*, Irishmen, and rally for the dear old Tongue
Which, as ivy to a ruin, to the dear old land has clung;
Oh, snatch this relic from the wreck, the only and the last,
To show what Erin ought to be, by pointing to the Past!

5.28 'A Dialogue in the Ulster Dialect', *Ulster Journal of Archaeology*, anon., 1858

'WROTE DOWN, PRENTET, AND PUT OUT, JIST THE WAY THE PEOPLE SPAKES'

Introduction

One day in the month of December, in the 'dark days' that happen at Christmas, a farmer of very small holding returned from his daily employment. He was known as 'wee Jemmy McCreedy,' of the town of Ballinastarvet, which lies on the side of a mountain. His crop of potatoes had failed him; his Hollantide was unpaid yet, and the agent had sent him a notice. Poor man, he felt age creeping on him; besides, he was weak and desponding, and troubles had made his wife peevish. Though it's wrong to 'come over' what's private, or 'let on' 'ins an' outs' of a quarrel, yet the story may prove to be useful, and they suffer nothing by scandal.

JEMMY

Auch! auch! there's another day over,
An' the year's comin' fast to an endin';
But two or three sich will desthroy me,
For my cough's gettin' worse, an' I'm waker.
Oh! Betty McCreedy, what ails ye,
That ye can't keep a wee bit o' fire on?
Go 'long, bring some clods from the turf-stack,
For my toes an' my fingers is nippin'.

BETTY

What's the manin' ov all this norration,
An' me llokin' after the childhre?
A'm sure, both my ancles is achin'
With throttin about since the mornin'.
If ye hev been outside for a wee while,
It's many another's condition.
An' the says is n't long; A can tell ye,
It's har'ly an hour since yer dinner.
An' Jemmy, A may as well say it,
There's no use at all in desavin',
It's crosser an' crosser ye're gettin'
Till my very heart's scalded wi' sorra.
Deed an' doubles A'll bear it no longer.

JIMMY

Well, Betty bad luck to the liars,
But there's one of us greatly mistaken.
From mornin' till day-lit-goin workin',
Cleanin' corn on the top if the knowe head,
The wine whistled roun' me like bag-pipes,
An' sut me in two like a razure.
A thrim' let an' shuck like an apsy,
While the dhraps from my nose, o' coul wather,
Might a' dhrownded a middle-sized kitlin'.

BETTY

Och! indeed yer a scar-crow, that's sartin;
Lord help the poor woman that owes ye;
But ye needn't be cursin' an' swearin'
An' still castin' up an upbraidin'.
If ye think there's a liar between us,
Jist look in the glass an' ye'll see him.
(Oh! the bitterest words in his gizzard
Is the best A can git thram my husband.)

JIMMY

Will ye nivver lave aff aggravatin'?
Now quet an' hav done. A forbid ye –

170

BETTY

Oh, indeed 'twas yerself 'at begun it,
So A'll give ye back-talk till ye're tired.
There was Johnny Kincaid in the loamin',
Was aafther me more nor a tewel'month,
When you hadn't yit come across me,
But A hedn't the luck for to git him.
He's a corpolar now on a pension,
An' keeps up his wife like a lady,
An's nate an' well dhrest on a Sunday.

JIMMY

Well, well! but there's no use in talkin',
His crap disn't fail him in harvest;
An' forby, Paddy Shales isn't paid yet
For makin' the coat that I'm wearin'.
More betoken, it wants to be mended,
But ye nivver touch needle nor thim'le.
There's my wais'coat is hingin' in ribbons,
With only two buttons to houl' it;
An' my breeches in dyuggins an' totthers,
Till A' can't go to meetin' on Sunday.

BETTY

Och! have done with yer schamin' religion,
For ye nivver wos greedy for Gospel.
Deed, bad luck to the toe ye'd go near it,
If we cloth'd ye as fine as Square Johnston.
Ye wud slung at the backs o' the ditches,
With one or two others, yer fellas,
A huntin' the dogs at the rat holes.

JEMMY

But I'm used to be clanely an' dacent,
An' so wos my father afore me;
An' how can a man go out-bye, when
His clo'es is all out at the elbows?

BETTY

Well, yer hat disn't need any patchin',
An A'm sure it's far worse nor the t'others;

I bought it myself in the market,
From big Conny Collins, that made it,
For two shillins, an' share of a naggin.
See, the brim is tore off like brown paper,
Till ye're jist like a Connaughtman nager.
An' then, as for darnin' yer stockin's,
As well thinkov mendin' a riddle.
Why a woman's kep throttin' behine ye,
Till she can't do a turn, nor a foundet.

JEMMY

Now, jist let me alone; an' believe me,
If ye don't houl' your tongue in one minute,
An' git me my supper o' sowins,
The same as ye say'd in the mornin',
A'll warm all the wax in your ears,
An' we'll see which desarves to be masther.

BETTY

Och! ye mane-hearted cowartly scrapins,
Is that the mischief that ye're up to?
Ye wud jist lift your hand to a woman,
That ye ought to purtect an' to comfort.
See, here, — ye're a beggarly cowart;
If ye seen yer match sthript an' fornenst
Ye wud wish to creep intil a mouse-hole.
So, ye needn't be curlin' yer eyebrows,
An' dhrawin' yer fist like to sthrek me.
God be thankit the tongs is beside me,
An' as well soon as syne, A may tell ye,
If ye offer to stir up a rippet,
An thinks that ye're imperance cows me,
All the veins in ye're heart ye shall rue it.
If ye dar for till venthur to hit me,
See, by this an' by that, ye'll repent it.
A'll soon comb yer head with the crook-rod,
Or sen' its contents shinin' through ye.

5.29 *An Irish Translation of the Holy Bible from the Latin Vulgate*, Archbishop MacHale, 1861

The want of a complete Catholic version of the Canonical Scriptures, in our own native language, has long been felt and deplored in Ireland. Though this want is to be obviously ascribed to the religious persecutions to which so many of our privations can be traced, it must be confessed, that it could even now have been supplied by vigorous exertions. The hostility with which the Catholic church has been so long assailed in this country, was not confined to its members, whether lay or ecclesiastical, but involved Priests and Churchmen, Professors and Colleges, together with the ancient language of Ireland, in the same indiscriminate persecution. It is some time now since the fury of that tempest, spent by its own violence, has subsided. But though our ecclesiastics have come forth, displaying a zeal and learning worthy of any period of the Church, and though our Colleges and Temples are once more covering the land, it is to be regretted that our language, has not yet been made the vehicle, of conveying the entire wisdom of the inspired writings, to the people. . . .

The Irish language, from its insular position, as well as the freedom of the Island from Roman invasion, was not exposed, it is true, to the vicissitudes of the other European tongues. It had acquired full maturity, when those were yet almost unshapen. Still an Irish version of the Scriptures, prior to the Sixteenth Century, would not be generally understood in the present day. Its copious vocabulary was loose and fluctuating, and not sufficiently arrayed under the grammatical discipline, that has distinguished beyond all others, the languages of Greece and Rome. During the three centuries of the active conquests of its missionaries abroad as well as at home, the Irish church had but little leisure to devote to the cultivation of its literature, and to that didactic style of writing, in which correct logic and precise language, are found harmoniously exemplified. And when they might be permitted to repose from the extraordinary toils and successes of their missionary career, and to enjoy collegiate leisure; the harassing inroads, now of the Danes, and again, the more protracted hostility of the English settlers, denied them such an opportunity.

After printing had brought literature within ordinary reach, there is little doubt but an Irish orthodox translation of the Scriptures, by a competent hand, would have contributed much to the fixity of a standard language, among a people so remarkable for the uniformity of their faith. A person so qualified would have been found in Geoffrey Keating, whose pure idiomatic style so familiar to this day, whilst later writers are unintelligible, has thrown a rare charm over his romantic pages, and rescued from ridicule some of those trivial legends, which may seem unsuited to the grave tone of history. But, alas! the leisure, the books, the expenses, and the encouragement necessary for such an arduous work, were denied to the learned ecclesiastic, by the adverse fortune of those times. To have been collecting and embellishing the scattered traditions of the country, was more congenial to his erratic life, whilst flying from the persecutions of Elizabeth's deputy; and had his lot been thrown amidst more fortunate circumstances, his writings would surely have been distinguished by a more discriminating judgment. But how unequal any private individual, however zealous, would have been to the arduous work of publishing a translation of the Scriptures, we may learn from this circumstance, that the first Irish translation of the New Testament, early in the Seventeenth Century, by some ascribed, to Nehemia Donnelan, and by others, to William O'Donnell, both Protestant Archbishops of Tuam, is said to have been printed at the expense of the people of Connaught, one of the many and heavy subsidies, to which Catholic Ireland has since been doomed, to sustain a hostile establishment. Towards the close of the same century, an Irish version of the Old Testament was issued, fraught with all the errors of the English authorised version.

6

1876–1922

INTRODUCTION

In political terms the final section of this history covers the shift from the consequences of the defeat of the Fenian rebellion to the constitution of the Saorstát in
1922. The commencement of the Land War in 1879 saw the development of
another mass nationalist movement which wrought important political conces-
sions from the British Government. This in turn had a revitalising effect on the
Home Rule campaign which dominated Irish politics in the period 1870–1914.
Under the leadership of Butt, the Home Rule movement had attracted support
from the Protestant middle class, particularly after the disestablishment of the
Church of Ireland in 1870. Once Parnell had succeeded Butt, however, the political nature of Home Rule altered with the gaining of the support of the Catholic
clergy and the inclusion of activists experienced in earlier struggles. Notwithstanding its slow progress, and the fall of Parnell, the passing of the third
Home Rule Bill in 1914 appeared to be a significant victory for constitutional
nationalism. By then, however, the development of militant forms of both
Republicanism and Unionism meant that the constitutional route was to be
bypassed. Pearse's prophecy of 'the coming revolution' was to be realised in
three outbreaks of war: the Easter Rising of 1916, the Anglo-Irish War of
1919–21, and the Irish Civil War of 1922–23. The constitution of 1922 gave
the Saorstát the status of Dominion within the Commonwealth; when Home
Rule, as previously understood, was achieved on the island of Ireland, it was
ceded to its most bitter opponents, the Unionists of Northern Ireland.

The split between the cultural and political wings of nationalism which had
appeared in the early to mid-nineteenth century developed further towards it
end. Cultural nationalists of all shades castigated the leaders of the Irish Parliamentary Party for their neglect of the language question in particular. The
matter was now urgent: the 'poor Irish peasant', described by McSweeny in
1843 as having 'preserved his language triumphant', was, though frequently
invoked, proving rather hard to find. The Annual Report of one of the Commissioners of Education in 1856, Keenan, a man sympathetic to the teaching of
Irish, declared simply of the rural poor: 'the knowledge which they search for

in the school is, therefore, confined to a speaking use of the English language.' If, as the lament was to be heard in the twentieth century, there was 'the shame of Irish dying in a free Ireland', in the nineteenth century the evidence indicates that the shame was felt by monolingual Irish speakers.

To redress that situation a number of societies were founded, non-religious in nature and non-party political in constitution, to prevent the further decay of Irish and to attempt its revival. None, however, at least at the level of the leadership, appeared to dissent from Thomas Davis' appraisal that the achievement of a Gaelic-speaking Ireland was as good as impossible. The Society for the Preservation of the Irish Language (founded in 1876) included in its rules the goal of 'the preservation and extension of Irish as a spoken language'. An advertisement of the inauguration of the Society showed its more modest aim to be

> to create such a tone of public feeling as will utterly banish the ignorant and unpatriotic notion (of foreign origin), that our native tongue is one which no Irishman of the present day should care to learn, or be willing to speak.

Such an aim was evidently too unambitious for some of the Society's members who left to form the Gaelic Union (1880), which published the influential and bilingual *Irisleabhar na Gaedhilge/Gaelic Journal* (1882–1909). The most important of these societies, however, was founded in 1893: the Gaelic League (Conradh na Gaeilge). Based to a large degree upon Douglas Hyde's inaugural presidential address to the National Literary Society, 'The Necessity for De-Anglicising Ireland' (1892), the League flourished and, as well as taking over *Irisleabhar na Gaeilge*, the League published a weekly newspaper *Fáinne an Lae* (*The Dawning of the Day*) and its successor *An Claidheamh Soluis* (*The Sword of Light*). The League was undoubtedly successful in attracting a large membership (there were 593 branches in 1904) though its efficiency in the teaching of Irish was minimal, as Synge savagely pointed out. As a largely urban and lower-middle-class movement with negligible take-up in the Gaeltacht, it stood little chance of defeating the forces which were causing the decline of Irish. What it did successfully, however, was to act as a focus for cultural nationalism and to channel energies which were later to appear in the leadership of the Rising of 1916 and the events thereafter. Picking up on the populist tactics of earlier language activists (Nolan's setting of Irish Grammar to verse, for example, or his acrostic 'Plea for Our Mother Tongue') the League organised Language Sunday processions and published a Gaelic League Catechism. No doubt all this was part of Yeats' 'casual comedy', but the League played its part in the transformation to the 'terrible beauty' of political war.

The Gaelic League's most immediately practical success was its intervention in education debates. As noted previously, the teaching of English in the National Schools was considered to be one of the prime causes of the eradication of

Irish. To tackle this, the Society for the Preservation of the Irish Language had campaigned for the teaching of Irish in primary schools outside of school hours, and achieved success in 1879. The Society had also been victorious in its attempt to have 'Celtic' accepted as a possible subject for examination in the Intermediate (secondary) Schools. The Gaelic League's achievement, which gave an enormous boost to its status, lay in its engagement in the controversy over the issue of Irish in Intermediate education, prompted by the investigation of the Royal Commission into the system of secondary schooling. Taking on the cultural establishment, which was hostile to the teaching of Irish, in the persons of Trinity College dons Mahaffy and Atkinson, the League, led by Hyde, ridiculed the evidence of their opponents to the Commissioners. Mahaffy's flippant rejection of Irish, and Atkinson's weakness as a scholar in the language, were exposed by the League and brought them to humiliating defeat. Perhaps the League's most daunting test, however, was not that posed by the enemies of Irish, but by a force which had, albeit late in the day, supported the revival campaign: the Catholic Church. The issue which caused the conflict was the compulsory inclusion of Irish as a Matriculation subject for the new National University (founded in 1908). It was a battle which the League won in 1909, but the bitterness caused by it was a foretaste of things to come.

The historical and contemporary roles of the Catholic Church were in actuality matters of heated dispute. The Synod of Catholic Bishops at Tuam in 1858, with Archbishop MacHale in the Chair, exhorted the clergy to strive 'to have in every parish where Gaelic is the vernacular a class in your school where all pupils shall learn it'. MacHale, Patron of the Society for the Preservation of the Irish Language, contributed to the Catholic wing of cultural nationalism with his translation of the Pentateuch. Others, reflecting on the Church's record over the nineteenth century, blamed the clergy for the parlous state of the language. O'Donnell put it succinctly: 'Priests kill the language and Irish studies.' In the main, however, towards the end of the century Irish Catholicism, both lay and clerical, supported the language movement, at times to such an extent that it was to the embarrassment of prominent Protestants in the Gaelic League – including its President Douglas Hyde. The League's declared non-sectarian stance, troubled by the excessive identification with Irish Catholicism, was threatened by an incident involving Canon Hannay, the Protestant minister better known as George Birmingham. In 1906 Hannay was barred from a local Gaelic League Committee by a Catholic priest on the basis of his objection to Hannay's non-Gaelic League writings. To its credit, the organ of the League, *An Claidheamh Soluis*, issued a denunciation of the priest (penned by Pearse) declaring his actions to be 'the first gross instance of intolerance of which a Gaelic League Body has been guilty'. Hyde, whose political acumen was often greatly underestimated, remained silent; Hannay continued to contribute valuable work to the League.

Gaelic League pamphleteers in the main followed the strict line that the League's position was strictly non-political. Kavanagh, for example, insisted that the language movement offered 'to unite Irish people of all creeds and classes in a common effort to save their country' and made a clever reference to the 'gifted patriots of our past'. Others such as Moran insisted on the uniqueness of Irish culture and the 'isolating power' of the language. Trench, writing in 1912, made a distinction between a 'peaceful process of evolution' in which languages are merged and perhaps disappear, and the 'forcible extermination' of cultural difference. This was a point also made by Agnes Farrelly in her politically radical attack (in direction if not always content) on 'cosmopolitanism', the term used in the 1890s to describe the same process which is known today as 'globalisation'. Despite these arguments, however, the non-political stance of the League was always in danger and in a sense was something of a fiction in any case (as Ó hEigceartaigh pointed out later). For the cultural nationalist, nationality superseded politics since the nation was formed by things held in common. But the greater the stress on language, history, literature, institutions, joys, hopes and aspirations which constituted the commonality of the Irish nation, the less the Irish nation appeared as anything but a political ideal of one section of the total population. It was a repetition at the cultural level of the difficulty caused by the Home Rule Bill: a commonality was presupposed where in reality divisions existed. The inevitable politicisation of the League's activities was also hastened by the declarations of 'the language war' and 'the struggle between the civilisations which these languages represent'. The dangers were compounded by the fall into the lurid discourse of racial miscegenation, which recalled nothing more clearly than the Anglo-Irish Chronicles and their fear of 'degeneration'. Pearse at least had the good sense to see it as a straight political and military fight.

It was not of course that Pearse himself was entirely above the temptations of the fray – the dismissal of Yeats as a poet of the third or fourth rank makes him sound petulant. And his rejection of literature written in English as 'Irish' literature (composed before he was 20) masks what was in general a positive, though always conservative, attitude towards the Irish Literary Theatre. Yeats argued against Irish-Ireland on the question of writing in English on the untypically astute basis of the practical point which he shared with the Gaelic Leaguers in their campaign for the teaching of literacy in Irish in Irish-speaking districts: 'no man can write well except in the language he has been born and bred to.' It must be noted too that he recommends the English of the 'Irish-thinking people of the west' as 'the only good English' spoken in Ireland; this, of course, was the language in which Synge sought to write. This new form, made in the crucible of Hiberno-English history one way and another over centuries, had been commented upon many times before, usually with contempt or mockery. But a positive interest in it had begun to emerge, as the dialogue in 'Ulster dialect' of 1858 and P.W. Joyce's *English as We Speak it in Ireland* (1910) indicate. As Thomas MacDonagh, one of the signatories to the Proclamation of the Irish Republic (later executed by the British) put it, this was a 'new language' created by the breaking and remaking of English, and forged in living speech.

6.1 *An Cheud Leabhar Gaedhilge. First Irish Book,* Society for the Preservation of the Irish Language, 1877

The mistakes of past generations and the apathy of centuries cannot be remedied easily. The Nation must help, but above and beyond all the hearty support of the clergy is indispensable, as they, in a great measure, are the guardians of what remains of our mother tongue. A language so rich and expressive as ours ought to have strong claims on the teachers of religion, for it is wondrously adapted for giving utterance to devotional feelings, and is an admirable vehicle of praise and prayer. . . .

The efforts of the Society will be strongly put forth to have our language taught in the National and Christian Brothers' Schools, so that at no distant date there may be a current literature in Irish. . . . No matter what the political state of Ireland may be, she can boast of glories that can never be taken away by force, however they may perish by neglect.

6.2 *Irish Grammar Rules in Prose and Verse,* Revd John Nolan, 1877

['Prepositions':]
Ar and air, with de and do
Aspirate; as you must know
Fa, fo, and also faoi
Do the same, as all agree.
O, from, and im, about,
Are of same rule, without a doubt.
Mar, tar, and likewise tre
Follow here in like array. . . .

'Plea for Our Mother Tongue'

Do justice to Irish, and give it a chance
On its own native soil, as the French has in France;
No honey so sweet as it drops from the leaf
Or so thrilling a sound for the bard and the chief.
The gift of our fathers from sire to son
Despite the proud Saxon, his steel, and his gun.
Erin's St Patrick through it spread the good news,
Securing salvation to men if they choose.
Proud Brian in Gaelic charged his brave men,
And smote the barbarian on Cluan Tairb fen.
Ireland shall weep if this tongue you don't cherish
Repel the disgrace which is yours if it perish. . . .

'How to learn Irish, and be Irish'

One letter, then another,
And the alphabet is gained;
One word, then another,
And the language is attained;
One speak it, then another,
And 'tis spoken as before;
One man, then another,
And we're Irish as of yore.

'Bearla Na bfeinne, The language of my land', anon.,
The Irish American

To neglect is a crime, in the Celt of our time,
To learn the language of my land, –
As a stream in its order, flowing over its border
Irrigates the bright meadows of my land –
As the full force of Sol upon my land –
On the fruit of the earth, of the island,
There was friendship and mirth between neighbours of birth,
Through the sway of the language of my land.

Though late it is better than further to fetter
But cling to the language of my land.
It was music to the chief, and the sage found relief
When he spoke in the language of my land.
Tis as old as the green hills of my land;
Tis as true of the friendships of my land:
Tis urgent in pleading, and sharp in degrading;
Oh, forcible language of my land.

When prayer should be given, at morning and even',
Use you the language of my land:
It is better by far than the Sassenach's jar,
Who hates the sweet language of my land.
Now show to the world, in my land,
You determine and will through the island,
You'll embrace, with a will, the last heritage still
That is left in the language of my land.

6.3 *Annual Report of the Commissioners of Education,* P.J.Keenan, 1879

Even in places where all social communication is carried on in Irish, and where, in short, few or none of the adult population know a word of English, the language of the National Schools, the books, the teaching, etc., are entirely *English*. The children of parents who at present speak Irish only, will, through the course of education pursued in the National Schools, and the experience of home, speak English and Irish when they grow up, but their children will, in nine cases out of ten, speak English only. In this way the Irish language will gradually fall into disuse, and be, perhaps, forgotten. Many good men would rejoice at this; but they seem to me to forget that the people might know both Irish and English, and they also forget that by continuing to speak Irish, *and learning English through its medium*, the latter language would be enriched by the imagery and vigour of the mother tongue. . . . The shrewdest people in the world are those who are bilingual: borderers have always been remarkable in this respect. But the most stupid children I have ever met are those who were learning English while endeavouring to forget Irish. . . . The real policy of the educationist would, in my opinion, be to teach Irish grammatically and soundly to the Irish-speaking people, and then to teach them English through the medium of their native language.

6.4 *Memo of Commissioners of National Education to the Chief Secretary*, 1884

In [bilingual children's] own interests, and in the interests of the country, there can therefore be no question whatever but that the language of the education of these English-speaking children should be English. . . . In a country where all the interests, social, commercial, and political, combine to favour the acquisition of the English language by the people, it would certainly be neither natural nor rational to impose upon children who know English an imposition to study Irish. . . .

It is utterly impracticable to make Irish the language of the schools in any part of the country, or to interfere with the free current of progress, under the auspices of the local managers of the schools, in the education of the people in the English language.

6.5 *Proceedings of the Congress Held in Dublin, 1882,* Society for the Preservation of the Irish Language, 1884

[There is a need] to remove the prejudices of the unenlightened *shoneen* who is said to be ashamed to speak his mother's tongue. . . . The chief obstacle is caused by the indifference, or apathy of the people generally as to the necessity of preserving the National Language. . . . Our success can be deemed but partial until the parents heartily desire that their children should be familiar with their native tongue, and cherish and promote its cultivation, by regarding it as an essential part of their children's education . . . [rather than] the slavish notion that the knowledge of the country's ancient and noble language is something, if not to be wholly ashamed of, at least to be indifferent about . . . it is well known that more Irish may be heard spoken at present in New York, London, Liverpool, or Glasgow than in Dublin.

6.6 'Practical Hints Towards Preventing the Decay of Irish in Irish-Speaking Districts', Donal Flaherty, 1884

The greatest danger which threatens the language, and one from which it is certain to suffer, is the prejudice entertained against it by the illiterate Irish-speaking peasant, whose phraseology it is. They fancy it is the synonym of poverty and misery, and that many of the evils from which they suffer are traceable to its continued use; that, if they could dispose with it altogether, they would elevate themselves socially, and be much more respectable members of society.

6.7 'The Necessity for De-Anglicising Ireland', Douglas Hyde, 1892

When we speak of 'The Necessity for De-Anglicising the Irish Nation', we mean it, not as a protest against imitating what is *best* in the English people, for that would be absurd, but rather to show the folly of neglecting what is Irish, and hastening to adopt, pell-mell, and indiscriminatingly, everything that is English, simply because it *is* English.

This is a question which most Irishmen will naturally look at from a National point of view, but it is one which ought also to claim the sympathies of every intelligent Unionist, and which, as I know, does claim the sympathy of many.

If we take a bird's-eye view of our island today, and compare it with what it used to be, we must be struck by the extraordinary fact that the nation which was once, as every one admits, one of the most classically learned and cultured nations in Europe, is now one of the least so; how one of the most reading and literary peoples has become one of the *least* studious and most *un*-literary, and how the present art products of one of the quickest, most sensitive, and most artistic races on earth are now only distinguished for their hideousness.

I shall endeavour to show that this failure of the Irish people in recent times has been largely brought about by that race diverging during this century from the right path, and ceasing to be Irish without becoming

English. I shall attempt to show that with the bulk of the people this change took place quite recently, much more recently than most people imagine, and is, in fact, still going on. I should also like to call attention to the illogical position of men who drop their own language to speak English, of men who translate their euphonious Irish names into English monosyllables, of men who read English books, and know nothing about Gaelic literature, nevertheless protesting as a matter of sentiment that they hate the country which at every hand's turn they rush to imitate.

It has always been very curious to me how Irish sentiment sticks in this half-way house – how it continues to apparently hate the English, and at the same time continues to imitate them; how it continues to clamour for recognition as a distinct nationality, and at the same time throws away with both hands what would make it so. If Irishmen only went a little farther they would become good Englishmen in sentiment also. But – illogical as it seems – there seems not the slightest sign or probability of their taking that step. It is the curious certainty that come what may Irishmen will continue to resist English rule, even though it should be for their good, which prevents many of our nation from becoming Unionists upon the spot. It is a fact, and we must face it as a fact, that although they adopt English habits and copy England in every way, the great bulk of Irishmen and Irishwomen over the whole world are known to be filled with a dull, ever-abiding animosity against her, and – right or wrong – to grieve when she prospers, and joy when she is hurt. Such movements as Young Irelandism, Fenianism, Land Leaguism, and Parliamentary obstruction seem always to gain their sympathy and support. It is just because there appears no earthly chance of their becoming good members of the Empire that I urge that they should not remain in the anomalous position they are in, but since they absolutley refuse to become the one thing, that they become the other; cultivate what they have rejected, and build up an Irish nation on Irish lines.

But you ask, why should we wish to make Ireland more Celtic than it is – why should we de-Anglicise it at all.

I answer because the Irish race is at present in a most anomalous position, imitating England and yet apparently hating it. How can it produce anything good in literature, art, or institutions as long as it is actuated by motives so contradictory? Besides, I believe it is our Gaelic past which, though the Irish race does not recognise it just at present, is really at the bottom of the Irish heart, and prevents us becoming citizens of the Empire, as, I think, can be easily proved.

To say that Ireland has not prospered under English rule is simply a truism; all the world admits it, England does not deny it. But the English retort is ready. You have not prospered they say, because you would not settle down contentedly, like the Scotch, and form part of the empire. 'Twenty years of good, resolute, grand-fatherly government,' said a well-known Englishman, will solve the Irish question. He possibly made the period too short, but let us suppose this. Let us suppose for a moment – which is impossible – that there were to arise a series of Cromwells in England for the space of one hundred years, able administrators of the Empire, careful rulers of Ireland, developing to the utmost our national resources, whilst they unremittingly stamped out every spark of national feeling, making Ireland a land of wealth and factories, whilst they extinguished every thought and every idea that was Irish, and left us, at last, after a hundred years of good government, fat, wealthy, and populous, but with all our characteristics gone, with every external that at present differentiates us from the English lost or dropped; all our Irish names of places and people turned into English names; the Irish language completely extinct; the O's and the Macs dropped; our Irish intonation changed, as far as possible by English schoolmasters into something English; our history no longer remembered or taught; the names of our rebels and martyrs blotted out; our battlefields and traditions forgotten; the fact that we were not of Saxon origin dropped out of sight and memory, and now let me put the question – How many Irishmen are there who would purchase material prosperity at such a price? It is exactly such a question as this and the answer to it which shows the difference between the English and the Irish race. Nine Englishmen out of ten would jump to make the exchange, and I as firmly believe that nine Irishmen out of ten would indignantly refuse it.

And yet this awful idea of complete Anglicisation which I have here put before you in all its crudity, is, and has been, making silent inroads upon us for nearly a century. . . .

What we must endeavour to never forget is this, that the Ireland of today is the descendant of the Ireland of the seventh century; then the school of Europe and the torch of learning. It is true that Northmen made some minor settlements in it in the ninth and tenth centuries, it is true that the Normans made extensive settlements during the succeeding centuries, but none of those broke the continuity of the social life of the island. Dane and Norman drawn to the kindly Irish breast issued forth in a generation or two fully Irished, and more Hibernian than the Hibernians themselves, and even after the Cromwellian plantation the children of numbers of the English soldiers who settled in the south and midlands, were, after forty years' residence, and after marrying Irish wives, turned into good Irishmen, and unable to speak a word of English, while several Gaelic poets of the last century have, like Father English, the most unmistakably English names. In two points only was the continuity of the Irishism of Ireland damaged. First, in the north-east of Ulster, where the Gaelic race was expelled and the land planted with aliens, whom our dear mother Erin, assimilative as she is, found it difficult to absorb, and in the ownership of the land, eight-ninths of which belongs to people many of whom always lived, or live, abroad, and not half of whom Ireland can be said to have assimilated.

During all this time the continuation of Erin's national life centred, according to our way of looking at it, not so much in the Cromwellian or Williamite landowners who sat in College Green, and governed the country, as in the mass of the people whom Dean Swift considered might be entirely neglected, and looked upon as hewers of wood and drawers of water; the men who, nevertheless, constituted the real working population, and who were living on in the hopes of better days; the men who have since made America, and have within the last ten years proved what an important factor they may be in wrecking or in building the British Empire. These are the men of whom our merchants, artisans, and farmers mostly consist, and in whose hands is today the making or marring of an Irish nation. But, alas, *quantum mutatus ab illo!* What the battleaxe of the Dane, the sword of the Norman, the wile of the Saxon were unable to perform, we have accomplished ourselves. We have at last broken the continuity of Irish life, and just at the moment when the Celtic race is presumably about to largely recover possession of its own country, it finds itself deprived and stript of its Celtic characteristics, cut off from the past, yet scarcely in touch with the present. It has lost since the beginning of this century almost all that connected it with the era of Cuchullain and of Ossian, that connected it with the Christianisers of Europe, that connected it with Brian Boru and the heroes of Clontarf, with the O'Neills and O'Donnells, with Rory O'More, with the Wild Geese, and even to some extent with the men of '98. It has lost all that they had – language, traditions, music, genius, and ideas. Just when we should be starting to build up anew the Irish race and the Gaelic nation – as within our own recollection Greece has been built up anew – we find ourselves despoiled of the bricks of nationality. The old bricks that lasted eighteen hundred years are destroyed; we must now set to, to bake new ones, if we can, on other ground and of other clay. Imagine for a moment the restoration of a German-speaking Greece.

The bulk of the Irish race really lived in the closest contact with the traditions of the past and the national life of nearly eighteen hundred years, until the beginning of this century. Not only so, but during the whole of the dark Penal times they produced among themselves a most vigorous literary development. Their schoolmasters and wealthy farmers, unwearied scribes, produced innumerable manuscripts in beautiful writing, each letter separated from another as in Greek, transcripts both of the ancient literature of their sires and of the more modern literature produced by themselves. Until the beginning of the present century there was no county, no barony, and I may almost say, no townland which did not boast of an Irish poet, the people's representative of those ancient bards who died out with the extirpation of the great Milesian families. The literary activity of even the eighteenth century among the gaels was very great, not in the South alone, but also in Ulster – the number of poets it produced was something astonishing. It did not, however, produce many works in gaelic prose, but it propagated translations of many pieces from the French, Latin, Spanish, and English. Every well-to-do farmer could read and write Irish, and many of them could understand even archaic Irish. I have myself heard persons reciting the poems of Donogha More O'Daly, Abbot of Boyle, in Roscommon, who died sixty years before Chaucer was born. To this very day the people have a word for archaic Irish, which is much the same as though Chaucer's poems were handed down amongst the English peasantry, but required a special training to understand. This training, however, nearly every one of fair education during the Penal times possessed, nor did they begin to lose their Irish training and knowledge until after the establishment of Maynooth and the rise of O'Connell. These two events made an end of the Gaelicism of the Gaelic race, although a great number of scribes and poets existed even down to the forties and fifties of the present century, and a few may linger on yet in remote localities. But it may be said, roughly speaking, that the ancient Gaelic civilisation died with O'Connell, largely, I am afraid, owing to his example and his neglect of inculcating the necessity of keeping alive racial customs, language, and traditions, in which with the one notable exception of our scholarly idealist, Smith O'Brien, he has been followed until a year ago by almost every leader of the Irish race. . . .

In fact, I may venture to say, that, up to the beginning of the present century, neither man, woman, nor child of the Gaelic race, either of high blood or low blood, existed in Ireland who did not either speak Irish or understand it. But within the last ninety years we have, with an unparalleled frivolity, deliberately thrown away our birthright and Anglicised ourselves. None of the children of those people of whom I have spoken know Irish, and the race will from henceforth be changed; for as Monsieur Jubainville says of the influence of Rome upon Gaul, England 'has definitely conquered us, she has even imposed upon us her language, that is to say, the form of our thoughts during every instant of our existence'. It is curious that those who most fear West Britonism have so eagerly consented to imposing upon the Irish race what, according to Jubainville, who in common with all the great scholars of the continent, seems to regret it very much, is 'the form of our thoughts during every instant of our existence.'

So much for the greatest stroke of all in our Anglicisation, the loss of our language. I have often heard people thank God that if the English gave us nothing they gave us at least their language. In this way they put a bold face upon the matter, and pretend that the Irish language *is* not worth knowing, and has no literature. But the Irish language *is* worth knowing, or why would the greatest philologists of Germany, France, and Italy be emulously studying it, and it *does* possess a literature, or why would a German savant have made the calculation that the books written in Irish between the eleventh and seventeenth centuries, and still extant, would fill a thousand octavo volumes.

I have no hesitation at all in saying that every Irish-feeling Irishman, who hates the reproach of West-Britonism, should set himself to encourage the efforts which are being made to keep alive our once great national tongue. The losing of it is our greatest blow, and the sorest stroke that the rapid Anglicisation of Ireland has inflicted upon us. In order to de-Anglicise ourselves we must at once arrest the decay of the language. We must bring pressure on our politicians not to snuff it out by their tacit discouragement merely because they do not happen themselves to understand it. We must arouse some spark of patriotic inspiration among the peasantry who still use the language, and put an end to the shameful state of feeling – a thousand-tongued reproach to our leaders and statesmen – which makes young men and women blush and hang their heads when overheard speaking their own language. Maynooth has at last come splendidly to the front, and it is now incumbent upon every clerical student to attend lectures in the Irish language and history during the first three years of his course. But in order to keep the Irish language alive where it is still spoken – which is the utmost we can at present aspire to – nothing less than a house-to-house visitation and exhortation of the people themselves will do, something – though with a very different purpose – analogous to the procedure that James Stephens adopted throughout Ireland when he found her like a corpse on the dissecting table. This and some system of giving medals or badges of honour to every family who will guarantee that they have always spoken Irish amongst themselves during the year. But, unfortunately, distracted as we are and torn by contending factions, it is impossible to find either men or money to carry out this simple remedy, although to a dispassionate foreigner – to a Zeuss, Jubainville, Zimmer, Kuno Meyer, Windisch, or Ascoli, and the rest – this is of greater importance than whether Mr.Redmond or Mr.McCarthy lead the largest wing of the Irish party for the moment, or Mr So-and-So succeed with his election petition. To a person taking a bird's-eye-view of the situation a hundred or five hundred years hence, believe me, it will also appear of greater importance than any mere temporary wrangle, but, unhappily, our countrymen cannot be brought to see this.

We can, however, insist, and we *shall* insist if Home Rule be carried, that the Irish language, which so many foreign scholars of the first calibre find so worthy of study, shall be placed on a par with – or even above – Greek, Latin, and modern languages, in all examinations held under the Irish Government. We can also insist, and we *shall* insist, that in those baronies where the children speak Irish, Irish shall be taught, and that Irish-speaking schoolmasters, petty sessions clerks, and even magistrates be appointed in Irish-speaking districts. If all this were done, it should not be very difficult, with the aid of the foremost foreign scholars, to bring about a tone of thought which would make it disgraceful for an educated Irishman – especially of the old Celtic race, MacDermotts, O'Conors, O'Sullivans, MacCarthys, O'Neills – to be ignorant of his own language – would make it at least as disgraceful as for an educated Jew to be quite ignorant of Hebrew.

6.8 'The Loss of the Irish Language and Its Influence on the Catholic Religion in Ireland', Henry Morris, 1898

[I note] the veneration that is due to [Irish] by reason of its close and inseparable connection with holy Faith, with which it has travelled hand in hand, influencing and being influenced, through the long span of fourteen hundred years. . . . This is why it behoves Irish Catholics of today to pause and consider is it their duty, is there any moral obligation on them to preserve the Irish language merely and solely *for the sake of their religion* . . . I will not speak here of the baneful effects of English literature – Protestant, infidel, immoral; or of subjecting the intellect of a soulful, spiritual people like the Irish to that of a sordid, worldly race like the English by adopting their language and literature . . . Irish is pre-eminently the language of prayer and devotion. Its dignity and impressive majesty admirably suit the themes of religion . . . it has for Catholics an altogether peculiar interest common to themselves alone.

6.9 'The "Irish" Literary Theatre', P.H.Pearse, 1899

Ireland is notoriously a land of contradictions and shams, and of Irish contradictions and shams Dublin is assuredly the hot-bed. We have in the capital of Ireland 'Irish' national newspapers whose only claim to nationality is that they run down – whilst they imitate – everything English; we have 'Irish' politicians who in heart and soul are as un-Irish as Professor Mahaffy; we have a 'national' Literary Society, which is as anti-national, without being so outspoken, as Trinity College. Apparently, the only thing necessary to make a man or an institution Irish is a little dab of green displayed now and again to relieve the monotony, a little eloquent twaddle about the 'children of the Gael,' or a little meaningless vapouring about some unknown quantity termed 'Celtic glamour.' Take away the dab of green, strip off the 'leafy luxury' of words, and what have you? The man or the institution is as English as Lord Salisbury. Newspapers, politicians, literary societies, all are but forms of one gigantic heresy, a heresy of the deadliest and most insidious kind, a heresy that, like a poison, has eaten its way into the vitals of Irish nationality, that has paralysed the nation's energy and its intellect. That heresy is the idea that there can be an Ireland, that there can be an Irish literature, an Irish social life, whilst the language of Ireland is English.

And lo! just as the country is beginning to see through the newspapers and the literary societies, here we have the Anglo-Irish heresy springing up in a new form, the 'Irish' Literary Theatre. Save the mark! Much ink has been spilled in our newspaper offices over this same 'Irish' Literary Theatre, but I note that not a single 'national' daily impeaches it on the only ground on which, details apart, it is impeachable – namely, that literature written in English cannot be Irish. Why waste time in criticising stray expressions when the whole thing is an imposture, a fraud, a heresy? Had Mr.Yeats and his friends called their venture the 'English Literary Theatre,' or simply 'The Literary Theatre,' I should have been the last in the world to object to it. But in the name of common sense, why dub it 'Irish?' Why not select Hindoo, Chinese, Hottentot, or Eskimo? None of these, of course, would be true, for a play in English, if it is literature at all, must be English literature; but any one of them would be quite as appropriate as 'Irish.' What claim have these two English plays to be called Irish literature? None in the world, save that the scene of each of them is laid in Ireland. Is, then, 'Timon of Athens' Greek literature? Is 'Romeo and Juliet' Italian literature? Is 'Quentin Durward' French literature? Is the 'Vision of Don Roderick' Spanish literature? When Greece, Italy, France and Spain claim these works as their respective properties, then may Ireland claim 'The Countess Cathleen' and 'The Heather Field' as her own.

The 'Irish' Literary Theatre is, in my opinion, more dangerous, because less glaringly anti-national than Trinity College. If once we admit the Irish literature in English idea, then the language movement is a mistake. Mr.Yeats' precious 'Irish' Literary Theatre may, if it develops, give the Gaelic League more trouble than the Atkinson-Mahaffy combination. Let us strangle it at its birth. Against Mr.Yeats personally we have nothing to object. He is a mere English poet of the third or fourth rank, and as such he is harmless. But when he attempts to run an 'Irish' Literary Theatre it is time for him to be crushed.

6.10 'Irish in County Wexford', Donnchadh Ruadh, *An Claidheamh Solius*,1899

For my own part I believe the priests are more to blame for the decay of Irish than any other class of the population. . . . The priests are to blame as a body for their attitudes towards English . . . I would not have the people look expectant to their Parish Priests to take the initiative in the language movement. As a spiritual guide the Irish priest needs little defence in this world or the next, but they who speak of him as a leader in any political or allied sense talk pure nonsense. He never even joins any secular movement till it is well under way, and then, in order to retain his spiritual influence, he places himself in front and gets pushed along. Consequently the Irish people are better trained to die than trained to live. Let the language move therefore; the priests will soon be its greatest helpers. Up to this they have had sore temptation to be English. They are gentlemen by position and education, and 'tis long since Irish was fashionable in Ireland. . . .

I may here remark that the W.D.& L. Railway seems to have trailed something of English taste right through the county, and the influence is felt on both sides of the line to a breadth of some miles. . . . There is nothing necessarily English about a railway of course, but 'tis a mark of progress, and so is English thought to be unfortunately.

6.11 Letter to *The Leader*, W.B.Yeats, 1900

Dear [D.P.Moran],

I look upon THE LEADER as of importance, for it will express, I understand, and for the first time, the loves and hates, the hopes and fears, the thoughts and ideals of the men who have made the Irish language a political power. *Claidheamh Soluis* and *Fainne an Lae*, because of their preoccupation with the language itself, have been unable to make that free comment on the life about them, which the times require, if illusions that were, perhaps, truths in their day are not to cling about us and drown us. Ireland is at the close of a long period of hesitation, and must set out before long under a new policy, and it is right that any man who has anything to say should speak clearly and candidly while she is still hesitating. I myself believe that unless a great foreign war comes to re-make everything, we must be prepared to turn from a purely political nationalism with the land question as its lever, to a partly intellectual and historical nationalism like that of Norway, with the language question as its lever. . . . We must not feel anxious because the new movement has taken a firmer hold in the towns than in the country places, for very many of the priesthood are coming to understand that the Irish language is the only barrier against the growing atheism of England, just as we men of letters have come to understand that it is the only barrier against the growing vulgarity of England; and the priesthood can do what they like with the country places. In ten years or in fifteen years or in twenty years the new movement will be strong enough to shake governments, and unlike previous movements that have shaken governments, it will give continuity to public life in Ireland, and make all other righteous movements the more easy.

I do not think that I am very likely to differ very seriously from you and your readers about this movement, and for the very reason that it is a national movement, a movement that can include the most different minds. I must now, however, discuss another matter, about which I have differed and may still differ from you and from many of your readers.

Side by side with the spread of the Irish language, and with much writing in
the Irish language, must go on much expression of Irish emotion and Irish
thought, much writing about Irish things and people, in the English language, for no man can write well except in the language he has been born
and bred to, and no man, as I think, becomes perfectly cultivated except
through the influence of that language; and this writing must for a long
time to come be the chief influence in shaping the opinions and the
emotions of the leisured classes in Ireland in so far as they are concerned
with Irish things, and the more sincere it is, the more lofty it is, the more
beautiful it is, the more will the general life of Ireland be sweetened by its
influence, through its influence over a few governing minds. It will always
be too separate from the general life of Ireland to influence it directly, and
it was chiefly because I believed this that I differed so strongly in 1892 and
1893 from Sir Charles Gavan Duffy and his supporters, who wished to give
such writing an accidental and fleeting popularity by uniting it with politics
and economics. I believe that Ireland cannot have a Burns or a Dickens,
because the mass of the people cease to understand any poetry when they
cease to understand the Irish language, which is the language of their
imagination, and because the middle class is the great supporter and origi-
nator of the more popular kind of novels, and we have no middle class to
speak of; but I believe that we may have a poetry like that of Wordsworth
and Shelley and Keats, and a prose like that of Meredith and Pater and
Ruskin. There will be a few of all classes who will read this kind of literature, but the rest will read and listen to the songs of some wandering
Raftery or of some poet like Dr.Hyde, who has himself high culture, but
makes his songs out of the thoughts and emotions he finds everywhere
about him, and out of the circumstances of a life that is kept poetical by a
still useful language, or they will go to perdition with their minds stuffed
full of English vulgarity; till perhaps a time has come when no Irishman
need write in any but his own language.

We can bring that day nearer by not quarreling about names, and by not
bringing to literary discussion, which needs a delicate and careful temper,
the exasperated and violent temper we have learned from a century of
political discussion. You have decided, and rightly, considering your purpose, to call all 'literature concerning Ireland written in English,' 'Anglo-
Irish literature,' and I shall certainly do the same when I would persuade a
man that nothing written in English can unite him perfectly to the past
and future of his country, but I will certainly call it Irish literature, for
short, when I would persuade him that 'Farewell to Ballyshannon and the
Winding Banks of Erne' should be more to him than 'The Absent-Minded
Beggar,' or when I am out of temper with all hyphenated words, or with
all names that are a mixture of Latin and English. Such things are governed
by usage and convenience, and I do not foresee a day when there will not be
Englishmen who will call Walt Whitman English literature, and merely

because they like him, and Englishmen who will call him American literature, and merely because they dislike him. And I would be sorry to see a
day when I should not find a certain beautiful sermon of St.Columbanus,
which compares life to a roadway on which we journey for a little while,
and to the rising and falling of smoke, in accounts of Irish literature, as
well as in accounts of the Latin literature of the Early Church. . . .

In Ireland, too, it may be those very men, who have made a subtle
personal way of expressing themselves, instead of being content with
English as it is understood in the newspapers, or who see all things reflected
in their own souls, which are from the parent fountain of their race, instead
of filling their work with the circumstance of a life which is dominated by
England, who may be recognised in the future as most Irish, though their
own time entangled in the surfaces of things may often think them lacking
in everything that is Irish. The delicate, obscure, mysterious song of my
friend, 'A.E.,' which has, as I know, comforted the wise and beautiful when
dying, but has hardly come into the hands of the middle class – I use the
word to describe an attitude of mind more than an accident of birth – and
has no obviously Irish characteristics, may be, or rather must be, more Irish
than any of those books of stories or of verses which reflect so many
obviously Irish characteristics that every newspaper calls them, in the
trying phrase of 1845, 'racy of the soil!'

6.12 *The True National Ideal*, Revd M.P.O'Hickey, n.d. [?1900]

This brings us once more face to face with the question proposed at the
outset – what is a nation? Or, in other words, what is nationality? I reply
by two quotations – one from a former lecture of my own; the other from a
passage in the lecture referred to: 'Nationality is not anything actually
concreted. It is the soul, "the very breath," the vivifying principle, the
whole atmosphere and environment of a distinctive people. It is the outcome, the resultant, the culmination of many things, of which political
autonomy is but one – very important doubtless, but by no means the
only, or even the chief, thing to be considered. You may have a nation without political autonomy – not, I admit, a nation in all its fullness and
integrity; but I emphatically insist that autonomous institutions, failing all
the other elements and landmarks of nationality, do not constitute a nation
in the true sense'. So far I quote my own words; I now proceed to quote
from those of another: 'Nationality . . . is the spirit which makes men
citizens, which knits them together for the common weal. The nation is
the sum of all the characteristics of all the individuals now existing within
it. But it is more. It is the heir of all the ages, and it is the resultant of all
the generations that lived and worked since the nation began to be.

A common tradition, a common history, a common language, a common literature, common institutions, common sorrows and common joys, common hopes and common aspirations – these things make up a nation, these things shape its destiny, these things determine its place in civilisation. If a people grow weak in any of these essentials, it is losing its nationality, it is drifting from its moorings. It may succeed in politics, in manufactures, in commerce, but the nation is passing away.'

The elements of nationality, therefore, are numerous. All are useful. All in greater or less degree, colour nationality, influence it, mould it, make it more distinctive. But to the essence of nationhood some are vital. Amongst the essentials of nationality, understood aright, none is more fundamental, none more important, none strikes deeper roots, none is more far-reaching in its results, than a national language. This truth the Dutch clearly grasped, and have enshrined in a proverb – 'No language, no nation.'

But a nation's language is more – much more – than a mere element of nationality. It is its most striking symbol – the one invincible barrier against national disintegration. A distinct language is the surest and most powerful bond of a distinctive nationality; its most effective bulwark; the most certain – indeed, the only certain – guarantee of its continuance and perpetuation. But a nation's language thus regarded, should not be looked at merely in itself. It should be looked at in conjunction with all that it imports, holds and enshrines – all that it carries down the stream of time from the dim and distant, the storied and centuried past. It should be regarded as the vehicle of the people's history; the key to their polity and jurisprudence; the mirror in which their mind, manners and customs are reflected; the shrine of their legends, myths, beliefs and superstitions; the repository of their literature; the only reliable index to the national life of the past. For all this, and much more, a people's language is. . . .

One thing is fairly certain. The Anglicisation of Ireland can never be absolutely completed. The Celt can never be wholly merged into the Saxon. History, divergent interests, and a thousand things beside, forbid it. Should we lose our national identity, we shall become at best but a mongrel race – neither Celts nor Saxons. We may, to all intents and purposes, cease to be Gaels; we may, in a sense, become West Britons; further we cannot go – Saxons we cannot become. Should the worst befall, it were better, in my opinion, to be something that could be clearly defined and classed; for anything at all would seem preferable to a mongrel, colourless, nondescript racial monstrosity evolved somewhere in the bosom of the twentieth century. If then the process of change is to continue, better far that the assimilation or absorption should be complete. We should then be something definite and distinctive. But complete absorption being, as I conceive, impossible, we are compelled to choose between retaining our national identity, and becoming a mongrel race – without a history and without a future, without the good qualities or special characteristics of Celt, or Saxon, or any other people. 'They who trample upon the past,' says Davis, 'do not build for the future.'

Do I wish then that we should go back upon the past? In a certain sense, I do wish it most assuredly – wish it with all my heart and soul. I wish that we should study the past; that we should safeguard our national continuity. I wish that, as a race, we should ever remain in all essentials what the past has made us; that we should guard and perpetuate our national landmarks; that we should preserve our national and racial characteristics; that we should cherish and revere our past – study it, know it, love it.

6.13 *The Irish Language and Irish Intermediate Education*, Gaelic League, n.d. [?1900]

[Extract from the evidence of Revd J.P.Mahaffy, D.D., F.T.C.D., Professor of Ancient History, Trinity College Dublin.]

653. CHAIRMAN. – I see, Dr.Mahaffy, that in your paper you refer to the subject of Celtic as one of the subjects for examination? – Yes.

654. Now, Celtic is, of course, a very interesting study from a philological point of view? – Yes.

655. In your opinion, viewing it as a living language, has it any educational value? – None. I am corroborated by the experts in this book, one of whom finds fault with the text books at present used, or one of them, on the grounds that it is either silly or indecent. I am told by a much better authority than any in Irish, that it is impossible to get hold of a text of Irish which is not religious, or which does not suffer from one or other of the objections referred to. Another specialist is the Todd lecturer in the Royal Irish Academy, Mr.Gwynn. He states that the twenty years' study under the Intermediate system has, in fact, diminished the knowledge of Irish in this country, and that there is less knowledge of Irish at the present time than there was twenty years ago.

656. I don't want at all to undervalue Irish as a subject of study if studied in the proper way, but is it your view that its only real value as a study is in a philological sense, as it is taught, I believe, in some of the German universities? – It is sometimes useful to a man fishing for salmon or shooting grouse in the West. I have often found a few words very serviceable.

657. But as a subject to be seriously taken up by students whose time is of importance to them, whose condition in life, does not permit their parents to allow sufficient time for their education, so that every moment is of importance, are you not of the opinion that Celtic is

a subject that should be entered on at all by them? – I think it is a mischievous waste of time.

6.14 *Irishwomen and the Home Language*, Mary E.L.Butler, n.d. [?1901]

As an Irishwoman, I appeal to Irishwomen on a subject of vital importance to the country to which we have the honour to belong. . . .

A spiritual possession can only be taken from us by our own free will, and the language is a spiritual possession. To their bitter shame and grief the Irish people stood passively by while the language, that priceless heritage, was 'slipping into the grave'. But what they lost they may regain by the exercise of will power. No government, no 'Educational' Board, no dolts or bigots of an alien ascendancy party, can thwart their purpose. The people, as they have been recently told, have the power in this case absolutely in their own hands.

What then remains to be said when this view has been forcibly and convincingly put before the public? One thing remains to be said. This power is in the hands of the whole people of Ireland, it is true, but it is in an especial manner in the hands of the women of Ireland. Why? because this language movement is not an academic one. It is a living one. What is wanted is to make the language living in the land; to do this it is necessary to make it the home language; and to make it the home language it is necessary to enlist the co-operation of woman – the home maker. Home makers of Ireland, make Irish the home language. You, and you alone, can do it. This is the issue to be placed before our countrywomen. The heavy responsibility rests with them of deciding the fate of the language, and with it the fate of the nation, the existence of which is inextricably bound up with it. How are they going to acquit themselves of this responsibility?

This movement in which Irishwomen are now earnestly asked to join, is frequently described as 'the language war,' and rightly so. It is a war to the death between Irish ideals and British sordid soulessness.

Now, the women of our race are dignified and decorous; they shrink from mingling in a melee, and retiring into the inner courtyard, they leave the scene of strife in the outer world to the sterner sex. They may think, therefore, that in this language war they have no place. But they are mistaken, for it is warfare of an especial kind, warfare which can best be waged not by shrieking viragoes or aggressive amazons, but by gentle, low-voiced women who teach little children their first prayers, and, seated at the hearth-side, make those around them realise the difference between a home and a dwelling. To most Irish people it is extremely distasteful to see a woman mount a platform and hold forth in public. We are the most conservative people in the world, and the deeply rooted conviction regarding the desirability of women acting a retiring part is not likely to be eradicated.

195

Let it then be thoroughly understood that when Irishwomen are invited to take part in the language movement, they are not required to plunge into the vortex of public life. No, the work which they can best do is work to be done at home. Their mission is to make the homes of Ireland Irish. If the homes are Irish the whole country will be Irish. The spark struck on the hearth-stone will fire the soul of the nation. . . .

The man of the house goes abroad every day for business or pleasure, the woman stays at home, as a rule. What is she doing all day long? Many things; but one thing incessantly. Let it be written in capital letters – TALKING. When the man of the house goes out in the morning he leaves her talking, and when he comes home in the evening he finds her still talking to those about her. It must be recognised, therefore, that what this indefatigable talker talks about, and through what medium she conveys her ideas, is important. She is bound to talk about something in some way or other. It is necessary to ensure that she is talking about the right things in the right way. Verily, a language movement is of all movements one in which woman is fitted to take part. . . .

What an inspiriting work for Irishwomen to put their hand to. When they have nationalised the home circle – it is here that their work must start – they may then nationalise the social sphere, and convert the atmosphere of an imitative, petty, provincial town, into that of a proud capital, living its own life, originating its own ideas and customs, speaking its native speech, setting not following a lead in every sphere of life, literary, artistic, industrial and social. While the men are striving for a native seat of government, the women might so mould the tone of life in the metropolis, that when the day of political independence arrives, it may be found that the parliament House is situated in a genuine capital, the home of a true nation. . . .

It may be useful to give in conclusion a summary of a few of the methods by which Irishwomen may help the Irish language movement. One thing must be borne in mind – 'The only gift is a portion of thyself'. Let Irishwomen then not only advocate the following principles but act up to them.

SOME SUGGESTIONS AS TO HOW IRISHWOMEN MAY HELP THE IRISH
LANGUAGE MOVEMENT

1. Realise what it means to be an Irishwoman, and make others realise what that means by being Irish in fact as well as name.
2. Make the home atmosphere Irish.
3. Make the social atmosphere Irish.
4. Speak Irish if you know it, especially in the home circle, and if you have no knowledge of the language, set about acquiring it at once. If you only know a little, speak that little.
5. Insist on children learning to speak, read, and write Irish.

6. Insist on school authorities giving pupils the benefit of a thoroughly Irish education.
7. Use Irish at the family prayers.
8. Give Irish names to children.
9. Visit Irish-speaking districts. If Irish people who are students of the language go among their Irish-speaking fellow country-people in the right spirit, and instil the right principles into them, they will be conferring a benefit upon the people, and the people will in return confer a benefit on them by imparting their native knowledge of the spoken language to them.
10. Encourage Irish music and song.
11. Support Irish publications and Irish literature.
12. Employ Irish-speaking servants wherever possible.
13. Join the Gaelic League and induce others to do so.
14. Spread the light among your acquaintances.
15. Consistently support everything Irish, and consistently withold your support from everything un-Irish.

6.15 *The Irish Language Movement: Its Philosophy*, Revd Patrick Forde, n.d. [?1901]

The science of Ethnology, as you know, enquires into the laws that govern the origin and growth of racial diversities, how the many races of men who now inhabit this globe differ, and came to differ, from one another. For it is noticed that each nation has a character and a language of its own, has its own peculiar and characteristic gifts of body and soul, of mind and heart. In this science two principles are looked on as fundamental: that of Environment, which explains how national character is influenced by the soil, climate and scenery of the common Fatherland; and that of Heredity, which tells that children are like their parents, that each generation hands on to the generations that follow the total racial character, the whole national inheritance, as modified by its own peculiar experience. One of the most valuable means of studying national character is the national language; scientists find a real intrinsic connection between the two. To appreciate the significance of this last point you should bear in mind that science deals with the fixed laws of nature, not with accidental or random conventions.

We learned from Aubrey de Vere the important lesson that each nation has been sent by God to do a special and peculiar work, for which the whole circle of its characteristic endowments is but the qualifying equipment, while its actual history is merely the fulfilment of that work. Therefore, each nation has its own country and its own soul, its own language and its own liberty given to it by Almighty God, as the means whereby the Divine plan is to be wrought out. This view of the subject, which is perfectly true, and which contains in itself all that I have to say upon it, should give pause to the good people who say that a nation's language is an unimportant matter. Still, it is contended that after all, language in general is but a secondary thing, that words are merely conventional instruments which we may use as we like, that ideas are wholly independent of them, and that ideas alone are our prime concern. Men who speak thus plume themselves upon their sound common sense and practical wisdom, and therefore they cannot reasonably shrink from a friendly debate on the merits of the question.

Rational language in general is the expression of human thoughts and emotions by means of articulate sounds; it is the use you make of your own organism to show forth what you think and feel in your own soul. Now, thought and feeling are evidently of their very essence wholly personal and characteristic things, the kind and quality of which will necessarily depend upon the special gifts and susceptibilities of each individual; each man will think and feel in his own way, which will be unlike that of other men, except in so far as those others resemble him in constitution, physical, mental and moral. Now, it is noticed that there is a very special resemblance of this kind between members of the same race, a likeness of physical confor-mation, and a likeness of thought, feeling, general behaviour, and deport-ment. The sum total of all these peculiar resemblances constitutes the racial type, the peculiar racial endowment in body and soul, in mind and heart. Ultimately these likenesses are family likenesses, resemblances between men who are in a true sense brethren. They are descended from a common ancestry, they live together on the same land which is their common home, they have the same things to think about, they look at things from the same standpoint, and so there is a racy way of looking at things and being affected by them, modes of thought and feeling that are racy of the soil. But how is the living multitude to be bound together in social unity without a common language? This is the first and chief function of language – to be the bond of social unity, to give rational coherence to the dumb voiceless crowd. Clearly, therefore, language will not only share in the social peculiarities, but will also be in itself one of the most prominent of those peculiarities, and the most important of their sustaining causes. But how is racial unity of speech determined? Members of the same race, as we have seen, have quite the same things to say – the same peculiar thoughts and feelings that demand utterance; and, on the other hand, their organs of speech are alike also, and will, therefore, under pressure of similar inward experiences, be likely to utter similar articulate sounds. But will they be certain to do so in virtue of any definite natural law? . . . God gave us language for this precise purpose of conveying our ideas and feelings to one another; it is, as we shall see, a practical necessity of man's intellectual and social nature; moreover, every nation has ever had a distinct language of its own. It is hard to conceive how these things can be all accounted for by mere random caprice without any definite law. . . .

Clearly then it cannot be a wholly indifferent matter what language is used for the education of an individual or a nation. National education is the natural, and therefore, the best system of education, both for the individual and the community. It is the only possible preservative of national continuity. National continuity consists in the abiding presence of national thought and feeling – of national ideals and ways of realising them, of national ways of looking at things and being affected by them. These things form a nation's soul, and the nation lives in them while generations of men pass away; they are handed down from generation to generation; they are learned in the home, in the schools, in the crowded thoroughfares, in the highways and by-ways, wherever man meets and speaks to his brother man. Like some subtle essence they pervade every utterance of men; they live in proverb and song and tale; they are taught in history and romance, in art and music, in business and in recreation. Without these things the nation cannot live. But they cannot live without the nation's language. The nation lives not, the nation does not energise among men unless she utter forth her message in her own authentic voice. . . .

But what are we, what is the Irish nation? Are we simply a badly treated crowd of English colonists, whose highest ambition is to be even as Yorkshire or Surrey? Do the so-called blessings of Protestant English liberty suffice for us? Or are we on the other hand, a totally distinct and wholly superior race, ever zealous for the better gifts that God made the soul of man to desire and enjoy, clinging ever to the spirit-world, ever willing to yield up for the good things unseen, not alone the grosser clay, in virtue of which inferior souls are proud and boastful, but every sweet and goodly thing in God's fair world, aye, even the fair hills of holy Ireland? Are we mere planters and marchmen of the Pale, or are we Celts, Gaels, Irish? Oh, thank God, we know what we are; and may we realise the pressing duty that springs from that knowledge.

Gaels we all are, and therefore our only possible perfection consists in the development of the gaelic nature we have inherited from our forefathers. Centuries of real development, of true civilisation, of noble fidelity to all the ideals that men can worship, have fixed for ever the national character of Ireland; and if we be not true to that character, if we be not genuine Irishmen, we can never be perfect men, full and strong men, able to do a true man's part for God and Fatherland.

6.16 *The Threatening Metempsychosis of a Nation*, Revd John M. O'Reilly, 1901

The situation is this: that the English mind is coming upon us, slowly and unperceivedly, it may be, but with a fateful certain progress that can only prosper by our denial or doubt of it. By little and little that which made us ourselves is being erased in us, and its place being taken by the erasing force. The erasing force is the English mind. This process is sometimes called assimilation; but we shall not pause upon words – the thing meant is the same.

The Irish mind, away back in its most pagan days, was emphatically and eminently a mind inclining towards religion. It was chaste, idealistic, mystical. It was spiritual beyond the ways of men; and it could not rest, or live, without contact with the other world; without the conviction of some ideal hereafter. It was clean of heart, and saw God darkly, and from afar, if you will, but with the invincible conviction of the clean heart's instinct. It was most dutiful and docile to parents. It was passionately loyal to chief, whether earthly lord or spiritual shepherd. Nor was loyalty a worded principle, whose terms might be questioned or cavilled at. It was a thing beyond words; it was a life-instinct; a force infinitely stronger and more enduring than theoretical convictions. The Irish mind was the most kindly and towardly soil ever known under the sun for the seed of the Gospel to fall upon. That seed fell at last and it grew, and it endured, and it remains, and we are here today in the strength of it, and our country is still a trumpeting witness for Christ in the wilderness of an almost re-paganised world. By an incomparable man the Word was planted upon incomparable soil – the mind of our race and nation. That mind has come down to us unstained by memories of revolt, unblemished by scoff or sarcasm against a solitary tittle of doctrine, in a language unpolluted with the very names of monstrosities of sin which are among the commonplaces of life in English-speaking countries. That Irish mind was loyalty itself to spiritual authority. It knew no envy of the influence of its pastors, and it never dreamt of invidious, malicious distinctions between the man and his office, between the doctrine and the person of the preacher; and this is a great part of the secret of the sound and splendid endurance of our faith to this day . . . and this is exactly what the English mind has always been jealous of. If England could destroy that loyalty of the Irish people to their pastors, there would be no further trouble about Home Rule. For she knows full well the truth of what Johnson said in effect: 'If you want to ensure infidelity, introduce disrespect of the ministers of religion.' But she has not succeeded very far in this direction yet in Ireland. The practical religion of the people's everyday life cannot be described, cannot be compared. The word sincere would be but a feeble and foolish word to apply to it. In fact their religion was not a thing to be reached by impersonal adjectives; it was part of their existence indissociable from their very selves. God joined it to their nature, and hence it has proved so hard for man to sunder it from their lives. The Catholic Church was the mistress of the Irish peasant.

It was in such minds and in such mouths the Irish language lived, and came down the centuries to our own day; and, as will be natural and inevitable to expect, the language that conveyed those minds into articulate sound, stands unmatched and unapproachable under the sun of living, breathing faith, for fecundity of religious thought, for a vocabulary incredibly copious and capable for religious expression. . . .

It may be objected that the actual splendid faith of our people was learned in the English tongue; but I answer, it was not learned in English, for it was not learned at all. You might nearly as well say we learned to be born, or learned to be our parents' children. Other people learn the faith – and forget it. That is the frequent fate of things learned. The Irish people do not forget their faith, just because they never learned it. Of course, we learned the articles and the doctrines of our creed, and we might forget the precise terms in which some of these doctrines are formulated; but the spirit and soul of the faith itself – that was in us in some deeper way than learning. The mind of this nation is still to a great extent the Irish language mind. But sixty years ago, the Irish language was the engine and factory of the people's thought, as well as the organ of its conveyance; and those people and the men who came immediately after them were Irish and Catholic in a way that we are undoubtedly not. It may have been in English they taught us our prayers, or our catechism; but it was not their words, it was their minds we felt; and their minds were Irish by race and root and constitution, and by the heredity of scores of centuries, and by all these forces combined in that one great soul-making force, the Irish language. Those minds imprinted not their words, but themselves on us. And this is the true explanation of the strong, sound faith which is still among us – the fact, namely, that though we speak English now, we got our faith direct from the Irish language mind.

But that state of things is most certainly changing, and faster than even a pessimist might believe, as the nature and stamp of the Irish mind is being gradually palimpsested, gradually erased and over-written by the spirit of the English tongue.

The character of the English mind ought to be fairly understood in Ireland, and yet I am half afraid to sketch it even slightly to this meeting. But it is a natural and unavoidable part of the trend of my argument to set forth something of the nature of that spirit, and how it is coming upon us, and I cannot shrink from doing so. If the English mind has virtues, it has enough tongues and pens to publish them, and can dispense with my services there. But as it bears on my purpose – and I speak not of exceptions, but of a general fact – as it bears on my purpose, it is a mind without God in the world. It is a fleshy spirit, bent towards earth; a mind unmannerly, vulgar, insolent, bigoted; a mind whose belly is its God, yet which cannot endure the world belly; a mind to which pride, and lust, and mammon are the matter-of-course aims of life, the only objects conceivably worthy of pursuit; a mind to which real Christian virtue is incredible, and sure to be set down as clever hypocrisy, or stark imbecility; a mind where every absurd device, from grossest Darwinism to most preposterous spiritualism, is resorted to and hoped in, to choke the voice of eternity in the conscience;

a mind to which the idea of a churchman possessing real, efficient, spiritual authority over his flock, would be unspeakably ludicrous. . . .

Present-day Irishmen of the noisy type, usually known as politicians, are mostly as prompt as the English themselves to see provoking absurdity and pernicious tendency in any attempt to hamper business with religion. Wherever they find religion a usable force, conducive in any way to their purposes, then religion is a good thing enough, and may be connived at in a politic sort of way. But these men are baited and exasperated to meet it in their path in its quality of a power claiming to question the methods, or the machinery of their purposes. They say it should be confined to a department, to preclude the chance of its becoming a nuisance, to insure its good behaviour. They formulate this in a phrase somewhat remote in sound from its real purpose – no priests in politics. That phrase means simply, keep religion out of life; it means the English mind. For the English mind is aptly summed up in that blotting out of 'Thou shalt not steal' from the Decalogue by the pirate in the play. When asked why he erased that precept, the pirate replied: 'Why, it was a commandment to command myself and my men from our functions – we put forth to steal.' Quite so, it was an obstacle to business, and had to be removed. The way of business must be kept clear, and business means just whatever we like, just whatever we want to do. This is exactly the English mind, and no less exactly the mind of 'No priests in politics.' That phrase could not be rendered into Irish idiom. The genius of the Gaelic tongue could no more assimilate it, than the human system could assimilate a dagger in the stomach.

In all this connection I have been viewing the Irish language as a barrier, and the only possible barrier, against the invading tide of English ideas. If this nation is to live on, or the Church of this nation, the Irish mind will have to be preserved; and to try to preserve it without the Irish tongue, is to endeavour to hold it while choosing the best means for letting it go. It is an imbecile dream, unworthy of the intelligence of a nation; and yet we seem unable to see it.

6.17 *The Reign of Humbug*, Agnes O'Farrelly, 1901

There is a vague something called 'cosmopolitanism' and it so happens that the educated youth of Ireland sigh after its dreamy expanse. It is the most senseless, yet, to my mind, the most elusive of present-day problems. I asked one of these 'cosmopolitans' one day what he meant exactly by the word. 'Well! you see,' he said, 'I can't say exactly what I mean, but it is something like this. I think it too petty to be talking of nationality when one belongs to the world in general. The people of every country should be the same to us as the people who happen to be about us.'

Then I asked him if he would advocate a universal kingdom. He thought that impossible, natural boundaries and different climates taken into consideration. 'Universal laws, then?' 'No; the same laws would not suit different races,' and he finally agreed that a universal language was the maddest of all Utopian schemes, the Volapuk, Esperanto, and other jargons being possible only in dreamland. But he still insisted on the idea of a 'universal brotherhood,' a fair-sounding phrase which might mean anything or might mean nothing.

Cosmopolitanism is a beautiful sentiment in theory, but it never works for the good of nations nor for the good of the world in general. A nation works out its own destiny after its own fashion. God must have willed it so when He gave to each country its peculiar atmosphere, and to each people peculiar habits of thought and action. Destroy this individualism and you destroy the soul of the world. In being true to the duties which come in our way in our own corner of earth we are thus working for the general good. This sentiment of 'universal brotherhood' can only mean that in the largeness of human nature there is room for all of the kind outside the immediate interests of our own race. It means that having fulfilled our duties to ourselves and to the land where God has thrown our destinies, we are ready to stretch the hand of friendship to all men. It means that having developed the individualism that is our birthright we are ready to give and take in the mutual action of nations. It means that we love with a personal love the land of our fathers first, and the broad track of the world after. . . .

We have been wont for many years to mix up nationality and politics in a sad way, until now, to the popular mind, one word is synonymous with the other. And yet they are two distinct things. A movement free from all political bias and outside of party spirit, may yet be the national movement of the country; and such the Irish language revival claims to be. Political weapons are not to be despised, nor can they well be dispensed with; but we must not forget that politics are but a means to an end, and that end is nationhood; nor must we forget that the political ideal may fall far short of nationhood. There are many men and many minds in this country. We are all Irish, Tory and Nationalist, and yet there is every chance, mean-spirited as we are, that, while we squabble about politics and foreign wars, what remains of the native language may go, and, once gone, there is no hope of rekindling its dead fires. If we give our sympathy to the weak and oppressed of other nations should we not see to our own fireside? We are all Irish, some of us pinning our faith in a separate legislative assembly to take its stand in College Green, some of us building up a glorious future for our country on the fulness of time which may give strange zest to things unwont, to wit, the union of shamrock and rose – and some of us again believing neither in one nor the other of these panaceas for our ill, but thinking in all good faith that the disease is deeper than the surgeon's eye can reach or the physician's plaster heal, and that internal bleeding can only be stopped by internal remedies. But most of us are blind to the internal cancer that is eating away the heart and the soul of Ireland. That cancer is anglicisation, and the root of the cancer is in the English language, or rather, in the loss of the Irish language, and the sole use of English over the greater part of the country. . . .

Look at the book-stalls in the city, at the railway stations, in the country towns – everywhere you go through the length and breadth of the land – English books and English journals, not the best or second-best of English literature. Think of it and all it portends – the purity of the Celtic mind coming in contact with London's exhalations. The philosophic spirit of the thinking Irishman being nourished on the third-rate literature of England. Think of the fair soul of the grey-eyed Irish maiden in some remote village of Kerry brooding over the fate of the gallant English lord, who gets tired of society life ('blasé' they always call it in these penny novelettes) and his conquests there, and finds solace in hunting Indian tigers, until at length a native princess asks him to share her throne and her slaves! Think of the first spark of sentiment in the heart of a winsome lad who whistles after his plough in the wild Connemara homestead being awakened by the mis-fortunes of ''Arriet Jane' or 'Sarah Anne'. . . .

In the streets the young men discuss the merits of a Langtry when she idealises vice in all the glory of histrionic genius. 'The acting is perfect, and then, you know, such is life as it is lived beyond the water.' 'It is narrow-minded to shut our eyes to facts.' This sort of misplaced broad-mindedness is blunting our moral principle from day to day. Soon our power of distinguishing good from ill will have passed in 'cosmopolitan' vapours, and weakness of soul will be ours – the last sign we are not to be redeemed. . . .

These are only a few of the many signs of a mighty change in our outlook on life. We are being touched by the influence of a material race. Here can be seen the evils of commercialism without any of the solid benefits. We grow sordid, and yet we are as poor as we were in our prouder and happier days, when we recognised our poverty as the price of our mental independence, for after all ''tis in the heart that freedom lies.' In the cities and towns, along the country roads, and – worst of all – in the homes, we speak a new language other than the language our fathers spoke. How we mouth and twist it out of all shape as we try to make it fit in with the requirements of our peculiar mental attitude which two or three generations of English speakers cannot turn away from a Celtic standpoint. And there lies the root of all the evil that has befallen our race in its march to anglicisation – the root of all the vulgarity and all the humbug.

6.18 *Ireland's Defence – Her Language*, Revd P.F.Kavanagh, n.d. [?1902]

The language of a people, said a great writer, is their pedigree – a true saying. Language marks a race of men as distinct from other races, and determines their rank among them by its antiquity, its purity, and its excellence as a means of expressing thought. The mind of a people is mirrored in their language. A people's language tells us what they were even better than their history. So true is this that even if the people had perished and their history had been lost, we might still learn from their language – and in language I include literature – to what intellectual stature they had attained, what was the extent and direction of their moral development, and what their general worthiness. . . .

An enslaved nation can call nothing its own but its mind, but the mind of a nation must in time follow its language, and when the National language is lost the national mind cannot long survive. When both are lost it is easily absorbed and assimilated by its enslaver. This change may not come quickly, but it comes surely; one or two generations may pass before it is accomplished, but it is certain to come in time. Such a change of language might possibly be an advantage to an enslaved or a conquered people if it were a barbarous one with an obscure or inglorious history, but in the case of a highly civilised and gifted race with an illustrious history and an ancient, beautiful and vigorous language, such as our language and history are, who would not account it a misfortune, not alone for the nation itself, but for the whole human family?. . .

I have said our language is our pedigree, but not from printed books or manuscripts alone can we trace the pedigree of the Gael. It is inscribed upon every plain and river, every hill and dale that bears the name of some famous worthy of our race, and the memory of many long departed kings and legislators, of bards and Brehons, of Saints and scholars, has been eternized by being imprinted upon the face of nature itself. These names carry us back through the ages to the period when the outlines of history begin to grow dim and uncertain in that mist that ever shrouds the remote past of a country. They help to confirm the truth of our written annals, and transport us in imagination to those days whose story the pen of the historian has been unable to record. They live only in legends and traditions.

If the very *soil* of our country is thus eloquent of the past, can the people of Ireland be forgetful of *it* or the language in which its story is enshrined?

WHAT THE IRISH LANGUAGE MOVEMENT WILL DO FOR IRELAND

It will, I believe, help to unite Irish people of all creeds and classes in a common effort to save their country. Yes the revival of the Irish language may do for our country what the most gifted patriots of our past have striven, but failed to do for her. It may unite Irish people of all creeds and classes (save those who look for personal aggrandisement in the degradation of their country) in a strenuous and generous effort to promote her welfare.

It will help to create an atmosphere in which the anti-Irish Irishman will breathe with difficulty and in which he will feel himself ill at ease, nor will the additional misery be spared him for knowing that he is despised, nor the more painful consciousness that he deserves to be so. . . . The language movement will help to raise Irishmen in their own esteem and in that of other nations, even the English. Is it not true that Irish men and women educated in English or Anglicising schools, are in the eyes of English people but servile copyists of their own ways and fashions? Although this servile imitation by certain classes of the Irish may flatter the vanity of Englishmen, they do not respect their copyists – who could? Who could respect those who do not respect themselves? . . . The young Englishman leaves his college loving his country and proud of her. The young Anglicised Irishman leaves his without any love for the land of his birth, nay he considers it a misfortune to be born an Irishman. He takes no pride in being an Irishman, and is immensely flattered if someone mistakes him for an Englishman. He is not an Englishman by birth, he is not an Irishman in spirit. What is he, then? He is a self-degraded and denationalised being who is proud of being mean and who glories in the subject. Such is the anti-Irish Irishman trained in our Anglicising University. . . .

If the rising generation are taught both the language and the history of their country, then indeed we may hope for a new Ireland. Then the men and women of Ireland will be Irish indeed, and not as too many of them are today, mere imitators and copyists of a foreign people, a people with whom they have nothing in common but a common humanity. A people between whom and them nature itself has drawn a broad line of separation, I may say a triple line, geographical, moral and intellectual, a nation never really great or good even in its best days, and which is now descending to the lowest grade among civilised peoples – poor in wit, poor in literature, and feeble in arms – a decaying and decadent nation whose apparent greatness is but the swelling of putrefaction. We must hasten to quit this nation or go down with it. In other words, our country must cease to be an anglicised Ireland or our place amongst the nations will be forever lost.

6.19 *Samhain*, W.B.Yeats, 1902

As we do not think that a play can be worth acting, and not reading, all our plays will be published in time. Some have been printed in *The United Irishman* and the *All Ireland Review*. I have put my *Cathleen ni Houlihan* and a little play by Dr.Hyde into this SAMHAIN. Once already this year I have had the noble pleasure of praising, and I can praise this *Lost Saint* with as good a conscience as when I wrote of *Cuchulain of Murthemne*. I would always admire it, but just now, when I have been thinking that literature should return to its old habit of describing desirable things, I am in the mood to be stirred by that old man gathering up food for fowl with his heart full of love, and by those children who are so full of the light-hearted curiosity of childhood, and by that schoolmaster who has mixed prayer with his gentle punishments. It seems natural that so beautiful a prayer as that of the old saint should have come out of a life so full of innocence and peace. One could hardly have thought out the play in English, for those phrases of a traditional simplicity and of a too deliberate prettiness which become part of an old language would have arisen between the mind and the story. . . . Even if one could have thought it out in English one could not have written it in English, unless perhaps in that dialect, which Dr.Hyde had already used in the prose narrative that flows about his *Love Songs of Connaught*.

Dr.Hyde has written a little play about the birth of Christ which has the same beauty and simplicity. These plays remind me of my first reading of the *Love Songs of Connaught*. The prose parts of that book were to me, as they were to many others, the coming of a new power into literature. I find myself now, as I found myself then, grudging to propaganda, to scholarship, to oratory, however necessary, a genius which might in modern Irish, or in that idiom of the English-speaking country people, create a new region of the mind to wander in. . . .

I cannot judge the language of his Irish poetry, but it is so rich in poetical thought, when at its best, that it seems to me that if he were to write more he might become to modern Irish what Mistral was to modern Provençal. I wish too, that he could put away from himself some of the interruptions of that ceaseless propaganda, and find time for the making of translations, loving and leisurely, like those in *Beside the Fire* and *The Love Songs of Connaught*. He has begun to get a little careless lately. Above all I would have him keep to that English idiom of the Irish-thinking people of the west which he has begun to use less often. It is the only good English spoken by any large number of Irish people today, and one must found good literature on a living speech. English men of letters found themselves upon the English Bible, where religious thought gets its living speech. . . . The translation used in Ireland has not the same literary beauty, and if we are to find anything to take its place we must find it in the idiom of the poor, which mingles so much of the same vocabulary with turns of phrase which have come out of Gaelic. Even Irish writers of considerable powers of thought seem to have no better standard of English than a schoolmaster's ideal of correctness. If their grammar is correct they will write about 'keeping in touch,' and 'object lessons,' and 'shining examples,' and 'running in grooves,' and 'flagrant violations,' of various things, with a light heart. Yet, as St. Beuve has said, there is nothing immortal except style. One can write well in that country idiom without much thought about one's words, the emotion will bring the right word itself, for there is everything old and everything alive and nothing common or threadbare. I recommend to the Intermediate Board – a body that seems to benefit by advice – a better plan than any they know for teaching children to write good English. Let every child in Ireland be set to turn first a leading article and then a piece of what is called excellent English, written perhaps by some distinguished member of the Board, into the idiom of his own countryside. He will find at once the difference between dead and living words, between words that meant something years ago, and words that have the only thing that gives literary quality, personality, the breath of men's mouths.

The habit of writing for the stage, even when it is not country people who are the speakers, and of considering what good dialogue is, will help to increase our feeling for style. Let us get back in everything to the spoken word, even though we have to speak our lyrics to the Psaltery or the Harp, for, as A.E. says, we have begun to forget that literature is but recorded speech, and even when we write with care we have begun 'to write with elaboration what could never be spoken.' But when we go back to speech let us see that it is either the idioms of those who have rejected, or of those who have never learned the base idioms of the newspapers.

6.20 *The Ruin of Education in Ireland and the Irish Farmer*, F.H.O'Donnell, 1903

Priests kill the Irish language and Irish studies . . . from the beginning of the century, if not earlier, increasing multitudes of the Irish priests addressed their Irish-speaking congregations in the finest Maynooth English. If the knowledge of religion, as well as the traditions of the race, suffered by the confusion of the tongues, that appears to have been the least of the anxieties of a patriotic and electioneering clergy. . . . The destruction of the national tongue is a serious moment in the existence of any race. When that destruction is precipitated by the priests of the national worship itself, need we wonder that the results may be abidingly calamitous for the race and the religion.

6.21 *Lectures on the Irish Language Movement*, Revd P.Dinneen, 1904

The Irish Language Revival movement is attracting a good deal of attention of late. The main plank in the platform of the movement is the Irish language in one form or another, but with the cultivation of the language there is associated an effort to revive Irish games and pastimes, Irish manners and customs, as well as Irish industries. The language is the root on which all the other elements are grafted, and it is the language in its living state, and not the language as found in books and manuscripts, that is the true basis of this general national revival. If the Irish language were to become extinct as a living speech, as, say, Cornish is extinct, even though it should be studied in every school in Ireland, it could not be taken as the basis of a national regeneration. It is the living word, and the living word alone, that possesses the spell that is powerful enough to call back the nation as a whole from the degrading life of foreign imitation, and give it strength and nerve to develop a native civilisation. For this object, it is not necessary that the language should be vernacular throughout the entire country. It is sufficient that it exist in a flourishing condition as a real vernacular, that it have every facility for growth and extension, and that it be studied everywhere, and be held in high esteem in the schools and councils of the land. It is impossible, however, for the language to exist and thrive at the present time without growth and extension. It must be made the vehicle of education, it must be used for all the purposes of civilised life, it must be cultivated to the point of spontaneous literary expression, it must produce a literature that will be able to hold its own against contemporary English literature. To produce such a literature, an audience of Irish readers must be created sufficient to ensure a reasonable circulation for Irish books and newspapers and magazines, and the Irish-reading public must be of sufficiently wide range to insure a healthy diversity to the literary output.

In an age like the present, it is no easy thing to maintain a cultivated living speech in such a state of vitality that it can hold its own against the living, highly cultivated languages of the great modern nations. Irish has, indeed, several advantages over English. It has long lain dormant, and has never been spoiled by excessive printing. Its lack of scientific terminology, though a serious shortcoming, from the utilitarian point of view, renders it more suitable as a vehicle of pure literature. Its study is interesting to the antiquarian and comparative philologist, and it has preserved its identity more completely than perhaps any other European language. It is even at the present day a strongly inflected language and its grammatical structure is so precise and so unlike that of most other modern languages, that its study may become an important element in a liberal education. It is so closely bound up with our historical documents, and with the very topography of the country that a knowledge of it is indispensable for even an elementary study of our history. It is, no doubt, deficient in literature of general interest, and this deficiency must continue for a long time. . . .

National character is influenced and moulded by the events and circumstances that mould a nation's history, and is wounded deeply whenever there is a violent or sudden change in the circumstances under which it grew and strengthened. Each succeeding age, introducing, as it does, a new set of circumstances, tends to stamp its own image on the national character, tends to inoculate it with its own peculiar virtues and vices. It is only permanent national institutions that will give it steadiness amid the fluctuations of taste, of manners, of habits, and that will check the undue influence of foreign teaching and foreign example. Among these institutions it is obvious that religion holds a foremost place, and it is equally obvious that the national language is of far-reaching importance. The language in which a nation has lisped in the infance of its civilised life, that has given expression to its most glowing enthusiasm, to its wisest reflections, to its sweetest melody, that has grown and developed step by step as the nation grew and developed, whose very words and phrases breathe the breath of history and legend, such a language is a powerful factor in moulding the national character, and being of its nature a permanent factor, cannot be destroyed without irreparable loss to that character. The national language is the poor man's literature and folk-lore, it is his history and tradition, it reflects what he knows of his own country and of the outer world, it is his fund of music and song, it is the repertory of his prayers, it is the source of his wise maxims, in it he gives vent to his feelings, to his hopes and fears, in it he hears words of consolation and encouragement from his friends, and in it the minister of his religion soothes his soul in its passage to eternity. He teaches that language to his children, not by any system of pedagogy, but in the school of nature and parental affection, with the infant pupil reclining on his breast and the tender hand stroking his rugged cheek. But in teaching that language he makes his infant child a denizen of an empire that embraces the past and present, he makes him heir to the thought, the wisdom, the imagination, the melody of his ancestors, he supplies him with a medium in which he can continue the interrupted conversation of those that went before him, add to their store of wisdom and revel in their sallies of wit and humour; and all this in as kindly and natural a manner as if long generations of his forefathers still inhabited the earth, and sang their songs, and repeated their words of wisdom in his ear. That language is suited to every age from the lisping of childhood to the slow and solemn utterances of grave seniors. It can give expression to the warmest desires, to the most ardent piety, to the sincerest patriotism. It is the nurse of piety, of love of home and country, of every social and domestic virtue. . . .

The struggle between the languages, is a deeper, a more far-reaching struggle than appears on the surface, it is a struggle between the civilisations which these languages represent, and of which they are the most natural channels of expression. The extinction of Irish as a living speech, would mean the predominance of foreign civilisation, of foreign ideals, of foreign customs, of foreign vices. I shall not now say anything hard of what English civilisation was in its prime. Let us grant that it was excellent. But it is no longer in its prime, it is fast breaking up and giving place to vulgarity. It is a mighty wreck that threatens to submerge the smaller crafts that are battling with the waves. It is a ruin that is fast debasing the minds and enfeebling the bodies of the people, it is wiping out the great landmarks of morals, it is creating difficulties that may become insurmountable for the ruler and statesman. . . . It is the simple old-world virtues of our ancestors that alone can save us from the ruin with which we are threatened, and these virtues grow up and flourish wherever our language exists. The Irish language is their natural guardian, it is the natural medium for their expression. Remove it from the scene, and the virtues are certain to drop and die.

6.22 *The Philosophy of Irish Ireland*, D.P.Moran, 1905

We must retrace our steps, and take as much as possible from our own country and its history. We must be original Irish, and not imitation English. Above all, we must re-learn our language, and become a bi-lingual people. For, the great connecting link between us and the real Ireland, which few of us know anything about, is the Gaelic tongue. A national language will differentiate us from the rest of the world, and keep us ever in mind that we are an entity of original and historic growth, not a parasite stuck on to the side of England because our own heart was too weak to keep the vital spark in us. A distinct language is the great weapon by which we can ward off undue foreign influence, and keep ourselves surrounded by a racy Irish atmosphere. The value of such a language as a fount of a hundred inspirations; its direct and indirect influence on the character of a people; its potent isolating power, are things gone beyond the necessity of proof now. The state of Wales, where political union is not questioned, contrasted with the state of Ireland, where we have been working all the century to hoist the harp without the crown, bears its own eloquent witness; the language wars on the Continent proclaim them, and we have the echo of the voice of the Irish-hating Spenser ringing out from three hundred years ago – ' . . . for it hath ever been the use of the conquerors to despise the language of the conquered, and to force him by all means to learn his'. There is one great advantage which a language movement has over a political agitation, an advantage which must appeal to a people sick to despair with disappointed hopes – it cannot be betrayed by any leaders. The death of one man, or the stupidity and cowardice of a section in an hour of crisis, cannot render years of labour worse than useless; every move is a step forward and a step that cannot be blotted out. A movement of this kind stands like a cone upon its base, not like so many of our disastrous agitations, a cone upon its apex with one holding it in place. When the fashionable young Irishman and woman, not overburdened with strength of character – the type which in every community follows the tide whithersoever it may lead – can talk Irish as well as English, and knows more of the real Ireland than of modern London, then there will be a genuine Irish nation – whoever may be making the laws – which economic tendencies, battering rams, or the Queen's soldiers will be powerless to kill. If anyone is startled at this view, and decides that it is impossible of realisation, that the price is too much, the difficulties too great, then let him have the courage of his convictions, think things out to a rational conclusion, and cease playing the fool.

6.23 *The Aran Islands*, J.M.Synge, 1907

A branch of the Gaelic League has been started here since my last visit, and every Sunday afternoon three little girls walk through the village ringing a shrill hand-bell, as a signal that the women's meeting is to be held, – here it would be useless to fix an hour, as the hours are not recognised.

Soon afterwards bands of girls – all ages from five to twenty-five – begin to troop down to the schoolhouse in their reddest Sunday petticoats. It is remarkable that these young women are willing to spend their one afternoon of freedom in laborious studies of orthography for no reason but a vague reverence for the Gaelic. It is true that they owe this reverence, or most of it, to the influence of some recent visitors, yet the fact that they feel such an influence so keenly is itself of interest.

In the older generation that did not come under the influence of the recent language movement, I do not see any particular affection for Gaelic. Whenever they are able, they speak English to their children, to render them more capable of making their way in life. Even the young men sometimes say to me –

> 'There's very hard English on you, and I wish to God that I had the like of it.'

The women are the great conservative force in this matter of the language. They learn a little English in school and from their parents, but they rarely have occasion to speak with any one who is not a native of the islands, so their knowledge of the foreign tongue remains rudimentary. In my cottage I have never heard a word of English from the women except when they were speaking to the pigs or to the dogs, or when the girl was reading a letter in English. Women, however, with a more assertive temperament, who have had, apparently, the same opportunities, often attain a considerable fluency, as is the case with one, a relative of the old woman of the house, who often visits here.

In the boys' school, where I sometimes look in, the children surprise me by their knowledge of English, though they always speak in Irish among themselves. The school itself is a comfortless building in a terribly bleak position. In the cold weather the children arrive in the morning with a sod of turf tied up with their books, a simple toll which keeps the fire well supplied. I believe a more modern method is soon to be introduced.

6.24 'Can We Go Back Into Our Mother's Womb?', J.M.Synge, 1907

A Letter to the Gaelic League By a Hedge Schoolmaster.

Much of the writing that has appeared lately in the papers takes it for granted that Irish is gaining the day in Ireland and that this country will soon speak Gaelic. No supposition is more false. The Gaelic League is founded on a doctrine that is made up of ignorance, fraud and hypocrisy. Irish as a living language is dying out year by year – the day the last old man or woman who can speak Irish only dies in Connacht or Munster – a day that is coming near – will mark a station in the Irish decline which will be final a few years later. As long as these old people who speak Irish only are in the cabins the children speak Irish to them – a child will learn as many languages as it has need of in its daily life – but when they die the supreme good sense of childhood will not cumber itself with two languages where one is enough. It will play, quarrel, say its prayers and make jokes of good and evil, make love when it's old enough, write if it has wit enough, in this language which is its mother tongue. This result is what could be expected beforehand and it is what is taking place in every Irish-speaking district.

I believe in Ireland. I believe the nation that has made a place in history by seventeen centuries of manhood, a nation that has begotten Grattan and Emmet and Parnell will not be brought to complete insanity in these last days by what is senile and slobbering in the doctrine of the Gaelic League. There never was till this time a movement that was gushing, cowardly and maudlin, yet now we are passing England in the hysteria of old women's talk. A hundred years ago Irishmen could face a dark existence in Kilmainham Jail, or lurch on the halter before a grinning mob, but now they fear any gleam of truth. How are the mighty fallen! Was there ever a sight so piteous as an old and respectable people setting up the ideals of Fee-Gee because, with their eyes glued on John Bull's navel, they dare not be Europeans for fear the huckster across the street might call them English.

This delirium will not last always. It will not be long – we will make it our first hope – till some young man with blood in his veins, logic in his wits and courage in his heart, will sweep over the backside of the world to the uttermost limbo of this credo of mouthing gibberish. (I speak here not of the old and magnificent language of our manuscripts, or of the two or three dialects still spoken, though with many barbarisms, in the west and south, but of the incoherent twaddle that is passed off as Irish by the Gaelic League.) This young man will teach Ireland again that she is part of Europe, and teach Irishmen that they have wits to think, imaginations to work miracles, and souls to possess with sanity. He will teach them that there is more in heaven and earth than the weekly bellow of the Brazen Bull-calf and all his sweaty gobs, or the snivelling booklets that are going through Ireland like the scab on sheep, and yet he'll give the pity that is due to the poor stammerers who mean so well though they are stripping the nakedness of Ireland in the face of her own sons.

6.25 *What Is the Use of Reviving Irish?*, Dermot Chenevix Trench, 1912

From an Ireland that was mainly Irish-speaking, we are separated by one or at most two generations. That is but a trifle in the history of a nation. Is it to be believed that in fifty years the Irish brain has ceased to be convoluted in accordance with the subtle architecture of the Gaelic sentence, or that the Irish larynx has ceased to be the counterpart of Gaelic phonetics. Allusion has already been made of the Irishman who, quite indifferent to the subject of plovers, but whose mind was stirred to an interest by the thought of a pilbín – the Gaelic name for the same bird. It raises the interesting question as to whether an Irish word has not a greater inherent power of drawing forth an Irish mind than attaches to the word in any other tongue, quite apart from the question as to whether such mind has acquired a previous knowledge of the Irish language. At any rate you may ask any plain-minded Gaelic Leaguer who, perhaps, has spoken English from his cradle, and has only learnt Gaelic in the last few years, and he will tell you that 'pilbín' expresses his meaning with a truth to which the English 'plover' cannot attain. In the connection between the Irish language and the Irish mind lies an interesting study occupying the borderland between psychology and philology. In the interests of the Gaelic Revival, it is much to be desired that some student, let us say of the School of Ancient Irish Learning, should take it up and thus elucidate the philosophic basis underlying the practical success which the Gaelic League has achieved. So much for the soil of Irish psychology in which the movement is rooted. That Gaelic expresses the Irishman is a statement which, apart from all abstract theory, the work actually accomplished by the Gaelic League is there to testify. . . .

So little is it true that the trend of our time is against the smaller languages, that there are now far more languages spoken in Europe by educated people than there were a century ago. It may be destined that in the end the whole world will speak English, German, or Esperanto. The mingling of races, the increase of communication may cause national languages to disappear or be merged in a universal speech. If this is to take place through a gradual peaceful process of evolution no one will oppose its consummation. National language movements are not as a protest against the abolition of barriers of race in the interests of human solidarity, but against the forcible extermination of a racial genius through the pressure of political and economic circumstances. Language is not a matter of politics and economics, but of something far more important – namely, human idiosyncrasy. Ireland does not consent that she shall cease to be Irish in thought, simply because she happens to be governed from Westminster, or because the abnormal economic conditions that have prevailed in Ireland for the last half century have required that so large a portion of her people should emigrate to America. There can be no doubt that the violent and artificial suppression of a highly-developed language is a misfortune not only to the race primarily concerned, but to the whole human family.

Every nation has some contribution to make to the sum of human civilisation. Suppress a language and the Ethnic spirit which it preserves evaporates; you have, in fact, 'destroyed one of the original forms of the human mind.' No one who is aware that thirty years ago children in Ireland went to school with wooden tallies round their necks to be scored with a notch for every word of Irish spoken, and that they were beaten in accordance with the number of their notches, will deny that Irish has been violently and artificially suppressed. The melting of the snows is the only image which conveys the fact of its disappearance. It has not gone because of an intrinsic unfitness to compete with English. Douglas Hyde says that at the time of the conquest of 1172 it was a far more cultivated language than English, and its natural vigour is placed in evidence by the fact that for three centuries it constantly supplanted English among the colonists of the Pale. It has gone because sixty years ago all Ireland became obsessed with the notion that salvation for the race was only to be attained by emigration to New York, or for those who stayed at home through remedial legislation carried out at Westminster. To know nothing but Irish was a source of untold hardship to the exiles landed in their hundreds of thousands at the ports of America. The priest discouraged Irish because he wished to mitigate this hardship and to render, through a knowledge of English, his departing flock more effective missionaries of the Catholic Faith. The politi- cian ignored it because it was not the language of Westminster, and the people eagerly forgot their Irish in order to follow his speeches. The Press took its cue from the politician; we had a new-found system of primary education, planned by men who were not Irish, and who had no sympathy with the country's needs. They treated Ireland as a virgin page uninscribed by the hand of racial tradition, and on which the Anglicised pupils of the National Schools were to write for the first time an historical record of note and interest. . . .

The Gaelic League asks all Irish people to rally round the National language. It appeals to Firbolg, Milesian, Gael, or Cromwellian planter. It includes Catholic, Protestant, and Dissenter. Not by everyone in the same degree is the language felt to be his rightful and desired possession. There is, however, no excuse for defaulting from such a movement to be found by a Carlow or Wexford farmer, for example, in saying, 'It is all very well to get the Connemara people to speak Irish, but in this part of the country it has not been spoken for eighty years, and it is too late to return to it now,' or for a country gentleman to say, 'My ancestor was a Williamite planter, and I don't believe that he or his descendants ever spoke Irish, except for the purpose of dealing with the tenants.' To all such we put one question – 'Are you or are you not predominantly Irish, and do you not wish to live in an Ireland which reflects your racial type? If so, you will support the language which expresses the Irish nature and which will keep the Irish nation true to itself in all that it sets its hand to accomplish.'

6.26 'The Coming Revolution', P.H.Pearse, 1913

I have come to the conclusion that the Gaelic League, as the Gaelic League, is a spent force; and I am glad of it. I do not mean that no work remains for the Gaelic League, or that the Gaelic League is no longer equal to work; I mean that the vital work to be done in the new Ireland will be done not so much by the Gaelic League itself as by the men and movements that have sprung from the Gaelic League or have received from the Gaelic League a new baptism and a new life of grace. The Gaelic League was no reed shaken by the wind, no mere *vox clamantis*: it was a prophet and more than a prophet. But it was not the Messiah. I do not know if the Messiah has yet come, and I am not sure if there will be any visible and personal Messiah in this redemption: the people itself will be its own Messiah, the people labouring, scourged, crowned with thorns, agonising and dying, to rise again immortal and impassible. For peoples are divine and are the only things that can properly be spoken of under figures drawn from the divine epos.

If we do not believe in the divinity of our people we have had no business, or very little, all these years in the Gaelic League. In fact, if we had not believed in the divinity of our people, we should in all probability not have gone into the Gaelic League at all. We should have made our peace with the devil, and perhaps might have found him a very decent sort; for he liberally rewards with attorney-generalships, bank balances, villa residences, and so forth, the great and the little who serve him well. Now we did not turn our backs upon all these desirable things for the sake of *is* and *tá*. We did it for the sake of Ireland. In other words, we had one and all of us (at least, I had, and I hope that all you had) an ulterior motive in joining the Gaelic League. We never meant to be Gaelic Leaguers and nothing more than Gaelic Leaguers. We meant to do something for Ireland, each in his own way. Our Gaelic League time was to be our tutelage: we had first to learn to know Ireland, to read the lineaments of her face, to understand the accents of her voice; to re-possess ourselves, disinherited as we were, of her spirit and mind, re-enter into our mystical birthright. For this we went to school to the Gaelic League. It was a good school, and we love its name and will champion its fame throughout all the days of our later fighting and striving. But we do not propose to remain schoolboys forever. . . .

This is what I meant when I said that our work henceforth must be done less and less through the Gaelic League and more and more through the groups and the individuals that have arisen, and or are arising, out of the Gaelic League. There will be in the Ireland of the next few years a multitudinous activity of Freedom Clubs, Young Republican Parties, Labour Organisations, Socialist Groups, and what not; bewildering enterprises undertaken by sane persons and insane persons, by good men and bad men, many of them seemingly contradictory, some mutually destructive, yet all tending towards a common objective, and that objective: the Irish Revolution.

For if there is one thing that has become plainer than another it is that when the seven men met in O'Connell Street to found the Gaelic League, they were commencing, had there been a Liancourt there to make the epigram, not a revolt, but a revolution. The work of the Gaelic League, its appointed work, was that: and the work is done. To every generation its deed. The deed of the generation that has now reached middle life was the Gaelic League: the beginning of the Irish Revolution. Let our generation not shirk *its* deed, which is to accomplish the revolution.

6.27 'Politics and the Language', P.S. Ó h-Eigceartaigh, 1918

When the founders of the Gaelic League decreed that it should be non-political they made use of a somewhat misleading expression, what they had in their minds being non-party. The Gaelic League programme goes, in a revolutionary way, to the very roots of government in this country, and non-political in the literal sense it is not and it cannot be. But it was and it remains non-party. The accusations of being political which have been levelled at it in the past two or three years were similarly misapplied. What the accusers meant to convey was that they regarded the League as 'party'; but what they really meant was that the League had refused to commit itself to the particular Party they themselves were interested in.

Politics have, however, a very real connection with the fortunes of the language, and as it was political changes which banished the language, so it is political changes which will ultimately create the conditions which will restore it. And in the broad sense the language is, and it always has been, political – as political as Killarney's Lakes or Glendalough's Seven Churches – while remaining non-party. In the domestic quarrels of Ireland it takes no side, but it stands, as all national attributes in a nation must stand, with the nation in its international friendships and enmities.

Historically, the language has been one of the most potent of all political forces. It was through it that successive waves of foreigners were assimilated and Irishised. As Thomas Davis puts it:

> There came the brown Phoenecian,
> The man of trade and toil;
> There came the proud Milesian,
> A hungering for spoil;
> And the Firbolg and the Cymry,
> And the hard-enduring Dane,
> And the iron lords of Lombardy,
> With the Saxon in their train.

Until the eighteenth century none of the foreign elements projected into the Nation remained foreign. They, or their sons, married Irish wives, and in every case the third generation was Irish, with its foreign ancestry forgotten. 'When the tongue is Irish,' said Spenser, 'the heart is Irish also'; and the Irish language wiped out in a couple of generations even the Cromwellian Settlement, except in those places where a foreign language was definitely implanted by the planting of a complete social community, under no necessity of intermarrying with or holding close intercourse with the Irish. The eighteenth century saw the political subjugation of Ireland marked also by the subjugation of the language, and in addition to the superimposition on the Irish State of a foreign State there was superimposed on the Irish language a foreign language. With the establishment of English as the language of government, of the professions, of the municipalities, as the language of every function of the artificial State which was superimposed on the Irish State, began the political subjugation of the Irish language; and later on by the acceptance of the Irish-speaking people, after the Emancipation Bills of 1793 and 1829, of the framework of that State as the framework of their State, an acceptance of the English language as the language of government, the professions, and the whole public and collective life of a Nation still in the main Irish-speaking, the decay of the language began. The business of the country was done in English, and the country necessarily had to take to English. It was politics which brought about that change: which enabled the English government to establish and maintain in Ireland conditions which gave the Irish-speaking Irishman the choice of learning English, and using English, or of being shut out from every public function of life in his own country. There was no Irish leader from 1793, when the peril began, sufficiently clear-headed to see what was happening, and so a refusal to work the machine, the one thing which could have stopped it, was not forthcoming, and Irish gradually faded.

The Gaelic League seeks to reverse all that, to restore Irish as the living language of Ireland, to ensure that in all her public business, domestic and international, Irish shall be substituted for English. That is to say, it seeks to overturn the whole system of government in this country, and to substitute for it a system based on the Irish language. It cannot, therefore, be other than political, and the sooner the word non-political is altered to non-party the better. There is no public function of a Nation which does not affect, and is not affected by, its politics, and that will have to be frankly faced and acted upon if the work the Gaelic League has set itself to do is to be accomplished. Up to the present it has busied itself in creating an atmosphere, a public opinion. Now, to be effective, it must give expression in politics to that atmosphere, that public opinion: for the way to the machinery which controls the government machine in all countries is frankly political, and control of the government machine is essential if the revolutionary change in the spirit and practice of government in this country, which the fulfilment of the Gaelic League programme demands, is ever to be realised. That does not necessarily imply that the Gaelic League is to organise itself as a political party, but it must organise itself politically, and it must arrange to take within its purview every ramification of government, however obscure.

6.28 *Literature in Ireland*, Thomas MacDonagh, 1920

In Ireland a period intervened between the last days of the Gaelic literature that mattered and the beginning of the new literature in the English tongue, between the hope and admiration that captured the imagination of the people in the days of Hugh O'Neill and Hugh O'Donnell, then of Eoghan Ruadh O'Neill, then of the Jacobites, and the new hope and anticipation that dawned in the last century and is widened to morning in this. The old Gaelic polity and culture having lost their force and their integrity, Gaelic literature became decadent in the time of the Penal Laws. Whatever the fate of the Gaelic language and literature now may be – whether its long sickness end now in death without issue, or, as some of us confidently hope, in revival and vigorous life, with renewal of the same personality, a second youth, or in the birth of a new language to utter a new literature, destined to take after its Gaelic mother only in some parts, and for the rest to bear the name of bastard in its childhood and of true-born heir in its age, a well of English undefiled – whatever is to be in the unknown future, it would be folly to deny the sickness, the decadence of the immediate past. And while Irish was decadent, English was not yet able either to carry on the tradition, or to syllable anew for itself here. The English-speaking population in Ireland had none of the qualities – social cohesion and integrity, culture, enthusiasm, joy, high and brave emotion – to stammer and then to utter clearly the new word. That word came to the call of the country. It came in the new language and was heard in the new day. The Renaissance that stirred England to its greatest literature brought the mingling of the cosmopolitan with the national. Here the waters have been stirred by the breath of freedom; the alien language has stirred to expression on the lips of the native people.

The revival of nationalism amongst the Irish subject majority following the days of the Irish Volunteers, the United Irishmen, the independent Parliament; this nationalism, hardened by the austere independence of Parnell, by the land war and its victorious close; this, brought to full manhood by the renewed struggle for legislative freedom and the certainty of triumph and responsibility; this, free from alien hope and fear, craving no ease, hearing always the supreme song of victory on the dying lips of martyrs; this produced the unrest, the impetuous, intrepid adventure that shouts the song of joy for the sad things and for the glad things of life. The song in the new language demanded an intellectual effort that gave it a worth apart. English had to be broken and re-made to serve that song. The language that had been brought to perfection for English use, and then worn by that use, that had had the fixing of the printing press and had set the printer's word above the spoken, that language, in order to serve the different purpose of the new people, had to go back to the forge of living speech. King Alfred, in the first days of English prose, wrote long, awkward strings of words for sentences, with little syntactic order. The modern English author writes well-balanced, well-ordered sentences. But the Saxon King expressed more truly his thought; in him the word order imaged more truly the thought order. The modern writer uses counters where he used coin. The modern writer cannot distinguish between his idea and the set phrase that does duty for its expression, though its terms have other meanings. He alludes to things. His prose is a hint, perfectly understood no doubt by others who know the code, but not for all that a true language. Almost perfectly it does duty for a true language to the people with whom it has grown; better than perfectly in its poetry, which gains in suggestiveness more than its loss in concreteness. Compare the prose of this language with the superior prose of French. Compare its poetry with the far inferior poetry of French. It was, in a word, the English language, good for the English people, redolent of English history, even of the vagaries and absurdities of the history of the English people, with practical jokes and puns and stupid grammatical blunders smelling sweet with the aroma of some splendid verse – with golden lads and girls that come to dust, as chimney sweepers, and with deeds of derring-do. This language, now a courser of ethereal race, now a hack between the shafts of commercialism, serving Shakespeare and the stenographer, used efficiently in William Blake's lyrics and in telegrams; this differed in many of the ways of linguistic difference from the language of the Gael. In it the ideas of the Gael did not find easy expression.

But I have been led on a little too far. The language that was brought face to face with the Irish in the eighteenth and nineteenth centuries was not the language of English commerce. The Gaelic people had for English tutors the descendants of the old English settlers, in whose mouths the language was still the language of Shakespeare. The transplanted slip of a language does not develop as the parent tree. By comparison it rather ceases to develop. The descendants of the earliest English colonists here were found, by a new Englishman of Elizabeth's time, using 'the dregs of the old ancient Chaucer English.' So in our day we find in the mouths of the people what such a progressive might call the dregs of the old ancient Shakespeare English. And this was the English that had to be knit into a different complication from the modern complication of the central English language. For the rest, it is not only in Ireland that the phenomenon has occurred: analogous is the use of English by the American booster and by the mystic who has to express in terms of sense and wit the things of God that are made known to him in no language. . . .

My definite conclusions are three:

First, that an Anglo-Irish literature, worthy of a special designation, could only come when English had become the language of the Irish people, mainly of Gaelic stock; and when the literature was from, by, of, to and for the Irish people.

Second, that the ways of life and the ways of thought of the Irish people – the manners, customs, traditions and outlook, religious, social, moral, – have important differences from the ways of life and thought which have found expression in other English literature.

Third, that the English language in Ireland has an individuality of its own, and the rhythm of Irish speech a distinct character.

POSTSCRIPT

This history has returned finally to issues raised in the introduction. But neat closure would be entirely inappropriate; better to end with another turn of the story. In an article in *The Century Magazine* entitled 'The Irish Past is the Irish Language', the writer James Stephens asserted:

> Learn that you have enough of the past to last you for the entirety of your future and you will have done the one thing necessary to make this nation a nation, and to prepare for a literature, an art, and a culture, which will not be an abject imitation or a dishonest forgery.
>
> (Stephens 1922: 813)

This can be read as an expression of conservative nostalgia for the pure, integral past, embodied in the language, over and against the threat of historical and cultural difference in the future. It is all the more satisfying to know therefore that Stephens became a close friend of Joyce, and that Joyce nominated him to 'finish' *Finnegans Wake* if he were not able. *Finnegans Wake* of course being 'diverse tongued', written in 'desperanto', 'unglish' and 'nat language at any sinse of the world'. . . .

THEMES

As an alternative to chronological or period-based study I have outlined below a number of themes which appear in the texts in various forms. This is intended simply to be an illustration of another way of working with the materials. It is not an exhaustive list by any means.

Colonial language policy: 2.14, 2.17, 2.21, 2.22, 2.23, 2.25, 3.2, 3.3, 3.7, 3.10, 4.2, 4.13, 4.19, 4.26, 5.21, 6.7.

Representations of Hiberno-English speech: 2.6, 2.24, 2.26, 3.5, 3.6, 4.17, 4.27, 5.1, 5.28.

The origins of the Irish language: 2.12, 2.14, 2.23, 3.10, 3.15, 3.19, 4.1, 4.10, 4.22, 4.23, 4.24, 4.25, 4.28, 4.30, 5.21.

The politics of naming: 1.2, 2.23, 3.4, 3.6, 3.17, 4.1, 4.19, 5.22, 6.7.

Political leaders, attitudes to Irish and English languages: 4.31, 5.5, 5.14, 5.22, 6.7, 6.9, 6.16, 6.26, 6.28.

Women and the Irish language: 2.14, 5.16, 6.14, 6.23.

Irish language and Irishness: 2.23, 3.11, 4.6, 4.7, 4.20, 4.25, 4.29, 5.4, 5.6, 5.9, 5.10, 5.21, 5.22, 5.27, 6.1, 6.7, 6.9, 6.11, 6.12, 6.15, 6.17, 6.18, 6.21, 6.22, 6.25.

Degeneration of the (Old) English: 2.12, 2.14, 2.15, 2.22, 2.23, 3.3, 3.7, 3.8, 4.1.

Agencies responsible for destruction of Irish language: 3.1, 3.10, 4.1, 4.10, 4.14, 4.15, 4.20, 4.21, 4.26, 4.30, 5.8, 5.13, 5.19, 5.20, 5.21, 5.27, 5.29, 6.3, 6.7, 6.9, 6.10, 6.15, 6.16, 6.17, 6.20.

Irish spoken in the Pale: 2.2, 2.3, 2.14, 2.15, 2.23, 3.7, 3.14.

Education (in English or Irish): 2.2, 2.3, 2.11, 2.12, 2.17, 3.1, 3.3, 3.4, 3.8, 3.12, 4.2, 4.3, 4.5, 4.6, 4.7, 4.8, 4.16, 4.31, 5.5, 5.6, 5.7, 5.9, 5.10, 5.23, 5.26, 5.27, 6.1, 6.3, 6.5, 6.7, 6.13, 6.21.

The qualities of the Irish language: 2.14, 3.11, 3.15, 3.17, 4.1, 4.2, 4.8, 4.10, 4.13, 4.14, 4.20, 4.22, 4.23, 4.24, 4.25, 4.29, 4.30, 4.32, 5.2, 5.3, 5.6, 5.13, 5.16, 5.18, 5.21, 5.24, 5.25, 6.16, 6.21, 6.25, 6.28.

Irish language and Protestantism: 2.3, 2.5, 2.7, 2.9, 2.13, 2.17, 2.19, 2.21, 2.25, 3.1, 3.8, 4.2, 4.6, 4.7, 4.8, 4.9, 4.13, 5.4, 5.6, 5.9, 5.10, 5.17.

Irish language and Catholicism: 3.4, 3.11, 4.9, 4.18, 4.20, 5.9, 5.17, 5.19, 5.27, 5.29, 6.8, 6.10, 6.16, 6.21.

SELECT BIBLIOGRAPHY

1 Primary texts

Adams, Gerry (1986) *The Politics of Irish Freedom*, Dublin: Brandon.

Adamson, I (1982) *The Identity of Ulster: The Land, the Language and the People*, Belfast: Adamson.

An Claidheamh Soluis [*The Sword of Light*] (1899–1930) Dublin: Gaelic League.

Anderson, Christopher (1818) *A Brief Sketch of Various Attempts which Have Been Made to Diffuse a Knowledge of the Holy Scriptures through the Medium of the Irish Language*, Dublin.

anon. (1843) 'English Schools and Irish Pupils', *The Nation*, 26, Dublin.

—— (1843) 'The Irish Language', *The Nation*, 31, 35, Dublin.

—— (1858) 'A Dialogue in the Ulster Dialect', *Ulster Journal of Archaeology*, 6, Belfast.

—— [?G.Peele] (1605) *The Life and Death of Captain Thomas Stukeley* in *The School of Shakspere* (1878), New York: R. Simpson.

—— (n.d.) 'Diarmuid Mac Muiredhaigh Cecinti. Diarmaid Mac Muireadhaigh Sang This', in P. Walsh, *Gleanings from Irish Manuscripts* (1918), Dublin: Dollard.

Barron, P. (1835) *Ancient Ireland. A Weekly Magazine Established for the Purpose of Reviving the Cultivation of the Irish Language and Originating an Earnest Investigation Into the Ancient History of Ireland*, Dublin.

—— (1835) *Irish Sermons with Translations*, Dublin.

Begly, Conor and Hugh MacCurtin (Conchobar ó Beaglaoich agus Aodh Buidhe Mac-Cruitín) (1732) *The English-Irish Dictionary. An Focloir Bearla Gaoidheilge*, Paris.

Boorde, Andrew (?1547) *The First Book of the Introduction of Knowledge* (1870), ed. F.J. Furnivall, London.

Bourke, U.J. (1856) *The College Irish Grammar*, 5th edn (1868), Dublin.

Brooke, Charlotte (1789) *Reliques of Irish Poetry; Consisting of Heroic Poems, Odes, Elegies, and Songs Translated into English Verse*, Dublin.

Bunreacht na hÉireann. Constitution of Ireland (1937) Dublin: The Stationery Office.

Butler, Mary E.L. n.d. [?1901] *Irishwomen and the Home Language*, Dublin: Gaelic League.

Calendar of Ancient Records of Dublin, Vols I–V (1172–1692), ed. J.T. Gilbert (1889–95), Dublin.

Calendar of the Patent and Close Roles of Chancery in Ireland, Henry VIII to 18th Elizabeth (1861), ed. J. Morrin, Dublin.

Calendar of the State Papers Relating to Ireland, 1509–1573 [etc.] (1860–1912) 24 vols, London.

Cambrensis, Giraldus (Gerald of Wales) (1188) *Topographia Hibernica [Topography of Irelands]* (1863) London.

Campion, Edmund (1571) *A Historie of Ireland*, in *The Historie of Ireland Collected by Three Learned Authors* (1633), ed. James Ware, Dublin.

Carsuel, Seon (John Carswell) (1567) *Foirm na nUrrnuidheadh agus Freasdal na Sacramuinteadh* (1873), ed. and trans. T. McLauchlan, Edinburgh.

Céitinn, Seathrún (Geoffrey Keating) (1634) *Foras Feasa ar Éirinn [A Basis of Knowledge about Ireland]* (1902–14), ed. and trans. D. Comyn and P.S. Dinneen, London: Irish Texts Society.

Coneys, Revd (1842) 'The Irish Language', *The Nation*, 5, Dublin.

Connellan, Owen (1834) *A Dissertation on Irish Grammar*, Dublin.

Connellan, Thaddeus (1814) *An English-Irish Dictionary, Intended for the Use of Schools*, Dublin.

—— (1822) *The King's Letter, In Irish and English*, Dublin.

Conway, Richard (1612) 'An Account of the Decrees and Acts . . . in the Year 1611 in Dublin', trans. D.W. McDonald, *Irish Ecclesiastical Record*, 1874.

Corcoran, T. (ed.) *State Policy in Irish Education 1536 to 1816* (1916), Dublin: Fallon.

Cox, Richard (1689–90) *Hibernia Anglicana, or the History of Ireland from the Conquest thereof by the English to this Present Time*, 2 Pts, London.

Daniel, William (Uilliam Ó Domhnaill) (1602) *Tiomna Nuadh ar dTighearna agus ar Slánaightheora Iosa Críosd [New Testament]*, Dublin.

—— (1608) *Leabhar na nUrnaightheadh gComhchoidchiond [Book of Common Prayer]*, Dublin.

Daunt, W.J. O'Neill (1848) *Personal Recollections of the Late Daniel O'Connell, M.P.*, Dublin.

Davies, Sir John (1612) *A Discovery of the True Causes Why Ireland Was Never Entirely Subdued*, in *The Works In Verse and Prose of Sir John Davies* (1876) ed. Revd A.B. Grosart, London.

Davis, Thomas (1843) 'Our National Language', *The Nation*, 25, Dublin.

—— (1844) 'Repeal Reading Rooms', *The Nation*, 97, Dublin.

Dewar, D. (1812) *Observations on the Character, Customs and Superstitions of the Irish*, London.

Dinneen, Revd P.S. (1904) *Lectures on the Irish Language Movement*, Dublin: Gill.

Donlevy, Andrew (1742) *An Teagasg Críosduidhe do réir agus ceasda agus freagartha. The Catechism, or Christian Doctrine by way of Question and Answer*, Paris.

Edgeworth, M. (1802) 'Essay on Irish Bulls', *Tales and Novels by Maria Edgeworth*, 10 vols, Vol. IV (1870), London.

Fáinne an Lae (The Dawning of the Day) (1898–1900) 5 vols, Dublin: Gaelic League.

Flaherty, Donal (1884) 'Practical Hints Towards Preventing the Decay of Irish in the Irish Speaking Districts', *Proceedings of the [Society for the Preservation of the Irish Language] Congress Held in Dublin*, Dublin.

Flood, Henry (1795) 'Henry Flood's Will' in *Ancient Ireland* (1835), No. 5, ed. P. Barron, Dublin.

Forde, Revd Patrick, n.d. [?1901] *The Irish Language Movement: Its Philosophy*, Dublin: Gaelic League.

Gaelic League, n.d. [?1901] *The Irish Language and Intermediate Education. II*, Dublin: Gaelic League.

Gaelic Society of Dublin (1808) *Transactions*, ed. E. O'Reilly, Dublin: Barlow.

225

Gallagher, James (1736) *Sixteen Sermons in an Easy and Familiar Style on Useful and Necessary Subjects*, Dublin.

Gallduf, Teabóid (Theobald Stapleton) (1639) *Catechismus seu Doctrina Christiana Latino-Hibernica* [*Catechism, or Christian Doctrine in Latin and Irish*], Brussels.

Gilbert, J.T. (1885) 'Archives of the Municipal Corporation of Waterford', in *Historical Manuscripts Commission Report* 10, Appendix v.

Grattan, Henry (1812) 'Letter to the Secretary of the Board of Education', in T. Corcoran (ed.) *State Policy in Irish Education 1536 to 1816* (1916), Dublin: Fallon.

Gregory, Lady (1901) *Ideals In Ireland*, London: Unicorn.

Haliday, William (1808) *see* Edmond O'Connell.

Hardiman, James (1831) *Irish Minstrelsy, Or Bardic Remains of Ireland; with English Poetical Translations*, London.

His Majesty's Royal Charter for Erecting English Protestant Schools in the Kingdom of Ireland (1733), in T. Corcoran (ed.) *State Policy in Irish Education 1536 to 1816* (1916), Dublin: Fallon.

Holinshed, R. (1587) *The Chronicles of England, Scotland and Ireland* 3 vols, ed. John Hooker *et al.*, London.

Hughes, C. (1903) *Shakespeare's Europe: Unpublished Chapters in Fynes Moryson's Itinerary*, London.

Hutchinson, Francis (1722) *The Church Catechism in Irish, with the English Placed over it in the Same Karacter*, Belfast.

Hyde, Douglas (1892) 'The Necessity for De-Anglicising Ireland', in C.G. Duffy, G. Sigerson and D. Hyde *The Revival of Irish Literature*, (1894), London.

Irish Patent Rolls of James I; Facsimile of the Irish Record Commission's Calendar Prepared Prior to 1830 (1966) Dublin: Irish Manuscripts Commission.

Irisleabhar na Gaedhilge (Gaelic Journal) (1882–1909) Dublin: Gaelic Union/Gaelic League.

Jonson, Ben (1613) *The Irish Masque at Court*, in C.H. Herford Percy and Evelyn Simpson (eds) *Works*, Vol. VII (1941) Oxford: Clarendon.

Kavanagh, Revd P.F., n.d. [?1902] *Ireland's Defence – Her Language*, Dublin: Gaelic League.

Keenan, P.J. (1856) 'Annual Report of the Commissioners of Education', in *Irisleabhar na Gaedhilge. Gaelic Journal* (1884) Vol. 2, No. 15, Dublin: Gaelic Union.

—— (1879) 'Annual Report of the Commissioners of Education', in *An Treas Leabhar Gaedilge. Third Irish Book*, Dublin.

Keogh, John (1748) *A Vindication of the Antiquities of Ireland*, Dublin.

Ledwich, E. (1790) *Antiquities of Ireland*, Dublin.

Lewis, John (1712) *The Church Catechism. Explain'd By Way of Question and Answer; Caitecism na Heaglaise, Ar Mhodh Cheiste agus Fhreagra*, trans. John Richardson, London.

Lhuyd, Edward (1707) *Archaeologia Britannica, Giving Some Account Additional to What Has Hitherto Been Published, of the Languages, Histories, and Customs of the Original Inhabitants of Great Britain*, Oxford.

—— (1707) 'Focloir Gaoidheilge-Shagsonach', Preface trans. in W. Nicolson, *The Irish Historical Library* (1724), Dublin.

Lucius, Gratianus (John Lynch) (1662) *Cambrensis Eversus*, trans. as *Cambrensis Refuted* (1795), Dublin: Theophilus O'Flanagan.

Lynch, P. (1795) *Bolg An Tsaolair: Or, Gaelic Magazine*, Belfast.

Mac Aingil, Aodh (1618) *Sgáthán Shacramuinte na hAithridhe [Mirror of the Sacrament of Confession]*, Louvain.

MacCruitín, Aodh (Hugh MacCurtin) (1717) *A Brief Discourse in Vindication of the Antiquity of Ireland*, Dublin.

——— (1728) *The Elements of the Irish Language, Grammatically Explained in English*, Louvain.

——— (1732) *see* Begly.

MacDonagh, Thomas (1920) *Literature in Ireland*, Dublin: Talbot Press.

MacHale, Bishop John (1844) *An tIliad*, Dublin.

——— (1861) *An Irish Translation of the Holy Bible from the Latin Vulgate*, Vol. 1, Tuam.

McSweeny, Conor (1843) *Songs of the Irish*, Dublin.

Mason, H.M. (1829) *Facts Afforded by the History of the Irish Society*, Dublin.

——— (1844) *The History of the Origin and Progress of the Irish Society*, Dublin.

'Memo of Commissioners of National Education to the Chief Secretary' (1884) in *Irisleabhar na Gaedilge. Gaelic Journal*, 15, Dublin.

Moran, D.P. (1905) *The Philosophy of Irish Ireland*, Dublin: Duffy.

Morris, Henry (1898) 'The Loss of the Irish Language and Its Influence on the Catholic Religion in Ireland', *Fáinne An Lae*, I, 13, Dublin.

Moryson, Fynes (1617) *Shakespeare's Europe. Unpublished Chapters of Fynes Moryson's Itinerary* (1903), see Hughes, C.

Neilson, Revd W.M. (1808) *An Introduction to the Irish Language*, Dublin.

Nicolson, E. (1715) 'Letter to the Secretary, Society for Promoting Christian Knowledge', *Analecta Hibernica* (1931), 2, Dublin: Historical Manuscripts Commission.

Nicolson, Lord Bishop William (1724) *The Irish Historical Library*, Dublin.

Nolan, John (1877) *Irish Grammar in Prose and Verse*, Dublin.

Nugent, Christopher (Lord Delvin) (*c*.1584–85) *Queen Elizabeth's Primer of the Irish Language* in *Facsimiles of the National Manuscripts of Ireland* (1882), Pt. IV, i, ed. J.T. Gilbert, London.

O'Brien, John (1768) *Focalóir Gaoidhilge-Sax-Bhéarla, Or, An Irish-English Dictionary*, Paris.

Ó Bruadair, Dháibhidh (David O'Bruadair) (1910–17) *Duanaire Dhábhidh Uí Bhruadair. The Poems of David Ó Bruadair*, ed. and trans. J.C.MacErlean, London: Irish Texts Society.

Ó Cearnaigh, Seán (John Kearney) (1571) *Aibidil Gaoidheilge & Caiticiosma (Gaelic Alphabet and Catechism)*, Dublin.

Ó Cléirigh, Mícheúl (Michael O'Clery) (1643) *Foclóir na Sanasán Nua [A New Vocabulary or Glossary]*, in *Révue Celtique*, Vol. IV (1879–80), trans. A. Miller, Paris.

O'Connell, Daniel, *see* Daunt.

O'Connell, Edmond (William Haliday) (1808) *Uraicecht na Gaedhilge. Grammar of the Gaelic Language*, Dublin.

O'Conor, Charles (1753) *Dissertations on the Ancient History of Ireland*, Dublin.

Ó Domhnuill, Uilliam, *see* William Daniel.

O'Donnell, F.H. (1903) *The Ruin of Education in Ireland and the Irish Farmer*, London: Nutt.

O'Farrelly, A. (1901) *The Reign of Humbug*, Dublin: Gaelic League.

O'Flanagan, T. (ed.) (1808) *Transactions of the Gaelic Society of Dublin*, Dublin.

Óh-Eigceartaigh, P.S. (1918) 'Politics and The Language', in *Samhain*, Dublin: Curtis.

227

Ó hEódhasa, Giolla Brighde (Bonaventura Hussey) (1611) *An Teagasg Críosdaidhe*, Antwerp.

O'Hickey, Revd M.P., n.d. [?1900] *The True National Idea*, Dublin: Gaelic League.

Ó Maoilchonaire, Flaithrí (Florence Conry) (1616) *Sgáthán an Chrábhaidh [Mirror of Faith]*, Louvain.

O'Maolchraoibhe, Padraig (1984) *The Role of Language in Ireland's Cultural Revival*, Belfast: Sinn Féin.

Ó Rathaille, Aodhagáin (Egan O'Rahilly) (1911) *Dánta Aodhagáin Uí Rathaille. The Poems of Egan O'Rahilly*, 2nd edn, ed. and trans. P.S. Dinneen and T. O'Donoghue, London: Irish Texts Society.

O'Reilly, E. (1817) *Sanas Gaoidhilge Sagsbeurla. An English Irish Dictionary*, Dublin.

O'Reilly, Revd John M. (1901) *The Threatening Metempsychosis of a Nation*, Dublin: Gaelic League.

Orpen, Dr Charles (1821) *The Claims of Millions of our fellow Countrymen of Present and Future Generations To Be Taught In Their Own and Only Language; the Irish. Addressed to the Upper Classes in Ireland and Great Britain*, Dublin.

Ó Snodaigh, Pádraig (1995) *Hidden Ulster. Protestants and the Irish Language*, Belfast: Lagan Press.

Pairlement Chloinne Tomáis (1615) ed. N.J.A. Williams (1981), Dublin: Dublin Institute for Advanced Studies.

Pearse, P.H. (1899) 'The 'Irish' Literary Theatre', *An Claidheamh Soluis*, I, 10, Dublin.

—— (1913) 'The Coming Revolution', *Political Writings and Speeches* (1962), Dublin: Talbot.

Petty, William (1691) *The Political Anatomy of Ireland*, London.

Richardson, John (1711) *A Proposal for the Conversion of the Popish Natives of Ireland to the Established Religion: With the Reasons upon which it is Grounded: And an Answer to the Objections made to it*, 2nd edn, corrected and enlarged, 1712, London.

—— (1712) *A Short History of the Attempts that Have Been Made to Convert the Popish Natives of Ireland, to the Established Religion: With a Proposal for their Conversion*, London.

—— (1712) *see* John Lewis.

Ruadh, Donnchadh (1899) 'Irish in County Wexford', *An Claidheamh Soluis*, I, 29, Dublin.

Scurry, James (1827) *Remarks on the Irish Language*, Dublin.

Sheridan, Thomas (1780) *A General Dictionary of the English Language*, London.

Sidney, Henry (1585) 'A Discourse for the Reformation of Ireland', in *Calendar of the Carew Manuscripts Preserved in the Archiepiscopal Library at Lambeth* (1868), Vol. II, London.

Society for the Preservation of the Irish Language (1877) *An Cheud Leabhar Gaedhilge. The First Irish Book*, Dublin.

—— (1884) *Proceedings of the Congress Held in Dublin, 1882*, Dublin.

Spenser, Edmund (1596) 'A View of the Present State of Ireland', in James Ware (ed.) *The Historie of Ireland Collected by Three Learned Authors* (1633), Dublin.

Stanihurst, James (1570) 'The Oration of James Stanihurst, Speaker of the Parliament', in James Ware (ed.) *The Historie of Ireland Collected by Three Learned Authors* (1633), Dublin.

Stanihurst, Richard (1577) 'A Treatise Containing a Plain and Perfect Description of Ireland', in R. Holinshed *The Chronicles of England, Scotland and Ireland* (1587), 3 vols, ed. John Hooker *et al.*, London.

State Papers, Henry VIII, 11 vols (1830–52), London.

The Statutes at Large Passed in the Parliaments Held in Ireland . . . 1310–1761, 8 vols (1765), Dublin.

'The Statute of Kilkenny' (1366) in *Tracts Relating to Ireland* (1842), Dublin: Irish Archaeological Society.

Stephens, James (1922) 'The Irish Past is the Irish Language', *The Century Magazine*.

Stokes, W. (1799) *Projects for Re-Establishing the Internal Peace and Tranquility of Ireland*, Dublin.

Swift, Jonathan (*c*.1735) 'A Dialogue in Hibernian Style Between A and B', 'On Barbarous Denominations in Ireland', in *Prose Writings*, Vol. IV (1973), ed. Herbert Davis with Louis Landa, Oxford: Blackwell.

Synge, J.M. (1907) *The Aran Islands* (1979), Oxford: Oxford University Press.

—— (1907) 'Can We Go Back Into Our Mother's Womb?', in A. Price (ed.) *Collected Works* (1966), London: Oxford University Press.

Taylor, J.S. (1817) *Reasons for Giving Moral Instruction to the Native Irish, Through the Medium of their Vernacular Language*, London.

Thomas, Daniel (1787) *Observations on the Pamphlets Published by the Bishop of Cloyne, Mr. Trant, and Theophilus, On One Side, and Those by Mr. O'Leary, Mr. Barber, and Dr. Campbell On the Other*, Dublin.

Transactions of the Gaelic Society of Dublin (1808) ed. Theophilus O'Flanagan, Dublin.

Trench, D.C. (1912) *What is the Use of Reviving Irish?*, Dublin: Maunsel.

Vallancey, Charles (1772) *An Essay on the Antiquity of the Irish Language. Being a Collation of the Irish with the Punic Language*, Dublin.

—— (1773) *A Grammar of the Iberno-Celtic or Irish Language* (1782), 2nd edn, Dublin.

Walsh, Revd Paul (1918) *Gleanings from Irish Manuscripts Chiefly of the Seventeenth Century*, Dublin: Dollard.

Waterford (1885) 'Archives of the Municipal Corporation of Waterford', ed. J.T. Gilbert, in *Historical Manuscripts Commission, Tenth Report*, Appendix V, London.

Yeats, W.B. (1900) 'Letter to *The Leader*', in J. Frayne and C. Johnson (eds) *Uncollected Prose*, 2, (1975), London: Macmillan.

—— (1902) *Samhain*, 2, Dublin: Sealy Bryers and Walker.

Young, Arthur (1778) *A Tour in Ireland, with General Observations on the State of that Kingdom*, Dublin.

2. Secondary texts

Adams, G.B. (1964) *Ulster Dialects*, Holywood, Co. Down: Ulster Folk Museum.

Barnard, T.C. (1993) 'Protestants and the Irish Language, *c*.1675–1725', *Journal of Ecclesiastical History*, 44, 2, 243–72.

Belfast Agreement: An Agreement Reached at the Multi-Party Talks on Northern Ireland (1998) London: The Stationery Office.

Blaney, R. (1996) *Presbyterians and the Irish Language*, Belfast: Ulster Historical Foundation.

Bliss, Alan (1975) 'The English Language in Early Modern Ireland', in Moody *et al.*, Vol. III, 546–60.

—— (1979) *Spoken English in Ireland 1600–1740*, Dublin: Dolmen.

Breatnach, R.A. (1956) 'Revival or Survival? An Examination of the Irish Language Policy of the State', *Studies*, 45, 129–43, Dublin.

Cahill, E. (1935) 'The Irish National Tradition', *The Irish Ecclesiatical Record*, 46: 2–10, Dublin.

—— (1938) 'Norman French and English Languages in Ireland 1170-1540', *The Irish Ecclesiastical Record*, 51: 159–73.

—— (1939) 'The Irish Language and Tradition, 1540–1691', *The Irish Ecclesiastical Record*, 54: 123–42, Dublin.

—— (1940) 'The Irish Language in the Penal Era', *The Irish Ecclesiastical Record*, 55: 591–617.

Committee on Irish Language Attitudes (1975) *Report*, Dublin: The Stationery Office.

Corkery, D. (1925) *The Hidden Ireland: A Study of Gaelic Munster in the 18th Century*, Dublin: Gill and Macmillan.

—— (1954) *The Fortunes of the Irish Language*, Cork: Mercier.

Cosgrove, A. (1987) *A New History of Ireland*, Vol. II, *Medieval Ireland, 1169–1534*, Oxford: Clarendon.

Cronin, M. (1996) *Translating Ireland: Translation, Languages, Cultures*, Cork: Cork University Press.

Cronin, S. (1978) 'Nation-Building in the Irish Language Revival Movement', *Eire-Ireland*, 6, 7–14.

Crowley, T. (1996) *Language in History: Theories and Texts*, London: Routledge.

Curtis, E. (1919) 'The Spoken Languages of Medieval Ireland', *Studies*, viii, 234–54.

De Fréine, S. (1965) *The Great Silence*, Dublin: Foilseacháin Náisiúnta Teoranta.

Dolan, T. (1998) *A Dictionary of Hiberno-English*, Dublin: Gill and Macmillan.

Fitzsimons, J. (1949) 'Official Presbyterian Irish Language Policy in the 18th and 19th Centuries', *Irish Ecclesiastical Record*, 5th Series, 72: 255–64.

Greene, D. (1966) *The Irish Language*, Dublin: Cultural Relations Committee.

—— (1970) 'The Irish Language Movement', in M. Hurley (ed.) *Irish Anglicanism 1869–1969*, 110–19, Dublin: Allan Figgis.

Hindley, R. (1990) *The Death of the Irish Language: A Qualified Obituary*, London: Routledge.

Hutchinson, J. (1987) *The Dynamics of Cultural Nationalism: The Gaelic Revival and the Creation of the Irish Nation State*, London: Allen and Unwin.

Hyde, D. (1899) 'The History of Irish as a Spoken Language', in *A Literary History of Ireland From Earliest Times to the Present Day*, London: Fisher Unwin.

Jackson, D. (1973) 'The Irish Language and Tudor Government', *Éire-Ireland*, 8:1, 21–30.

Joyce, P.W. (1910) *English as we Speak it in Ireland*, Dublin.

Kiberd, D. (1979) *Synge and the Irish Language*, London: Macmillan.

—— (1996) *Inventing Ireland: The Literature of the Modern Nation*, London: Vintage.

Leersen, J. (1986) *Mere Irish and Fiór Ghael: Studies in the Idea of Irish Nationality*, Amsterdam: John Benjamins.

Macafee, C.I. (1996) *A Concise Ulster Dictionary*, Oxford: Oxford University Press.

Mahony, R. (1989) 'Yeats and the Irish Language', *The Irish University Review*, vol 19, 2, 220–3.

Moody, T., F.X. Martin and F.J. Byrne (eds) (1976) *A New History of Ireland*, Vol. III, *Early Modern Ireland, 1534–1691*, Oxford: Clarendon.

Mooney, Revd C. (1944) 'The Beginnings of the Irish Language Revival', *Irish Ecclesiastical Record*, 5th Series, 64, 10–18.

Ó Cuív, B. (ed.) (1969) *A View of the Irish Language*, Dublin: Stationery Office.

—— 'The Irish Language in the Early Modern Period', in Moody *et al.*, Vol. III, 509–45.

Ó Fearail, P. (1975) *The Story of Conradh na Gaelige. A History of the Gaelic League*, Dublin.

Ó Fiach, T. (1960) 'The Language and Political History', in Ó Cuív, 10–11 (1969).

O'Leary, Philip (1994) *The Prose Literature of the Gaelic Revival, 1881–1921 Ideology and Innovation*, Pennsylvania, PA: Pennsylvania University Press.

O'Muirithe, D. (ed.) (1977) *The English Language in Ireland*, Cork: Mercier.

O'Murchu, M. (1985) *The Irish Language*, Dublin: Government Publications.

O'Riordan, M. (1990) *The Gaelic Mind and the Collapse of the Gaelic World*, Cork: Cork University Press.

O'Tuama, S. (1972) *The Gaelic League Idea*, Cork: Mercier.

Paulin, Tom (1983) *A New Look at the Language Question*, Derry: Field Day.

Watt, J.A. (1987) 'Gaelic Polity and Cultural Identity', and 'The Anglo-Irish Colony Under Strain 1327–99', in Moody *et al.*, Vol. II, 314–51, 352–96.

INDEX